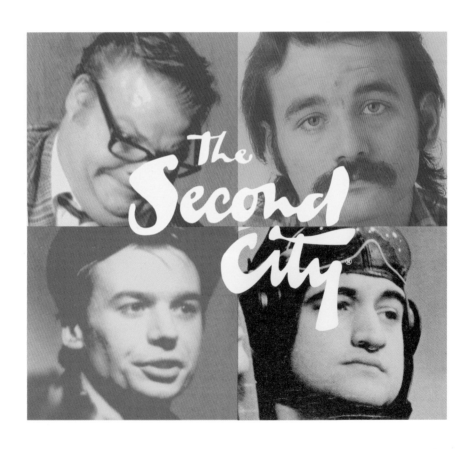

The Second City ®

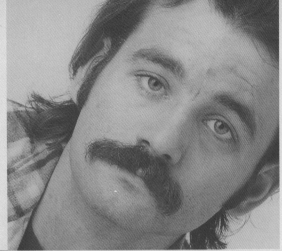

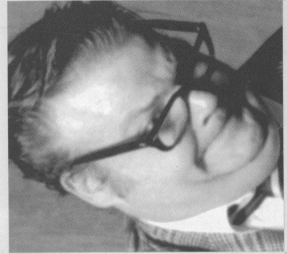

Backstage at
the World's Greatest
Comedy Theater

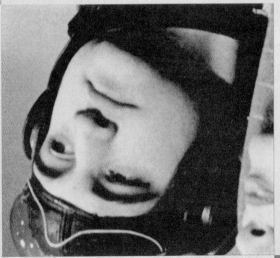

SOURCEBOOKS, INC.®
NAPERVILLE, ILLINOIS

Sheldon Patinkin
narrated by **Robert Klein**

foreword **Alan Arkin**
fiveword **Dan Aykroyd**
inword **George Wendt**
backword **James Belushi**
lastword **Harold Ramis**

Published by Sourcebooks, Inc.
P.O. Box 4410, Naperville, Illinois 60567-4410
(630) 961-3900
FAX: (630) 961-2168

Library of Congress Cataloging-in-Publication Data

Patinkin, Sheldon.
      The Second City: backstage at the world's greatest comedy theater/Sheldon Patinkin.
          p. cm.
      ISBN 1-57071-561-0 (alk. paper)
Second City (Theater company)—History. I. Title.

PN2277.C42 S452 2000
792.7'09773'11—dc21

                          00-057368
                          CIP

Printed and bound in the United States of America

DO 10 9 8 7 6 5 4 3 2 1

We would like to dedicate this book to the thousands of artists, technicians, staff, and audience members who have helped sustain The Second City for over four decades.

—Andrew Alexander & Len Stuart
Owners, The Second City

NBC National Broadcasting Company, Inc. Thirty Rockefeller Plaza
New York, N.Y. 10020 212-247-8300

March 7th

Dear Joyce and Jane and Bernie and the Entire Cast of Second
City and the whole audience and Everyone Involved from
the Ticket Taker to whoever sweeps up at night,

I had the best time being with you in Chicago. It was like
coming home and having ice cream and cookies in the kitchen
and laughing about stuff that happened in school that day.
So, this is a letter to say thank-you and a warning that I'll
be back to eat all your food and laugh at all your jokes.

I love you,

Gilda

Table of Contents

Foreword...

by Alan Arkin

My whole life turned around at Second City—every aspect of it. Before Second City I'd had one acting job. I was twenty-eight years old, and I'd had *a* job. I had about four lines in a play about Eloise and Abelard. I played the lute.

My first brush with improvisation came when David Shepherd hired me for a summer job at the "Crystal Palace" in St. Louis. I didn't think I was terribly good at improvising, but it kept me employed for the summer.

Paul Sills came down from Chicago to see the show. This was in 1959 when Second City was first being formulated. After the show I met Sills, and he said if I ever wanted a job in Chicago to call him up. I thanked him, but inside I was thinking, "Fat chance. I'm not going to bury myself in Chicago. I'll never do that."

So I went back to New York still thinking I was going to have a big career—but nothing happened. I starved for yet another year.

And then in desperation I called Sills and said if the job was still open, I'd come out to Chicago.

He hired me on the phone, and I went to Chicago thinking it was going to be the end of my life, that I'd be working for a hundred bucks a week at this tiny, insignificant, non-Equity club with the strange name for the rest of my life.

What I found in Chicago was an ensemble that was an amazing and eclectic mix of people. Paul Sills had an extraordinary sense of casting. He had a way of putting together very interesting groups of people.

I can't remember a single coherent sentence Paul Sills said. But as it often happens with talented directors—I've worked with a lot of talented directors who were totally incoherent, he was the first—somehow he got his message across.

I don't remember what the rehearsals were like, but somehow he yelled us into doing good work.

The first company I worked with at Second City consisted of Paul Sand, Severn Darden, Barbara Harris, Mina Kolb, Eugene Troobnick, Howard Alk, and Andrew Duncan. When I came into the group, they'd been working together for about six or eight months.

I was brought in to head a new company because the first company was going to go to New York. They brought me in to bridge the gap, but I got along so well with the first company, they decided to keep me with the original group.

My sense of the actors in the early years was that we were a diverse and multi-talented bunch of misfits. We all had broad interests and abilities, but no real specialties. We had nowhere else to go. We were saving our lives by being at Second City.

The way the show worked was that the evening was divided into two parts. At the beginning of intermission we would get suggestions from the audience. Current events, book titles, personalities in the news, movies— anything of current interest. Then we'd go backstage and scream at each other for fifteen minutes until we came up with about forty minutes of material, and that would be the second half of the show.

The first couple of months I thought I was in serious trouble. I wasn't getting laughs. I didn't feel funny; I didn't think I was going to make it.

Then one night I latched onto one character that worked. And as that character—no matter what I did—it was funny. So I just played that character for a while until I felt comfortable enough to add another character, then I found another one, and I ended up with a small library of characters.

At Second City, I felt like I had twenty-five years of pent-up stuff that finally exploded.

I'd wanted to be an actor since I was five years old. Second City was the first time I'd gotten any substantiation that this was a career I belonged in.

FiveWORD...

by Dan Aykroyd

I guess my first introduction to Second City–style humor was a Nichols and May album. It was the one for their Broadway show, *An Evening with Mike Nichols and Elaine May*. I remember hearing that on the radio, seeing them on Ed Sullivan, and being inspired by their work. When I was twelve, my parents sent me to study improv at the Ottawa Little Theater. I gave it up when I went to college in Carleton University, but I did have experience doing improv. At Carleton University, I studied sociology with courses that would have served a master's of criminology.

I dropped out before finishing at Carleton. My future comedy partner, Valri Bromfield, pulled me out of school, and when I was seventeen, we moved to Toronto. We performed as a two-person act, like Nichols and May. We had our own cable TV show and did a lot of shows in gay clubs. They would have comedy nights because there weren't a lot of comedy clubs in Toronto in the late 1960s, early '70s.

I was a mailman at the time. At the same time, John Candy was a Kleenex salesman. He had a brown suit and a car to match. I found out about Second City because I was a big fan of Alan Arkin after seeing him in *Wait until Dark*. In learning about him, I found out about Second City. Then I found out they were coming up to Toronto, opening up a club here. And people told me, "You would be perfect for this." So I auditioned.

We did the standard audition for Bernie Sahlins and Joyce Sloane, doing five completely different characters in five minutes. I was hired. And immediately, the learning began. Brian Doyle-Murray and Joe Flaherty were my primary teachers. They taught me Paul Sills and Viola Spolin's incredible psychological games. It was joyous. Those were beautiful days.

We learned generosity with your fellow actor, how to give onstage, how not to worry about failing, how to write, how to shape material. I think of all the "hyphenates" that came out of Second City, with Harold Ramis leading the pack, as an actor-writer-director.

We learned multiple skills, all the techniques of theater—a little parody Shakespeare, a little parody musical. You can see why Lorne Michaels has recruited so many out of The Second City, and why Second City's influence has been massive on comedy worldwide.

We set up in Toronto and performed from 1971 on. Then, in the summer of 1974, there was a switch: the Chicago comedy came to Toronto and we went down to Chicago. That was an incredible summer. That was the summer Nixon resigned, and I was doing Nixon at San Clemente Dodge-Chrysler, saying, "Now that I have some time on my hands, I am trying to move some Chryslers off my back lot."

We worked with Del Close, took classes from him. You knew you were touching the essence there, the real wellspring—they were wonderful days. He taught me so much. He taught me to write and be brave and do things that served me well at *Saturday Night Live*.

After that summer, I went back to Second City Toronto, and in 1975 I was invited to help open Second City Pasadena. John Candy and I drove thirty-eight hours from Toronto to Pasadena, straight through. We had a big Mercury Cougar, and we switched off driving. I went to only two rehearsals in Pasadena, and then Michaels called and had me in for an audition for *Saturday Night Live*. I went to New York and made it for the second interview. He kept calling me back for auditions. He vetted me two or three times before he hired me.

Second City was my college, and *Saturday Night Live* was my university. I had to go through Second City's baccalaureate program before I could get my master's degree.

Introduction

by The Second City

"[Second City is] the comedy empire that has made North Americans laugh for forty years."

—*New York Times*

On December 16, 1959, a 125-seat cabaret on the Near North Side of Chicago opened its doors for the first time. The space itself was nothing special. The theater was housed in a reconverted hat shop, with a former Chinese laundry storefront for a lobby next door. Eight performers—all young, all unknown—debuted a new form of theater. Using only a few small props and costumes, the cast presented comic and satiric scenes, blackouts, parodies, musical numbers, and on-the-spot improvisations. How could the cast have known that they would be creating the template for thousands of actors, comics, writers, and directors who would move from this simple stage to America's theaters, nightclubs, radio, television, and movies? They called themselves The Second City.

It only takes a sample list of Second City's alumni to recognize the tremendous influence this theater has had on the American entertainment industry: Alan Arkin, Dan Aykroyd, James Belushi, John Belushi, Peter Boyle, John Candy, Severn Darden, Rachel Dratch, Chris Farley, Aaron Freeman, Barbara Harris, Bonnie Hunt, Richard Kind, Robert Klein, Shelley Long, Andrea Martin, Tim Meadows, Bill Murray, Brian Doyle-Murray, Mike Myers, Bob Odenkirk, Catherine O'Hara, Gilda Radner, Harold Ramis, Joan Rivers, Paul Sand, Horatio Sanz, Avery Schreiber, Martin Short, David Steinberg, Ryan Stiles, Betty Thomas, Dave Thomas, George Wendt, and Fred Willard.

No other theatrical institution in the world can claim to have nurtured such an impressive number of successful and influential comic performers over such a long period of time. The Second City—the name taken from the title of a snotty *New Yorker* magazine piece about Chicago—is that rare place where commercial success has not meant the sacrifice of artistic integrity. Indeed, very few organizations can boast a foundation based on risk-taking, blind trust, and rebellion. At the heart of Second City lies improvisation. It is the root from which the talent is trained, the shows created, and the business conducted. The history of improvisation can be traced to The Second City and its predecessors, but Second City is improvising history itself—as generation after generation of Second City performer takes on the burden of making us laugh at ourselves.

The influence of The Second City, though celebrated by audiences in the millions and critics from all over the world, cannot be fully understood through sheer numbers. It is an influence that has permeated the skin of our culture. If you were collecting a list of the most significant films and television series in the last four decades, you would surely list *The Graduate*, *Young Frankenstein*, *M*A*S*H*, *Saturday Night Live*, *SCTV*, *Animal House*, *Hill Street Blues*, *Ghostbusters*, and *Cheers*. When you consider that each of these programs carries an important connection to The Second City, you understand the unique breadth of its influence upon not only the entertainment industry, but on North American culture in general.

The question may be, then, why The Second City? While there is no easy answer, the truth may lie in the unusual blending of highbrow and lowbrow culture that is developed by the theater. It would not be unusual, while attending a show at The Second City, to encounter references to Mike Ditka and Soren Kierkegaard—sometimes in the same breath. It is the marriage of these two types—a blue-collar, workingman icon and a figurehead of the intelligencia—that provides the most visceral example of this concept. The Second City has made its living on the unshakable belief that the audience is as smart as you let them be, that the actors need to work at the top of their intelligence, and that there is nobility in goofing off. How else does one explain how the audiences at The Second City have stayed the same age, even as the theater nears its middle years? The work speaks to the youth in each of us. It is laughter with bite and importance, and it reminds us how the value of that laughter becomes more vital with each passing year.

Over time, The Second City has become synonymous with a certain standard in comedy. Audiences, critics, and performers have all come to expect that The Second City will and must produce thoroughly funny work of the highest quality. While intimidating, it is a standard that inspires. It is not unusual for alumni of The Second City to look back on their years with the theater as the most fulfilling of their lives.

This book provides a glimpse inside this thoroughly unique and original enterprise, where the line between business and family has been consistently blurred; and where life-long friendships have been formed; where the individual voice is celebrated, as is the sacrifice of the individual spotlight for the greater good of the ensemble; and where so many success stories were born. It is not just the story of The Second City—it is the story of American comedy in the last half of the twentieth century.

The Second City Punch-Line

TIME

'60s

June 1971
John Belushi debuts in *No, No, Wilmette*, the forty-first revue.

June 1973
The Second City establishes a permanent home in Toronto on Adelaide Street, then in The Old Firehall, a nineteenth-century firehouse.

December 16, 1959:
The Second City opens at 1842 North Wells Street in Chicago's Old Town with *Excelsior & Other Outcries*.

'70s

August 197
Bill Murray, John Cand and Betty Thoma debut in *Phase 46 o Watergate Tomorrow Comedy Tonight*, th forty-sixth revue

May 1965
Robert Klein, Fred Willard, and musical director Fred Kaz debut in *Off the Road*, the eighteenth revue.

August 1974
The Canadian Show or Upper USA, the forty-eighth Chicago revue, opens with a cast that includes Toronto mainstage players Dan Aykroyd, Gilda Radner, John Candy, and Eugene Levy.

April 1963
The company makes the first of what will become an annual trek to Toronto's Royal Alexandra Theatre.

August 1967
The Second City moves two blocks south to its new, much enlarged home at 1616 North Wells, in Piper's Alley.

'80s

September 1993
A permanent Second City mainstage opens in a specially built new facility in Detroit.

November 1997
The Second City Toronto moves from its long-time home at The Old Firehall to a new state-of-the-art facility at 56 Blue Jays Way in time for its twenty-fifth anniversary in 1998.

September 1982
The Second City e.t.c. debuts next door to Chicago's mainstage in Piper's Alley.

'90s

March 1985
Andrew Alexander and Len Stuart acquire Bernie Sahlins' interest in The Second City.

December 16, 1999
The Second City Chicago celebrates its fortieth anniversary.

October 1975
Saturday Night Live debuts on NBC with Second City alums John Belushi, Dan Aykroyd, and Gilda Radner, with Bill Murray joining the cast the next season.

June 1988
Mike Myers joins Bonnie Hunt and Richard Kind at Second City Chicago in *Kuwait Until Dark or Bright Lights, Night Baseball*, the seventieth revue.

October 1976
The Second City Toronto produces *SCTV* for syndication in Canada. It would end up on NBC, then Cinemax, earning seven Emmy nominations and two Emmy awards along the way.

March 1989
Chris Farley and Tim Meadows debut in Chicago in *The Gods Must Be Lazy*, the seventy-first revue.

Chapter **1**

Before the Beginning

Predecessors to Second City

In the early 1950s, the Korean War was raging to its eventual stale-mate, people were becoming wary of an atomic attack by the Soviet Union, and Wisconsin Senator Joseph McCarthy was frightening America with his claims of communists all around us. Conformity and men in gray flannel suits were becoming the norm, post–World War II affluence and the birthing of babies were still on the rise, and the suburbs were becoming an attractive alternative to city living.

A black-and-white TV with an aerial on the roof or rabbit ears on top of the set was now a fairly commonplace sight in American living rooms, and people were discovering the joys of staying home to watch Milton Berle, Sid Caesar, and Ed Sullivan live, as well as

Groucho Marx, Jack Benny, Amos 'n' Andy, I Love Lucy, and Dragnet on film or kinescope. Hollywood was fighting the concurrent loss of business with widescreen and 3-D movies. Rodgers and Hammerstein were the reigning kings of Broadway. Pop songs tended to be about Tennessee waltzes and doggies in the window.

Comedy, mostly seen in nightclubs and on TV variety shows, was jokes, often about wives or mothers-in-law. What passed for political humor was best represented by Bob Hope's gags about President Truman's piano playing and his daughter Margaret's singing career or, later, Eisenhower's golf game and his wife Mamie's hats.

But the early 1950s were also when Arthur Miller was writing the anti–red-baiting drama The Crucible, the Beats were starting their protest against conformism by heading for the road, and Ernie Kovacs was playing with our minds on TV. White kids were finding black rhythm-and-blues on a few radio stations broadcast from remote spots on the dial (to their parents' dismay), and political satirist Mort Sahl's career, based on that day's newspaper, was taking off in nightclubs and on long-playing records.

In Chicago, there were fashionable nightclubs slightly north of downtown and popular jazz clubs on the South Side. Long a source of some national network radio programming, the city was now also sending out several locally produced shows on the newly formed TV networks, including Kukla, Fran, and Ollie; [Dave] Garroway at Large; and Studs' [Terkel] Place, all broadcast live. There was even a nationally televised soap opera called Hawkins Falls. But almost the only professional theater was Broadway road companies playing in downtown houses. Locally produced theater usually could be found only in summer tents and community, school, and church spaces and patronized, for the most part, by friends and family. There was, however, something brewing at that South-Side bastion of scholarly intellectualism, the University of Chicago.

Opening page (clockwise from top left): Andrew Duncan • Ed Asner and Leah Roshal in a scene from The Bespoke Overcoat • Mike Nichols • Bernie Sahlins

Above: The University of Chicago campus, home of University Theatre

University Theatre

In the late 1940s and early 1950s, among the people attending classes or hanging around at the University of Chicago were quite a few who were soon to become participants in Second City and/or its predecessor, The Compass. They included Paul Sills,

David Shepherd, Bernie Sahlins, Mike Nichols, Elaine May, Severn Darden, Andrew Duncan, Roger Bowen, Eugene Troobnick, Bill Alton, Zohra Lampert, Tony Holland, and me. There were also quite a few others who've made theater and film their careers, including Ed Asner, Fritz Weaver, and Joyce and Byrne Piven. The irony is that the University of Chicago had no theater department—or theater classes—and it still doesn't.

But there was University Theatre, a sort of after-school dramatic society for smart kids. It had a paid artistic director and a budget from the University. Everything else came from the students putting in the time around schoolwork or, as often happened, instead of schoolwork, leading to panic, craziness, and threatened suicides before final exams. The plays produced at UT were difficult, tending toward the obscure and the esoteric: Buchner, Wycherley, unfamiliar Shakespeare, the Capek brothers. And we had no instruction to help us over the rough spots, which were many. Some shows were considerably better than others.

In January 1952, Paul Sills directed and acted in UT's production of Cocteau's *The Typewriter*. The cast also included Mike Nichols and Joyce Piven. I learned how to run lights for it.

The Typewriter was a rebellion against the dominant fourth-wall method of acting. The concept of the fourth wall is part of the theory of acting developed by the enormously influential late-nineteenth- and early-twentieth-century Russian actor-director Constantine Stanislavsky and brought to America in the 1930s by Stella Adler, Elia Kazan, Lee Strasberg, and other members of the Group Theatre. In fourth-wall acting, you're pretending that the front of the stage is the fourth wall of the room you're pretending to be in. In other words, the actor tries to leave out any sense of performing for an audience. (Apparently Marlon Brando, a fourth-wall actor, couldn't even be heard in the back half of the theater when he played Stanley Kowalski in *A Streetcar Named Desire* on Broadway.) By the early 1950s, fourth-wall acting was the norm for any actor who wanted to be taken seriously. Thanks to Rodgers and Hammerstein, it was even starting to be expected in musicals. Comedy, however, doesn't bounce well off walls. You have to play the audience and their laughter—or silence—and therefore can't pretend to yourself that they're not there. It's one of the many reasons for the famous quote, attributed to several people, though most frequently to Groucho Marx: "Dying is easy; comedy is hard." It's also one reason why so many Strasberg-trained Method actors can't do comedy, or at least not very well.

The Typewriter became a box-office hit, and talk began about starting our own theater. Of course, none of us had any money,

Spotlight on
Joyce and Byrne Piven

Joyce and Byrne Piven, along with their acting and directing careers, are the heads of the Piven Theatre Workshop in Evanston, Illinois. Among the alumni are their son, Jeremy Piven; Lili Taylor; John and Joan Cusack, and Aidan Quinn.

Joyce remembers working on *The Typewriter*:

Mike Nichols, Paul Sills, and I spent six months rehearsing The Typewriter. *I wish I could recall what we did in those six months. We did a lot of improvising. We did a lot of drinking beer and all that, but we were very, very serious. We felt we were evolving a new form. I think in the Midwest, it was the first production where the audience was seated all around the stage, "in the round." Even at an early date, Paul [Sills] was pushing the envelope, breaking the so-called fourth wall between the actors and the audience. It was very exciting because we would enter through the audience. I remember many nights standing next to someone as I was emoting, with people sitting there either chewing gum right in my ear or knitting very diligently. Things like that.*

3

Top to bottom: *Estelle Luttrell, Tom Erhart, Anthony Holland, and David Shepherd perform* The Caucasian Chalk Circle *at the Playwrights Theatre Club.*
• *Elaine May and Byrne Piven in* A Midsummer Night's Dream *at Playwrights*

but when has that ever stopped the talk? (One big difference between then and now: there was no existing precedent in 1952 for starting your own theater company in Chicago.)

With the talk getting stronger, a bunch of us got together for five hours every Saturday afternoon during much of the 1952–53 school year, and Paul Sills taught us the improvisational games and exercises he learned from his mother, Viola Spolin. There are many of them. Exercises are usually used as warm-ups or to end a class and require no advance planning. Here's one: the group is divided into two teams who then have a tug-of-war, only the rope is mimed.

Each game has a single rule of play and, with few exceptions, is performed on an empty stage, with no costumes, and everything mimed except chairs. A game begins with the class counting off into two, three, or four people per team for that particular game. Then each team privately plans the three basic questions needed for any improvised scene: who? (who you are), what? (a mutual physical activity), and where? (the setting of the scene). After planning that much, and usually only that much, you're given the rule for the game you're about to play. It might be to do the scene in gibberish or as a silent movie. It might be to make as many entrances and exits as you can, but only while everyone else on stage is looking at you and without your saying anything about the fact that you're trying to make an exit or entrance. Or the teacher will side-coach you to heighten or explore any passing moment of your scene. Or your team will divide in half, with one half on stage acting the scene and the other half watching them behave and dubbing their dialogue while the actors on stage try to mouth the dubbed words as they're being said.

Some games and exercises help work on character (the who), some on the where, some on the what, some on focusing on the other, and there are many other kinds as well, all helpful to the actor in creating an individual character within an ensemble.

Paul, of course, had started learning the games from Viola when he was a child in Los Angeles (as had Elaine May, Paul Sand, and Alan Arkin). By 1953, he knew he was teaching us the games on those Saturday afternoons in order to build an acting ensemble for his dreamed-of new theater, and that's what happened to us. That's what always happens when a group plays Viola's improv games together for a while; they learn to trust each other, to more or less cope with each other's foibles, and to work off what's happening between them and the others instead of just off themselves. After all, in an improv, as opposed to a play, you don't know what you're going to say or do next, and whatever it is has to come off what you see and hear from the others, combined with what you want from them.

The last show of the 1952–53 University Theatre season was Paul's extraordinary production of Bertolt Brecht's *The Caucasian Chalk Circle* in its Chicago premiere and second production anywhere. (Given Brecht's communism, it opened, fittingly, on May Day.) The cast of twenty, between us, played about sixty characters without ever leaving the stage—a perfect chance to use the ensemble techniques we'd been learning in the workshops.

With the arrival of David Shepherd, who had as strong a vision as Paul's and a little money, talk also began on the possibility of opening a political cabaret for working-class audiences, which was David's dream.

Since no one was really ready for a political cabaret yet, Paul Sills, David Shepherd, and Eugene Troobnick opened Playwrights Theatre Club on June 23, 1953, with a restaged and somewhat recast production of *The Caucasian Chalk Circle*.

Playwrights Theatre Club

Playwrights was located at the corner of North and LaSalle (a block from the current Second City) on the outskirts of the area known as Old Town, far from the University of Chicago and slightly off the beaten track. Our space was a tile-floored reconverted Chinese restaurant upstairs from a drugstore and an all-night diner. (The building was later torn down and replaced by a Burger King.) We incorporated as a club because that was the only way you could be not-for-profit in those days—our lawyer had to invent a lot of that stuff as we went along. We sold memberships instead of tickets. The seats were wood-frame director's chairs with detachable red, blue, or yellow canvas seats and backs; each color was a different "membership" price.

There was a record heat wave on opening night and no air-conditioning, but the critics loved us anyway, and we were an instant hit in our 125-seat house with individual memberships priced at one to two dollars. (The diner downstairs sold an excellent barbecued-beef sandwich with fries, lettuce, tomato, and coffee for seventy-five cents, if that helps you understand the economy. Somebody always seemed to be playing Eartha Kitt's "I Want to Be Evil" on the juke box down there.) We were the first local theater in years, the beginning of a movement that wouldn't see its major growth until the late 1970s.

In two years, we did close to thirty productions, including *The Glass Menagerie, The Dybbuk, Murder in the Cathedral, Peer Gynt, The Sea Gull, Oedipus Rex, Juno and the Paycock*, the Chicago

David Shepherd came to Chicago in 1952, after getting his master's degree in theater history at Columbia University. Although he wasn't a student at the University of Chicago, he was soon hanging out at University Theatre. He became a producer and occasional director and actor at our first theater, Playwrights Theatre Club; producer, frequent director, and occasional actor at the first improvisational theater, The Compass, in all its incarnations; and advisor and occasional writer for Second City. He then created the ImprovOlympic, in which teams of improvisers compete. He now makes improv movies. David always has been in the vanguard of improvisational theater and, particularly because of The Compass (which is discussed later in the chapter), is as much a part of why there is a Second City as anyone.

Paul was the original director of Playwrights, Compass, and Second City; he was also one of the owners of Second City when it opened. He directed the first six shows there, all opening within the first eighteen months. He then directed the first several shows we did in New York, came back to Chicago to direct five more shows in the 1960s, and directed the first Second City show we did at the Royal Alexandra Theatre in Toronto. And through all that time he was also teaching many people the improvisational games he learned from his mother.

Paul's genius was transmitted as often as not with grunts, groans, mumbles, and hollering, accompanied by various kinds of body language and an occasional thrown chair. But transmit it he did and still does (although he's now far calmer and more articulate). He got more out of people than they knew was in them. He insisted that improvisers had to stay in the moment, never going into their heads to find what to say and do, but, by bypassing the intellect, keeping themselves free to react to just what's happening between them there and then. He also understood how to place all the separate scenes, songs, blackouts, and other material for a show into a seemingly seamless running order that made the whole show feel unified, while still managing to make all the performers look good, thus setting the standard for every Second City director to follow. He was the first, and he was the best.

In the mid-1960s, Paul and his mother, Viola Spolin, opened The Game Theatre in Chicago for a couple of years, where the audience itself was invited onstage to play the games. Paul then went on to create the Story Theatre form, where the characters in the story—usually fables, folk tales, fairy tales, or mythological tales—narrate their own parts of the story as well as participating in the action. He also brought the form to TV in a series shot in Canada in the early 1970s. In the 1980s, he formed Sills & Company, an improv group of mostly Second City alumni, with Paul coaching them in games in front of the audience. It played in L.A. and, for a short time, in New York. He's also the teacher of thousands, many of them famous, thus sending the work out to the world.

At this writing Paul is semi-retired, living with his family on his farm in Wisconsin. He continues teaching summer improvisational workshops there, as well as doing occasional guest workshops and lectures and directing once a year at the New Actors Workshop, the school he started in New York with Mike Nichols and George Morrison. (That's about as retired as Second City alumni get.)

Paul once said, "There's no laugh like the explosion of laughter after improvisation." Thanks to his unique genius, those explosions of laughter continue to this day at Second City and around the world.

Paul Sills works diligently on a Playwrights production.

premiere of *The Threepenny Opera*, some Shakespeare, a few originals—including one by Paul Sills and another by David Shepherd—an occasional evening of Poets' Theater, and a children's theater for which Elaine May wrote a very funny adaptation of "Rumpelstiltskin." The shows ran an average of three weeks each, some less, some more, depending on business. We did six performances a week, no matinees. We'd close on a Sunday and open the next show on Tuesday. We were young and didn't know you couldn't do all that. We were learning our craft by doing it six nights a week.

A lot of talented people were drawn to Playwrights in those days and by the opportunity it offered young actors to learn their craft and to work on a regular basis. Ed Asner (later of off-Broadway, Broadway, such TV shows as *The Mary Tyler Moore Show, Lou Grant, The Bronx Zoo,* and *Thunder Alley*) was one of them. He was in charge of cleaning up the theater before the show every night. He'd recently gotten out of the army and ran us like he was the master sergeant and we the buck privates. If Ed was angry with someone, that person got latrine duty that night.

We rehearsed daytimes and after the shows, and made sets, costumes, and everything else whenever we could. We lived communally off the take, earning five, ten, or fifteen dollars a week, each according to need. (Since Barbara Harris and I still lived more or less at home—we were both seventeen when Playwrights started—we were among those who got five bucks a week, as did those few with day jobs. I sometimes brought food from home for everyone, since my wonderful parents worried about whether anyone was getting enough to eat.) Many of the men in the company lived in little alcoves around the back and one side of the theater, separated from the main auditorium by curtains, not doors, leaving privacy at a premium.

As we were approaching our first anniversary, we decided to move to a bigger space and join Actors Equity, the actors' and stage managers' union, which provided a minimum guaranteed salary of fifty-five dollars a week, allowing

Top to bottom: Ed Asner • Ed Asner and Eugene Troobnick star in a Playwrights Theatre Club production of Widower's Houses.

the guys who'd been living in the theater to move into their own small apartments and still have enough money to eat. By then Bernie Sahlins—at the time a businessman with Pentron tape recorders and a travel agency and therefore someone with some money—had replaced Eugene Troobnick as one of the producers. Eugene didn't want to be a boss anymore, or at least that's what we were told.

The second Playwrights space—a two hundred–seat theater—was a reconverted photographer's studio at the corner of Division and Dearborn, upstairs from an expensive restaurant (which hated us) and across the street from *the* art-film house. We opened the new space with a four-play summer Shakespeare festival, which was mostly standing-room only, and we even brought in two "New York actors" to augment the ensemble. Membership prices went up a little. Business was usually excellent, but there were more seats to fill and more expenses. Actors started leaving for New York because there wasn't enough work in Chicago, and most of it didn't pay much better than Playwrights. (If you were going to make it, New York was the place to go. It had Broadway, it had the newly developing off-Broadway movement, it had many of the best teachers and most of the country's live dramatic TV

Top to bottom: The Playwrights Theatre Club cast: (top row) Eugene Troobnick, David Shepherd, Paul Sills (middle row) Sheldon Patinkin, Ed Asner, Marvin Peisner, Heyward Ehrlich, Bill Alton, Bob Smith, Byrne Piven, Phil Morini (bottom row) Sondra MacDonald, Joy Carlin, Helen Axelrood, Zohra Lampert, Joyce Piven, Ann Petrie • The entrance to the Playwrights Theatre Club

Bernard Sahlins owned Second City from 1968–1985.

Bernard (called "Bernie" by everyone who knows him) was one of the original owners of Second City and producer for its first twenty-six years. By 1968 he was, for all intents and purposes, the sole owner. The original owners were Bernie, Paul Sills, Howard Alk, and Bernie's father, Dr. Paul Sahlins. The deal was, if you decided to leave Second City, you had to sell your share to the remaining owner or owners, or to your replacement. Howard Alk sold his quarter to Bernie when he left; Paul sold his to me (his replacement as artistic director); and I sold mine to Bernie, making him basically the sole owner, since Dr. Sahlins had died the year before, leaving his quarter to Bernie and his brother Marshall.

Bernie began directing The Second City Chicago in 1969 while still remaining producer. (He also produced several Second City TV shows in the U.S., England, and Canada, as well as having been one of the producers of the first season of *SCTV*.) He co-directed his first show, *The Next Generation*, with Cyril Simon; he then solo-directed several shows before turning the job over to Del Close in 1973. He directed a couple of shows during Del's time, then took the job on again for five years when Del left in 1983.

Bernie was a more intellectually oriented director than those of us who'd come before him. Of course, like the rest of us, he insisted on keeping the reference level of the show material as high as possible and—also like every director before and after him—had his own agenda for the kinds of shows he wanted to have at Second City. He tended to stress writing over improvisation more heavily than we did as the means of achieving the material for the show. He also developed a structure for the running order, and then sometimes had to find pieces to fit the structure rather than finding the structure out of the pieces and who was in them, as had been more the norm before him. (Every director has had to struggle to develop pieces to open and close shows, something to close the first act, musical numbers—which often include any or all of the above—and full-company scenes. They're the hardest to improvise.)

Bernie sold Second City to Andrew Alexander and Len Stuart in 1985, but continued as artistic director until 1988, when he decided he'd done enough shows—close to twenty. By then he'd also helped his wife Jane Nicholl Sahlins organize Chicago's International Theatre Festival, which Jane produced for five seasons over ten years.

Bernie continues producing and directing around town, usually creating his own projects, including a show for Chicago's Museum of Science and Industry, and has published translations of several plays. He gives no sign of retiring and is currently at work on his memoirs, along with several other projects. Bernie is incredibly smart, deeply funny, and a good friend to have.

Backstage Passes

Bernie saved my life. Second City wasn't a theater ensemble to me, it was a halfway house. I think it was true of all of us for the first few years of the place. We didn't know that there was any future in it; we just knew that our lives were being saved by getting up and railing against everything we hated. When you ran out of things to hate, you went on and did something else with some other theater group. Bernie not only gave me a job, he took me in. I became his family, he became my family—the first family that I ever had and loved.

—Alan Arkin

• • •

I learned from Bernie that art is more important than money—but not by much. I learned that to be a good producer you have to know everything you can possibly know or hire someone who does. From Bernie, I learned the lessons of Moliere, Ibsen, and Shakespeare. Of course, Bernie learned these first-hand. From Bernie, I learned to marry a woman much smarter and much prettier than me. For Bernie and me that was actually pretty easy to do.

—Joe Keefe

shows.) Also, after eighteen months of productions, we were getting tired, especially Paul Sills, who'd directed most of the shows.

In early spring of 1955, the fire department descended. To this day, some people believe it's because we were suspected of being fellow-travelers and possibly even communists in that Joseph McCarthy era. Among other things, we'd started at the University of Chicago, which had been labeled "pinko" by anti-communist government investigators of the time. Quite a few of us came under suspicion because we were poor but Jewish. Also, we'd produced works by Brecht, who'd recently lied to the House Un-American Activities Committee, fleeing the country the next day to take up residence in communist East Berlin; and we'd just done an original play called *Rich But Happy*. Whatever started the investigation, we were certainly in violation of the outmoded fire codes and had been all along, and they closed us down. We did a few shows in rented spaces, but the spirit was gone, as were many of the original ensemble.

The Compass

During the nearly two years of Playwrights, we'd worked on Viola Spolin's improv games with her son Paul Sills whenever we could. Viola herself, who was living in L.A., came in toward the end, when excitement was building about opening David Shepherd's political cabaret theater. She arrived just in time to do improv workshops and help form the ensemble that became the first company of the new place, which David decided to call The Compass because he wanted it to point in whichever direction society was already going.

It was to be informal and close to where people lived so they could come without dressing up, where there'd be food and drink, and where they'd see shows dealing with the life they led, rather than

An improvised scene from the pre-Compass days. From left to right: Larry Kerkel, Roger Bowen, Sid Lazard, Ned Gaylin, and Leo Stodolsky

the illusions, dreams, and lies being put out by Hollywood, New York, and Washington. David wanted to open it in a working-class neighborhood in Gary, Indiana, a steel-mill town an hour's drive from Chicago, or in the neighborhood of Chicago's stockyards; fortunately (though not from David's point of view) neither of those worked out.

Fred Wranovics, a popular bartender at the Woodlawn Tap (known as Jimmy's) on 55th Street in the University of Chicago neighborhood, had just bought the Hi-Hat Lounge, also on 55th Street, and had also bought the empty store next door. After knocking a hole in the wall between the two buildings, the Compass ensemble, with a lot of hard work—especially by Andrew Duncan—converted the empty store into a playing space. The storefront windows were left unblocked so passersby could see the show—an excellent way of getting them inside. Fred re-christened the place The Compass Tavern, and the show opened on July 5, 1955. (It was supposed to open on the Fourth, but the air conditioner broke down.)

Paul Sills directed all the shows the first summer, and David Shepherd was the producer and one of the performers. Among the many performers that summer along with David and Andrew Duncan were Roger Bowen, Barbara Harris, and Elaine May.

The Compass began with a format that included a short opening piece or two to get the audience laughing, followed by "The Living Newspaper"—twenty minutes of improvs on and narrated reenactments of articles in that day's paper. Then came a fifty-minute or so, nine- to twelve-scene, politically or socially conscious play created from a written scenario—a scene-by-scene breakdown, usually without any of the dialogue—which was then improvised out by the cast in rehearsals and even in performance. The scenarios dealt with such subjects as teenage parental and peer pressure, high-powered salesmen, tax evasion, and the University neighborhood itself. (It was because he couldn't find new plays and playwrights to suit his purposes that David Shepherd settled on the idea of improvised scenarios instead.)

At the conclusion of the act, the actors would take suggestions from the audience in such categories as political events, authors, pet peeves, and so on and, after a short break, do a set of improvisations based on the suggestions. All this, done with some chairs and hats as the only props, was performed five nights a week, two shows on Friday, three on Saturday, with a new "Living Newspaper" every day and a new scenario every week or two.

David Shepherd and business manager Charley Jacobs moved the show on October 1, 1955, to The Compass at the Dock on Lake Park Avenue near 53rd Street, a larger space on the fringe of the University of Chicago area. There were some changes in the personnel: Paul Sills had gone to England on a Fulbright, taking his then-wife Barbara Harris with him; Roger Bowen was about to be drafted; David Shepherd was now the director; and Elaine May was running the improv workshops and performing along with Andrew Duncan and a company enhanced by the arrival of, among others, Mike Nichols and Severn Darden.

Andrew Duncan and Barbara Harris act out a story about women's fashion during a "Living Newspaper" scene.

Spotlight on
Sheldon Patinkin

I was production manager, musical director, box office manager, occasional assistant director, and very occasional actor at Playwrights while working toward my M.A. in English Literature at the University of Chicago. I worked on my Ph.D. until nearly a year after Second City opened, even though my desires lay elsewhere. (My parents were of the belief that if you weren't going to be a doctor, lawyer, or accountant, you could at least be a teacher.)

In November 1960, Bernie Sahlins called and asked if I wanted to be the manager of Second City and sort of assist Paul Sills as well. Since, by then, I was getting a stomachache every time I walked on the University of Chicago campus, I jumped at the offer. Six months later, I'd quit grad school, much to my parents' consternation. (It wasn't until my name started appearing in newspaper columns and relatives started calling them to try to get Saturday night tickets that they were able to accept my decision.)

One day, Paul Sills, back from New York to direct, was yelling at the actors more than usual, then finally turned around and said, "See what you can do with them, Sheldon," and walked out. Usually when he did that, he would come back after a while. After about half an hour, he hadn't come back. I called Bernie at home and asked if he knew where Paul was. Bernie said he was on a plane back to New York and that I was now the director. And that's how I became the artistic director. As director, I tended to depend more on ideas the actors came up with for material than did most of my predecessors and successors, out of a strong (and sometimes mistaken) belief that it really had to come out of them.

I remained artistic director until 1968, by which time I was getting a stomachache every time it was time to start rehearsals for a new show. By then, I'd directed about fifteen shows, plus

Sheldon Patinkin served as artistic director of Second City from 1960–1968.

touring company shows, a couple of our shows in New York, a couple of our shows at the Royal Alexandra in Toronto, including occasionally cooking the hamburgers, selling the tickets, seating the customers, and even filling in for the pianist a few times. I'd also begun teaching improv workshops.

In 1972, I moved to Toronto, where I directed a couple of shows at Second City, organized and taught classes, directed a few shows and revues in other places, acted in some commercials (for the money), and was one of the associate producers and writers for the first season of *SCTV*.

I moved back to Chicago in 1978. Since then, I've directed a couple more shows at Second City in Chicago and Toronto, helped form the first Second City Training Center, and am now Second City's artistic consultant.

In 1980, I took the job as chair of and a teacher in the theater department at Columbia College Chicago, where I still am. (We're now the largest theater department in the country, possibly the world, though we're not sure about China.) I'm also the acting faculty of the Lyric Opera Center for American Artists, director of the summer workshops at Steppenwolf Theatre, and I occasionally direct a play either at school or around town.

I doubt that I'll ever be talked into directing another Second City show. I'm too old, it's too hard, and I'm afraid of the stomachache returning.

Although I had directed numerous shows before arriving at 1616 North Wells, I soon found that none of my previous experience was adequate preparation for the singular process of staging a Second City revue. That's where Sheldon came in. He helped define the role of a director at Second City. He taught me that every scene should be about something and to trust the performers' instincts, because, at Second City, the actors are also the writers. If the choice the director is advocating feels wrong to the performer, then it is most likely wrong for the scene—and, therefore, will not ultimately serve the show. And, although it took me a couple of revues to learn this lesson, this simple advice has never betrayed me. With the exception of Bernie [Sahlins] and Joyce [Sloane], no individual has made a greater or more enduring contribution to Second City than Sheldon. Second City has always been a place to learn how to act, improvise, write, direct, and—sadly—move on. Sheldon's greatest influence has been as Second City's resident teacher. He is the most intelligent person I've ever met, yet he never makes me feel dumb. And he is generous with his ideas—he is constantly giving them away. Unlike most of us, however, I have never heard him ask for anything in return. By teaching everyone who has worked at the place—directly or indirectly—he has made the most important contribution of all: he has protected the artistic integrity of the work.

—Tom Gianas

● ● ●

Sheldon's the only person I know who gets younger. He's nine years younger now than he was when we met forty years ago.

—Alan Arkin

Mike Nichols and Elaine May formed their highly successful comedy team after leaving The Compass; it was popular in nightclubs, on radio, TV, on Broadway, and on records. (Comedy records became very big in the late 1950s and 60s; Mike and Elaine's *Improvisations with Music* was the first to be a bestseller). Mike went on to become the director of such plays as *Barefoot in the Park*, *The Odd Couple*, *Plaza Suite*, and *Hurlyburly*, and such movies as *Who's Afraid of Virginia Woolf?*, *The Graduate*, *Catch-22*, *Carnal Knowledge*, *Silkwood*, *Working Girl*, *Biloxi Blues*, *The Birdcage*, and *Primary Colors*. Elaine, who studied with Viola Spolin in L.A. when she was a kid, has been in several movies, including *Luv*, *California Suite*, and *Small Time Crooks*. She wrote and directed such movies as *A New Leaf* (which she also starred in with Walter Matthau) and *Ishtar*, and directed *The Heartbreak Kid*. Elaine has written several successful plays and has written or rewritten many hit movies, including *Tootsie*, *The Birdcage*, and *Primary Colors*.

When Severn Darden took an extended break, Shelley Berman replaced him and stayed on after Severn returned. Shelley Berman, like so many Compass and Second City players, began his career as an actor, not an improviser or a comedian, although, before joining The Compass, he'd done some freelance comedy writing for *The Tonight Show* when Steve Allen was the host. When The Compass closed in Chicago, Shelley began his career as a nightclub monologist, usually doing his end of phone conversations, a talent he developed while at The Compass. He became very famous in clubs, on TV, and on several bestselling records. After his popularity as a stand-up waned, he continued and continues doing theater and TV.

David Shepherd also decided they needed a pianist at the new Compass space. Allaudin (then William) Mathieu got the job.

By the time the company was performing at the Dock, the scenarios were getting more and more difficult and exhausting to create; and it was getting to a point where nobody liked anyone else's ideas for them, although Elaine May, in particular, kept coming up with new ones. At the same time, shorter, usually two-person behavioral scenes, many created in the improv sets, were proving to be repeatable, and Shelley Berman was already getting comfortable doing the phone monologues that eventually made him famous. Soon the show was usually two acts of scenes, with a set of improvs from audience suggestions at the end of the evening, which is still the basic Second City format. The material was, by now, rarely political; even "The Living Newspaper" had become "The Living Magazine." The show was mostly social satire, parody, and behavioral scenes. (They were called "people scenes" then and through the early years of Second City, which now calls them "relationship scenes.")

Allaudin Mathieu recalls the influence The Compass had:

There were many who came to see us who recognized The Compass as not only a new level of freedom in making theater, but also, more tellingly, a new level of creative social thought. We were the darlings of the University cognoscenti, especially the social scientists. One day, a scene of Mike [Nichols] and Elaine [May]'s even came up for discussion in my Social Sciences II class at the University. Something new was clearly in the air, something people found entertaining, intellectually stimulating, and useful in their lives.

Compass shows started running a good deal longer than a week or two each, but business was not great. In May 1956, David moved the show to the Argo Off-Beat Room on Broadway near Devon, on the other side of town, very far away from the University. By then, along with Mike Nichols, Elaine May, Shelley Berman, and Andrew Duncan, the cast included Mark and Bobbi Gordon, and music was now supplied by the Eddie Baker Trio. The show had become more professional in look and feel and was mostly two-person "people" scenes, occasional short scenarios, and Shelley's monologues. In July, Barbara Harris rejoined the

Mike Nichols as Tennessee Williams onstage at The Compass in 1955.

company, Paul Sills directed again for a while, a few other people came, a few went, and the show closed in January 1957. The now legendary and highly influential Compass had played in Chicago for only eighteen months, about the same length of time as Playwrights, although most audience members who remember those days are surprised when they're reminded that's all it was.

Meanwhile, in October 1956, Bernie Sahlins produced a season of plays at the Studebaker Theatre in downtown Chicago. (It's now part of the Fine Arts, a multiplex movie theater.) Among the shows were *Desire under the Elms, Summer and Smoke, Androcles and the Lion*, and the Chicago premiere of *Waiting for Godot*, with Mike Nichols as Lucky and Andrew Duncan as the boy (Harvey Korman was also in it). Bernie brought in name actors and directors to work with local talent. (Geraldine Page became a major

Backstage Pass

In late 1955, I found my way to Jimmy's Bar on 55th Street to audition for intermission pianist. Roger Bowen and a woman were onstage improvising a scene. They were apparently on the deck of a cruise liner, and the man, trying to pick up the woman, was casting about for an interesting activity that would engage their mutual interest. He placed two chairs side by side, and they stood on them, so as to be able to look down the ship's funnels. "What are those black things down there?" asked the woman with a shudder. "Those are the filters," answered the man, turning full-face to gaze wistfully at her, "like the hairs in your nose." I was impressed beyond words; the situation was so absurdly comical. Later, I did audition for David Shepherd, who heard a few bars and asked if I wanted to be the intermission pianist for The Compass Theater at The Dock, opening in a few weeks—five dollars a night, drinks at cost. I said yes. It never occurred to anyone, least of all me, that the club pianist should become part of the show. Once, for an improv with Elaine May set in a Parisian café, Mike Nichols asked if I would play "La Vie en Rose" in the background. It was the first time I'd been asked to accompany the action on stage, but I was so intent on playing the song correctly, I didn't follow the scene and played too loudly. Mike inserted into the dialogue a request to the café pianist to soften the music so the customers could hear themselves talk.

—Allaudin Mathieu

Del Close

Opposite page: Del Close willed his skull to the Goodman Theatre for use as Yorick in productions of Hamlet.

There are hundreds, perhaps thousands, of stories about Del, possibly only equaled by the number about Severn Darden. Del joined the Second City cast in 1961, having already done The Compass in St. Louis and his own stand-up act, and was in and out of the cast for several years, as well as directing the twelfth show, *20,000 Frozen Grenadiers or There's Been a Terrible Accident at the Factory*, and making such records as *How to Speak Hip* with John Brent, and *The Do-It-Yourself Psychoanalysis Kit*. Drugs eventually got the better of him and he left Chicago in 1964. (He finally gave them up in memory of John Belushi).

Del soon hooked up with The Committee, an improvisation group in San Francisco. It was there he invented the long-form improv he called "The Harold." He returned to Chicago in 1972, directed several more Second City shows and became one of the most important improv teachers in town. He also wrote comic books, pursued a successful acting career onstage and in a few films, including *The Untouchables*, was an advisor for *Saturday Night Live*, and joined Charna Halpern in running the Chicago ImprovOlympic where, among other kinds of comedy, teams compete in "Harolds." Many soon-to-be Second Citizens studied with Del, and The Upright Citizens Brigade first met and formed their ensemble in his classes.

Del, in an earlier life, had learned to eat fire. He once ate fire for a benefit being held at Second City. He wasn't at his best that evening and, as he was leaving the stage after doing his trick, the whole audience heard him saying, "Ice, gentlemen, ice!" He ended up in the hospital.

Del tried committing suicide one night while he was still a performer in the company. He did it shortly before curtain time so that we'd be sure to notice he was missing in time to save him, which we did, and got him to the E.R. to get his stomach pumped. The hospital authorities were insistent that he'd have to be committed, at least for observation, and they were going to send him to County. Bernie called a friend who called a friend, and we got Del committed to a private sanatorium about eight miles south of Second City. After a few days, we were informed that, if either Bernie or I was willing to come to the sanitorium, check Del out, take him to Second City, and bring him back to the sanitorium after the show, he could start performing again. So for several weeks it fell to Bernie or—usually—me to do exactly that six nights a week.

Once, John Candy and I helped Del move out of his apartment hotel room in Toronto when he was going back to Chicago. We found that he'd been using one of his dresser drawers as his kitty litter box, which he emptied into the toilet before we left for the airport early the next morning. Second City is banned from that apartment hotel to this day.

Del's marriage in the mid-1960s was a Buddhist ceremony. It didn't last. In the 1980s, he had an altar dedicated to Zeus in his apartment and would sometimes have his students invoke Zeus, sometimes Satan, before doing an improv.

Del died in 1999 at the age of sixty-four after holding a "living wake" in the hospital the night before he died, with saxophone players, white chocolate martinis, and a pagan ceremony. He willed his skull to Chicago's Goodman Theatre for use as Yorick in any productions they might do of *Hamlet*, with the understanding that his name would be listed in the credits. According to Charna Halpern, his last words were, "I'm tired of being the funniest person in the room."

It depended what cycle you got Del in. You never knew if you were going to get the most brilliant human being on the planet or this nightmare from hell. He was ectoplasmic, ever-changing, ever-revolving. He demanded excellence and would take you apart brick by brick. He would come back and throw shit at you if he thought you were not doing good work. He demanded that you be smart, that you be topical— you could not get away with just phoning it in. You had to be breaking new barriers all the time.

—Tim Kazurinsky

One of the things that he said to me that I loved was, "Don't ask for justice on the stage, create it." I'm not saying morality, but do justice, do right by the character you're playing.

—Kevin Dorff

Del stripped naked to show me his "track suit" just after Bernie Sahlins had talked me into signing a contract. All Bernie said was, "And this is your director…"

—Meagan Fay

Top to bottom: (left to right) Theodore J. Flicker, Joan Darling, Tom Aldredge, and George Segal • Alan Arkin, Jerry Stiller, Nancy Ponder, and Anne Meara

Compass fan while she was starring in three plays at the Studebaker.) Bernie also brought in the not-very-well-known actress Vicki Cummings to star in a production of Aristophanes' *Lysistrata*, which Paul took over directing about a week before opening. The cast for the show also included Eugene Troobnick, Andrew Duncan, Barbara Harris, and Elaine May, with Mike Nichols as leader of the men's chorus and Severn Darden as leader of the women's chorus. With that cast, it was hardly a traditional production of a classic Greek comedy, whatever that might be. Claudia Cassidy, the famed and feared critic of the *Chicago Tribune*, called it the worst production of the play in two thousand years.

On April 2, 1957, David Shepherd and his new partner Ted Flicker reopened the Compass at the Crystal Palace in St. Louis, by invitation of the owner, Fred Landesman. The cast was Ted, Nancy Ponder, Jo Henderson, and Del Close. During the summer, Jo Henderson left, Ted was in New York a lot working with David on trying to get a booking there, and Mike Nichols, Elaine May, and Severn Darden joined the cast. The show closed in September, presumably to reopen in New York, but the New York booking fell through so Mike and Elaine started their nightclub act. (Shelley Berman had already started his in Chicago.)

Ted Flicker opened his own New York improv place, The Premise, in November 1960 (eleven months after Second City opened). Among those who worked there during The Premise's more than three-year run were George Segal, Buck Henry, Gene Hackman, and Godfrey Cambridge. Ted Flicker later directed several movies including *The President's Analyst*, both wrote and directed for *The Dick Van Dyke Show* and *The Andy Griffith Show*, and was one of the creators of the sitcom *Barney Miller*. In 1964, Elaine May directed *The Third Ear* at The Premise, with a cast that included Peter Boyle (who later joined Second City in Chicago), former Compass performers Mark Gordon and Reni Santoni, Louise Lasser, and Renee Taylor.

David Shepherd produced other incarnations of The Compass in various places, using such performers as Alan Alda, Alan Arkin, Jack Burns, Diana Sands, and Jerry Stiller and Anne Meara, who formed their own act after leaving The Compass. They were soon popular in clubs, on records, and on TV, including a number of very funny commercials. Along with doing a lot of stage work, Anne has been seen on many TV shows, was a regular on *All My Children* and *Fame*, and was the title character in the TV series *Kate McShane*. She's also been in such movies as *The Boys from Brazil*, *Awakenings*, and *Kiss of Death*. Jerry's also been in several movies, including *Airport, Seize the Day,* and *Hairspray.* He's made many TV appearances and is probably best known as George Costanza's father Frank on *Seinfeld.* He is now a regular on the sitcom *King of Queens.* Jerry and Anne's son Ben Stiller is the star of such movies as *Flirting with Disaster, Reality Bites* (along with his parents), and *There's Something about Mary.*

In the late 1950s, nightclubbing was very popular, and comedy records were selling in the millions. Soon and suddenly, Mike Nichols and Elaine May were famous as a team, and Shelley Berman as a single. Moreover, comedy was changing: more personal, more laid-back, filled with ideas, characters, and stories rather than jokes. Some of it—Mort Sahl especially and Lenny Bruce eventually—was even political. Severn Darden and Del Close started doing stand-up acts. Paul Sills and his friend Howard Alk, who'd made occasional appearances at The Compass, got jobs at The Gate of Horn, a popular Chicago folk music and comedy club where Lenny Bruce appeared frequently.

Paul was house manager, and Howard ran the lights. They began talking a lot between themselves and with others about starting another Compass-like place in Chicago. Although David Shepherd was firmly into other ways of doing things and not interested in joining up, he gave them his blessings—though not the name—and whatever help he could supply from afar. ● ● ●

Jerry Stiller (left), Nancy Ponder, and Alan Arkin (right) spoof science fiction at The Compass on Gaslight Square in St. Louis, 1960.

Few areas of comedy or acting in general haven't been at least partly influenced by The Compass, Second City, and the work of Paul Sills, David Shepherd, and Viola Spolin.

Viola Spolin, as a teacher and through her seminal book *Improvisation for the Theater*, is the source of the work done by The Compass and Second City and their children and grandchildren. She developed her improv games as drama supervisor at Hull House, teaching children as part of the Recreational Project of the WPA. The book is also a standard text in many high school and college theater classes. The games are used in other fields as well, from social work to business management. Paul Sills and Viola's 1966 Game Theatre was, of course, the ancestor of today's burgeoning industry in improv clubs of various kinds, where the improvs are often treated as if they were competitive sporting events, which is about as far from the intentions of the games as you can get.

The improvisational games aren't games in the sense of winning and losing, and they aren't about being funny. They're about being in the moment; they're about being totally present to each other onstage—being "in play." If the rule of the game is that you have to mime eating a Thanksgiving dinner while having a continuous conversation without once mentioning food or the activities involved in eating, like "pass the cranberries," then that's what you have to do in order to have successfully played the game. And always work to serve your fellow players.

All the time Paul Sills was at Second City, he and Viola Spolin taught improv workshops, and then so did I, and so did Josephine Raciti Forsberg. Jo was an actor back at Playwrights who later became a student and disciple of Viola's. She began teaching workshops at Second City in the mid-1960s and later began our children's theater. Jo then created the Players Workshop at Second City, which she moved to its own space when the Second City

Viola Spolin teaches a group of aspiring actors about the art of improvisation. Alan Arkin is third from the left.

Training Center opened. Among the many people Jo taught were Bill Murray, George Wendt, Shelley Long, Robert Townsend, and even the late Brandon Tartikoff. Jo has sort of retired, and Players Workshop is now being run by her daughter Linnea.

Until Martin de Maat (Jo Forsberg's nephew and one of the foremost improv teachers in North America), Cheryl Sloane (Joyce's daughter), and I started the Second City Training Center in 1986, the only full-time place where you could study improvisational techniques was Jo Forsberg's Players Workshop.

The Second City Training Center has a beginning program, a Conservatory program, and a writing program. The beginning program is open to anyone interested in learning about improv. The Conservatory program is geared toward would-be pros and is entered through auditions. These students move through several different levels, each focusing on a different aspect of how to be a Second City performer, culminating in the presentation of a one-act revue of their own material. The writing program serves as a learning place for both performers and non-performers. (Many Second City alums have become TV writers: well over a dozen have written for *Saturday Night Live*; Jon Glaser and Brian Stack write for *Late Night* with Conan O'Brien; and Jenna Jolovitz has written for *MadTV* and *King of Queens*.)

Today, you can't swing a dead cat in Chicago without hitting an improv class. In addition to Second City and Player's Workshop, the late Del Close and Charna Halpern's ImprovOlympic has become an important school for long-form improvisation; Mick Napier's Annoyance Productions has its own take on the work and maintains a long waiting list for classes. And there are many more. However, The Second City Training Center is the largest and most well-known school of its kind. In the spring of 2000, the Chicago Training Center alone had an enrollment of more than nine hundred students per term. Nearly thirty instructors—many of them former or current cast members—were teaching seventy-five classes. Programs in Toronto, Detroit, New York, L.A., and Cleveland add almost another thousand students to the list of people using improv-based techniques to further their artistic and professional goals.

Only a handful of people will get into a Second City company. Quite a few of the others, especially in Chicago, will go off and form their own comedy acts and competitive comedy teams. There are lots of places for both studying and performing improv in Chicago now, several of them started in rebellion against Second City. Even in comedy or, perhaps especially in comedy, rebellion against one's elders is normal.

Backstage Passes

Paul Sills asked me to join Viola's workshop. Me, Dick Schaal, Hamilton Camp, Del Close, and John Brent—we worked with her every day. It was a five-days-a-week thing. She always had food for us. I carry that tradition on in my workshop; I bring food so that when the actors get a little low on energy, they can have something to come back with. She fed us as well as nurtured us in other ways. The most important thing she taught me was the necessity of being open and creative and true in everything you do.

—Avery Schreiber

When we asked Viola about particular points of improv games, she said, "I really don't know how that game goes—or any of them, really. I was in a state of revelation when I wrote them." I believe that, because everything about the games informs Second City, it informs interpretive work. It's about the job that the actor has to do. It's about being present, about being in play, about being an ensemble because of that combined energy. I think that's why Second City is enduring and probably will endure. It has that fluidity. It's connected to the art.

—Joyce Piven

The training at Second City—having to whip through scenes, putting them on stage and having them fail—teaches you that each idea isn't so important, it's knowing that you can create more ideas. That's really important in a room when you're writing TV comedy with people—not to suffer each pitch, but to be free enough to offer more things.

—Jenna Jolovitz

Chapter **2**

Second city Opens

A New Concept in Theater

By the end of the 1950s, Kennedy and Nixon were the front-runners for the next presidency of the United States. Alaska and Hawaii became the forty-ninth and fiftieth states.

Things were loosening up from the conformism of the 1950s, at least in the arts. The Post Office ban on D.H. Lawrence's sexually explicit 1928 novel Lady Chatterley's Lover was finally lifted. Among the influential new books were Günter Grass' The Tin Drum, Philip Roth's Goodbye, Columbus, Saul Bellow's Henderson, the Rain King, and William S. Burroughs' Naked Lunch. New plays included such landmarks as the first play by an African-American woman on Broadway—Lorraine Hansberry's A Raisin in the Sun—

Howard Alk, after leaving Second City, became firmly entrenched in the New York counterculture scene while devoting himself to independent filmmaking as a writer, editor, and director. He made the 1971 documentary *The Murder of Fred Hampton* about the charismatic Black Panther leader who was murdered by Chicago cops. He wrote and directed

the popular 1975 bio-pic of Janis Joplin, *Janis: A Film*, and was editor of Bob Dylan's *Renaldo and Clara* in 1978. Other editing credits include *You Are What You Eat*.

Allaudin Mathieu remembers Howard's influence on him: "Howard turned me on to dexy pills, then had to calm me down backstage. 'Be cool, Bill.' I thought of him at first as a kind of night-worker in the Intellectual Mafia, but after the actual Mafia bombed Second City for refusing to pay protection, Howard showed up to work packing a piece and peeking out of the newly replaced windows from behind the velvet curtains, like a film-noir scene."

Howard died in 1982.

Opening page (left to right): Paul Sand, Mina Kolb, and Eugene Troobnick

and Edward Albee's first play, The Zoo Story. *The two biggest hit musicals of the year were an odd pair: Ethel Merman's last new show,* Gypsy, *a tough and bawdy look at the American dream as reflected in the true story of a family during the last days of vaudeville who must play burlesque in order to make it, and Rodgers and Hammerstein's last show,* The Sound of Music.

Pop music was getting schizophrenic with Rodgers and Hammerstein's "Climb Every Mountain," Frank Sinatra's "High Hopes," and Elvis Presley's "A Big Hunk of Love" among the top hits of the year.

Provocative new films from Europe were the hits of the art-house theaters, including Federico Fellini's La Dolce Vita, *and the beginnings of the French "New Wave" in cinema: Francois Truffaut's* The 400 Blows *and Jean-Luc Godard's* Breathless. *Hollywood, too, was loosening up with films like Otto Preminger's* Porgy and Bess, *George Stevens'* The Diary of Anne Frank, *and Billy Wilder's* Some Like It Hot, *though more typical were William Wyler's* Ben Hur *and Disney's* Sleeping Beauty. *TV, of course, wasn't loosening up at all; the highest-rated shows of the year included* Gunsmoke, Father Knows Best, *and* Perry Mason. *Most network programming was out of Hollywood now, and hardly anything in prime time was still being broadcast live.*

But, in mid-December 1959, The Second City opened.

The First Year

Paul Sills and Howard Alk, both now having had experience running a night club, and Bernie Sahlins, who still had some money, opened The Second City in mid-December. They'd originally intended it as a coffeehouse where friends and other people could just sit around and talk, but then they decided they might as well put on a little show as well. Bernie was the producer and Paul the director; he directed the first six shows. (David Shepherd, Mike Nichols, and Del Close were among those who spelled Paul for a few days each during the rehearsals of those shows to give Paul a much-needed break.) The original eight performers were Howard Alk, Roger Bowen, Severn Darden, Andrew Duncan, Barbara Harris, Mina Kolb, Eugene Troobnick, and Allaudin Mathieu.

According to Andrew Duncan, Second City "was to be a lot like Compass, but more finished. We talked at that time about it being much more of a cabaret in the German sense and that it would hit politics much more" (Sweet, 1978).

We used the first of the two basically uninhabitable floors above the theater at 1842 North Wells as a dressing room, entered through a separate street door or from backstage. And we opened a summer beer garden in the vacant lot next door north, where we eventually also served ice cream and showed silent movies.

Within a few months, first Roger Bowen and then Howard Alk left the show. Howard continued as one of the producers, mostly just in name, and Roger continued sending in material, usually political in nature. They were replaced by Paul Sand and Alan Arkin. My first day at the club was the same day as Alan Arkin's (sometimes we referred to Second City as the "club," sometimes as the "theater." Nowadays it's always the theater). Most of us lived in the neighborhood, a few at a deservedly inexpensive rooming house (one dollar a day) around the corner run by a woman named Emma. Emma's was dark and dismal, with no cooking privileges and the bathroom down the hall—a good place for nurturing your angst, but otherwise a place you were usually glad to get out of to go to work.

Viola Spolin moved back to Chicago in 1960 to run the cast workshops and took up residence at the Lincoln Hotel (now a Days Inn), kitty-corner from the theater (David Mamet also lived there for a while later on, as did several Second City performers).

"The Compass scenarios," said Roger Bowen, "all seemed to have a theme in common—how society molds people into the shape it wants them to take. Now this is interesting because it characterizes society as an intelligent force with direction. Whereas the kind of picture you got of society at Second City a couple years later was that society was a blind, meaningless, unintelligent automaton and people would just get lost in it. Second City was about alienation" (Sweet). We began the first show on December 16, 1959, with Barbara Harris in a spotlight singing "Everybody's in the Know": Ⓒⅅ

> Everybody's in the know but me,
> Knows who Eisenhower has to tea;
> Knows what's wrong with education,
> Specialization, automation;
> Are clear as to what they would have done
> Had they been tempted by Twenty-One.
> Me, I'm not so sure of myself.
> No, I don't have it all clear.
> But
> If you don't like your drink,
> The next one will taste better…

Allaudin Mathieu, who composed the music for those lyrics, remembers his initiation into Second City:

Spotlight on
Roger Bowen

Roger Bowen wrote the outline for a stage story, "Enterprise," that was developed, through improvisation, by a group of University of Chicago actors into a play. By demonstrating the power of the improvisational techniques, this play served as the impetus for David Shepherd to create The Compass.

Roger excelled at playing pretentious characters at Second City. He was a pioneer in developing new improvisational forms, most notably the press conference in which audience members lobbed questions to him, playing President Eisenhower, one of his best roles.

Roger left Second City after the first show, but continued sending in scripts. He returned for a show in 1961, which is when he met his wife, Ann Raim Bowen, and then worked at The Committee in San Francisco for a while. After that he mostly pursued a writing career, including being the author of eleven novels. He appeared frequently on TV, but his most famous movie role was as Colonel Henry Blake in the 1970 movie *M*A*S*H*. Through improvisation, he and Gary Burghoff came up with the idea of Radar repeating Blake's orders almost as he was giving them. His last role was in *What About Bob?* with Bill Murray. Roger died in 1996.

Severn Darden's full name was Francis Xavier Severn Teakel Darden Jr. His father had been district attorney of New Orleans. He was an intellectual clown. What may define Second City clowns most clearly is that they're the ones audiences start laughing at by the second time they see them in the show, regardless of what's happening in the scene. The audience feels really comfortable laughing with or at them. Being a clown isn't anything that can be taught, and it can't be trained into you, either. It's part of your personality, your charisma, your sense of yourself, and you carry it with you wherever you go.

He was famous on the University of Chicago campus long before he became a performer at Compass and Second City. As a student, he drove around in an old Rolls Royce and often wore formal clothes (always with tennis shoes). The most famous of the dozens of stories about his antics at the University of Chicago is about the night he invaded Rockefeller Chapel, and when the guard saw him, he escaped through a side door shouting, "Sanctuary!" like Quasimodo, then hid out in a girls' dorm.

He once showed up at a fancy Chicago hotel in a sweatshirt, with a hard-boiled egg in a bag. At the hotel's lobby cafe, he asked for coffee to drink with his egg. The waiter refused, so Severn walked out of the hotel, blew a whistle he had dangling around his neck, and a friend pulled up in a Rolls and drove off with him.

He made one record, *The Sound of My Own Voice*, now a collector's item among comedy aficionados. He didn't like doing a solo act; even his record has other Second City people joining him.

Severn chewed on handkerchiefs, napkins, or anything else at hand, including, occasionally, people. During a full-cast press conference at the theater one afternoon, uncomfortable as usual at being interviewed, he polished the piano with a rag he'd found backstage. Since the polishing was finished before the press conference, he then sat on the stage floor chewing the rag.

Severn had the quickest mind imaginable; one of his favorite characters was the German professor who was an expert in whatever subject the audience suggested, Dr. Walter von der Vogelweide. The name came from a real medieval German tradesman, one of the title characters in Wagner's opera *The Mastersingers of Nuremberg*. Even in real life, Severn seemed a bit like an absent-minded professor, although he was anything but.

After Second City, Severn appeared often on TV and in movies, including a couple of the *Planet of the Apes* movies and, most famously, as the Russian in *The President's Analyst*. And he married Paul Sills' sister-in-law Heather. Severn died in 1995.

"Although scenes became set as we repeated them," remembers Shelley Berman, "there was no way that Severn would not surprise you. He was a true improvisationist."

Top to bottom: Darden bursts onto the scene in a creative way. • Darden has a run-in with the law during a scene from My Friend Art Is Dead.

Backstage Passes

Severn pinched my boobies the first time I met him. It was just madness. I could never relate to Severn. He wore a cape and carried a walking stick. He had a machine that projected the constellations on his ceiling. If you went to his house, you had to lie on your back and look up.

—Joan Rivers

• • •

Three days after my arrival in Chicago in 1961, Severn gently asked permission to tie me to a lamppost. "Why not?" I said. He then pulled out a rope. So this is Second City?

—Ann Raim Bowen

• • •

Severn could unhinge fellow actors because, while presenting a relatively normal visage to the audience, he could simultaneously twist his upstage profile into any of the Japanese mask repertoire. More than once did I leave my onstage seat more than a little moist.

—Judy Graubart

• • •

All Second City performers are good, but Severn Darden most personifies the quintessential Second City talent. One night he was in the audience and joined us in the set. He took off on one of the most imaginative improvs I've ever seen. Afterwards he said, "Boy, that was a bomb." It was then I felt I still had a long way to go.

—Fred Willard

Andrew Duncan was the quintessential straight man and interviewer at both The Compass and Second City. The straight man (or woman) is the person audiences feel is most like themselves and who serves as a kind of go-between between them and the comics. Unlike most straight men—Bud Abbott for Lou Costello and Dean Martin for Jerry Lewis, for example—Andrew was himself a little off-center—an Oliver Hardy to Stan Laurel or an Art Carney with Jackie Gleason. He didn't always play the straight role in scenes, as in "Great Books," where he played an

affected but rather stupid student. Because he was also very politically and socially conscious—he'd been a social worker—and had an organized mind, he was the glue that held together every company he was a part of. After his years at Compass and Second City, he did plays, movies, TV, and developed commercials and industrial shows through improvisations.

When I came off the road with The Stan Kenton Orchestra in late 1959, I met my old friend Roger Bowen. He said that a little theater company opening in December was looking for a musician, would I try out? I did, the next day. The moment I walked into the rehearsal and onto the newly built stage of The Second City, Paul Sills handed me a sheet of paper with lyrics on it, and said, "Can you make this into an opening song?"

I said, "Sure."

"Right now?"

"Okay."

There was a brand-new little Wurlitzer spinet tucked into an alcove stage left. I sat down at the keys, played a scale, and looked over the words: "Everybody's in the know but me...." Not bad. I began to tinker with ideas. The actors, only a few inches to my right, continued rehearsing, oblivious to my labors. I was suddenly a cog in a working machine. After five minutes, Paul yelled, "You done yet, Mathieu?" In ten minutes, I had enough to sing for him. Everyone stood in a semicircle around the piano and listened; there was instant acceptance. "Teach it to Barbara," said Paul. The actors broke for lunch. Barbara and I were alone in the theater. She was so drop-dead alluring that I could bear neither to look at her nor to look away. She learned quickly, almost instantaneously, and together we filled in the details of the song. In a few minutes, Paul was back and directing the blocking of the opening sequence. I composed two other songs, plus incidental music for all the scenes. In a week, we were in previews. Even though I was the youngest, I began to feel part of an accepting and engaging company. This was fun.

We opened three more revues during the first year, all well-reviewed and well-attended: *Too Many Hats* (a real backstage problem), *The Third Programme*, and *The Seacoast of Bohemia*. Titles have rarely had anything whatsoever to do with the content of the shows. Severn liked coming up with titles from Shakespeare; the seacoast of Bohemia is, for instance, a Shakespearean location—even though Bohemia doesn't have a seacoast.

It was nearly impossible to just go home and go to bed after a show, even though it was past midnight; the adrenaline was too high. So most nights, many of us would sit around in the theater after the audience was gone, the tables had been bussed, and the wait staff had been checked out and had finished moaning over the size of their tips. Sometimes the front-of-the-house employees would do parodies of the onstage employees and vice versa. Sometimes Allaudin would play and there'd be group singing.

We'd have a drink or two; everyone got a free drink after work. And there'd be talk—such talk—about the next show, about that night's audience, about politics, religion, sex, philosophy, books, movies (especially foreign ones), clothes, gossip, and whatever else anyone wanted to talk about. Opinions differed on almost everything, but rarely did they turn into serious arguments. When whoever was locking up that night wanted to go home, the ones who were left would often move across the street to the Lincoln Hotel for a snack or a meal and more talk.

The Lincoln Hotel had an all-night diner that was a major meeting place and hangout after the show, as well as a relatively cheap and convenient place for breakfast, lunch, or dinner, especially for those who were living at Emma's. The diner served hamburgers on white toast because they refused to carry buns. Steve, the counterman, was known to pull the ketchup bottle out of your hand when he felt you'd had enough or, if you were in a booth near the window, tell you to stop looking out the window and eat your food. And there was Marie, the waitress with sore feet who walked very very slowly and could only manage to carry one thing at a time, for instance, she'd bring you the bread, then the butter. The Lincoln was also a late-night hangout for some middle-rank Mafia types, who were incredibly nice guys once you got past being scared of them.

Paul Sand (left), Mina Kolb, and Eugene Troobnick (right)

Some balmy nights we didn't even get to the Lincoln, we just stood outside the darkened theater to continue talking. I remember two nights in a row in the summer of 1961 a few of us stood outside

Spotlight on Barbara Harris

Barbara Harris joined Playwrights when she was still a seventeen-year-old high-school student, went from there to The Compass, and then into the first Second City cast. Barbara was (and still is) beautiful and

clearly vulnerable. Nearly every man in the audience fell in love with her. An excellent actor with a terrific singing voice, her range of characters at Second City included everything from defensive teenagers to repressed soon-to-be spinsters, from little girls to strippers. After Second City, she starred off-Broadway in *Oh, Dad, Poor Dad, Momma's Hung You in the Closet and I'm Feeling So Sad*, and on Broadway in such shows as *Mother Courage*, *The Apple Tree*, and *On a Clear Day You Can See Forever*. Barbara won a Tony Award, directed plays both on and off-Broadway, and taught both acting and improvisation. Her film career includes roles in *A Thousand Clowns*, *Plaza Suite*, *Nashville* (she sings the song at the end of the movie), *The Seduction of Joe Tynan*, *Dirty Rotten Scoundrels*, and *Gross Pointe Blank*.

Backstage Passes

I remember rehearsals with Paul Sills and Mina Kolb. Paul would be rehearsing us, screaming and yelling and ranting and raving and wanting to plumb the depths of the intellectual climate of Chicago and the country. Mina was the only person in the group who was just sitting there, reading the newspaper. And I think it was the comics! She paid no attention, but it worked.

—Alan Arkin

• • •

Second City is about telling the truth. The reason Mina succeeded, and succeeded so beautifully, was that she always called them as she saw them. She told the truth.

—Bernie Sahlins

• • •

My favorite Second City memory is when Todd Cazeaux, the only male on our wait staff, ran to help some of his customers who were stuck in the snow. When he finally pushed their car out, he came back wet and cold and covered with snow, only to find they did not pay or tip him.

—Barbara Harris

the theater until five in the morning discussing and arguing about Federico Fellini's *La Dolce Vita*, which we'd all just seen.

Allaudin remembers those early days well:

The first few months of The Second City were special in the lives of those who lived it. A new societal mirror was being cast that enabled us all to see ourselves openly and critically in real time. The new theater was based not only on the immediacy of daily social and political life, and the humor to be found in those, but also on trust. The actors had to develop the capacity to tell themselves and each other the truth, and trust the audience to understand and accept it. The audience was in on the act, and as our audiences grew and our fame spread from local to national, the terrific feeling of good work well done grew also. This doesn't mean there weren't harsh words, or even fistfights, because there were, and often. But they didn't last long. What was at stake was too valuable. For me, one of the most important indicators of value was the temperament of the staff—waiters,

Mina Kolb and Avery Schreiber

cooks, ticket-seller, and hatcheck girl. We were all glad to get to work, glad to be in each other's presence, glad to be party to the audience's delight, and, especially, glad to party when the audience went home.

The Second City show was (and still is) a two-act satirical revue made up largely of scenes, blackouts, parodies, musical numbers, and an occasional on-the-spot improv taken from an audience suggestion. We did evening shows at 9:00 and 11:00 plus a set of improvs based on audience suggestions after the second show on Tuesday, Wednesday, Thursday, and Sunday; shows at 9:00 and 11:00 on Friday with no set; and at 9:00, 11:00, and 1:00 plus a set after the third show on Saturday—thirteen shows and five sets a week. It was an incredibly tough schedule, but, as Mina Kolb puts it, "We were young, you know."

In our first theater's very small lobby, which was extremely crowded between shows (especially in winter, when people wouldn't wait outside), there was a ticket-seller sitting at an unenclosed small table and working out of an unhidden small metal cashbox. (Why she was only robbed once is still a mystery.) The ticket table served as our office during the day. Also in the lobby were washrooms and an inadequate coat-check space usually run by a would-be actor who'd frequently get the coats mixed up, especially when it was overcrowded and some of the coats had fallen on the floor.

Past the ticket desk was a short flight of steps leading to (after we knocked a hole in the wall into the first floor of the building next door) the entrance to the theater where the hostess met you and took you to your table. The kitchen, which was also the bar, was through swinging doors behind the audience. The night office was a long, narrow closet behind the kitchen, which also served for liquor storage.

The lobby's and theater's walls were covered with old doors painted black, each door decorated with a glass-framed set of four black-and-white lithographs. The lobby windows were draped with red velvet. The tiny raised stage—it could look crowded when all seven actors were on—was also draped in red velvet. The piano was upstage left (audience right), tucked into a corner where Allaudin sat facing the audience. Since there was no stage-left exit, he was stuck there trying to look interested throughout each act, unable to take any breaks no matter how long a scene without music was, and many scenes were quite long in those days.

Seating capacity was 125, but Violet Torre, the hostess, claimed she could squeeze in 150 if everyone promised to breathe in unison. (It isn't a requirement of Second City that all employees have a sense of humor, but it helps.) The audiences at first were largely well-educated young professionals, many of them graduates of the University of Chicago—doctors, lawyers, psychiatrists, professors—in dressy-casual clothing. They surrounded the stage on three sides, seated on bentwood chairs at black-topped tables. Many of them smoked (not allowed in the theater anymore, though still possible in the bar), and all of them hopefully drank and ate before and during the show. We served half-pound burgers, grilled fresh and served on thick black bread, and pastries from the Bon Ton, a nearby Viennese bakery.

Spotlight on Mina Kolb

Mina Kolb was already a minor local celebrity when she was hired for the first Second City company. She and Ray Raynor had had a five-year run on a local TV show where she and Ray lip-synced live to

records while the teenage kids danced. Mina was not unlike Gracie Allen, a seemingly vague and perhaps even vacant-minded woman whose reasoning was perfectly logical once you accepted her basic premises—which were never like yours or mine. She'd never improvised before Second City.

"I didn't know what was going on," recalls Mina. "I grew up in a little town way out there somewhere. I didn't know what they were talking about. I never understood a word of it. All those people from the University of Chicago—my mother said, 'Don't get close to that.'"

Mina's onstage character was and is so clearly defined that, for a long time, Chicago ad agencies frequently asked for "Mina Kolb types." She eventually moved to Southern California, where she's done movies and TV, and where she still both teaches and performs as an improviser, sharing what she knows with the new kids.

Backstage Passes

Writer/director David Mamet, while still in high school, was the soda jerk and bus boy for Second City one summer. He hated the job, but was able to watch improvs and take workshops, all of which later helped him create his plays, including *Duck Variations*, *Glengarry Glen Ross*, and *Sexual Perversity in Chicago* (which was turned into the movie *About Last Night...*).

—S.P.

• • •

One of my most savored Second City memories was when I was playing Bach (the "Little F Major Prelude") and Barbara Harris was driving the men in the audience wild with a mimed striptease, with Severn Darden and Howard Alk looking on. Severn and Howard had entered arguing about whether or not something unstated could be done. They'd decided to find out, since they had an audience and a piano. They signaled me, and I began playing the Bach piece as Barbara entered and did her mimed strip. When the Bach was over and Barbara had run off-stage, mime semi-nude, Severn said, "You see, you can play Bach in a nightclub and people will listen."

—Allaudin Mathieu

• • •

It was a very repressive time. When we started—along with Lenny Bruce and Dick Gregory and Mort Sahl—we were very subversive. It was really easy because all you had to do was go onstage and say, "Eisenhower," and everyone would have an orgasm because it wasn't done. Now you can say anything.

—Bernie Sahlins

The only entrance onto the stage from backstage was stage right (audience left). Backstage was a long narrow corridor with, on one of the walls, the six rheostat dimmers which controlled all the stage lights. The lights were run by whoever wasn't onstage at

Severn Darden shows Andrew Duncan a midget during a scene at The Second City.

the time. The hostess or one of the wait staff had to squeeze through the audience to get backstage and run the lights for the end of the show and curtain calls.

Although stage-wear has become more informal over the years, in the beginning the men wore ties and brown corduroy suits, and the women wore three-quarter-length, full-skirted, black dresses from Jax, a now defunct fashionable women's store. Hats and a few small props (including many pairs of glasses) and costume pieces (furs, sweaters, and jackets mostly) were on hooks and ledges along the walls backstage, just to make it that much more crowded.

Also on stage were four bentwood chairs like the ones in the audience, helping to bridge the gap between them and the actors. Also bridging the gap and breaking the fourth wall was a lot of direct address to the audience. The show would begin with a mood-setting song or blackout or short scene (now called a "scenette"), followed by Andrew Duncan's welcoming of the audience and introduction to the first scene.

At the far end of the narrow backstage corridor was a door leading to a wider corridor which led to a staircase going up to the dressing room, a totally unpainted, unadorned, cold-in-winter, hot-in-summer room in the semi-decayed building over the club.

Here the cast dressed for the show, rested or argued between shows, and sometimes napped between rehearsals and performances. Rehearsals or Viola Spolin's improv workshops—we called them both workshops—were every day except Monday and sometimes Sunday, usually starting at 10:00 A.M. Everyone did get a few days off after an opening for doing laundry, renewing acquaintance with family and friends, sleeping. (Now rehearsals—and they're called rehearsals—are on Tuesday through Friday unless things are desperate right before an opening; and since we do far fewer new shows a year, we go several weeks without any rehearsals at all after an opening. And these days the cast only does improv workshops as preparation for creating a new show or when there's been a cast change.)

It was also in the upstairs dressing room that the cast planned the improv sets from suggestions taken in such categories as current events, fears, pet peeves, and authors. These fifteen-minute or so planning sessions were usually organized by Andrew Duncan. That night's suggestions, which had been written on a large sheet from a sketch pad, would be hung on the wall, and the actors would call out which ones they wanted to improvise on or which suggestions they wanted to try again and develop as scenes—especially those Paul Sills wanted to see again as possibilities for the next show. Then they gave the set-ups of the new ideas to the others they needed in the scene, and the scenes were put into a running order. Carbons (before the days of photocopiers) of the running order were made for Allaudin Mathieu, for the hostess, and for the kitchen, which needed to know when it was time to give last call and collect the outstanding checks. Meanwhile, those audience members who'd stayed—and it was usually most of them—and those who'd come for the improv set (for which we charged a dollar in the beginning, but which has for many years been free) were hopefully ordering a round of drinks or had gotten hungry and wanted a late snack.

The first time there was an empty table at a show—it was at an eleven o'clock show on a snowy Thursday night about a year after opening—Paul Sills was heard to moan that the end was near.

Breaking the Fourth Wall

Along with Andrew Duncan's welcome and introduction to the show, many scenes during the show—never called sketches or, even worse, skits—had introductions to tell the audience where they took place, to occasionally buy time for setting the stage, and to keep that fourth wall broken. Introductions were given by whoever wasn't changing from the last scene or for the

Spotlight on
Eugene Troobnick

Eugene Troobnick, one of the original producers and company members of Playwrights, played a wide range of characters at Second City. He played Business Man. He played Satan trying to tempt the richest man in the world into selling his soul, but who ends up working for him instead. He played an eager but obtuse University of Chicago theology student trying to learn how to play football. ⓒⒹ He played straight-man teacher to a group of boneheads trying to study the Great Books. He played bums, monkeys, knaves, you name it; Eugene was an accomplished comic character actor. (Character actors tend to disappear inside their characters, so that you don't always recognize them from scene to scene.) Eugene has worked extensively in movies and TV over the last four decades. From 1991–95 he played Stavros Kouperakis on the soap opera *The Guiding Light*. He's been seen in such movies as *All That Jazz*, *Funny Lady*, *California Split*, and *Deconstructing Harry*, as well as appearing on television shows too numerous to mention.

Allaudin Mathieu, the first Compass and Second City pianist/musical director, became a master not only at setting moods with the music he improvised to play scenes in and out, but also became very accomplished at heightening the effectiveness of scenes through occasional underscoring. Allaudin also sometimes played the trumpet in the show. (He'd written for and toured with The Stan Kenton Orchestra after quitting work on his master's in English studies under Norman McLean at the University of Chicago.) Occasionally, he'd play the trumpet with one hand and the piano with the other. He also wrote excellent music for the songs and musical and opera parodies which dotted the Second City shows, and patiently taught them to performers who didn't all learn music easily (though

usually easier than they learned dances). He and the cast also did spot improvs from audience suggestions like "Make-a-Song," "Make-a-Musical," and "Make-an-Opera." And he frequently made the decision about when to end an improvised scene by starting to play under the dialogue. (When the end of a scene hasn't been determined in advance, the decision rests between the pianist and whoever's running the lights.) Allaudin's talents made the same abilities necessary for every Second City pianist after him (except for the trumpet).

next one, or hadn't been onstage in a while. The length of a scene's introduction was determined by how long it would take the actors to get ready. Severn Darden once filled time leaning against the back wall and making strange mouth movements with his lips protruding; after a while, he stopped, stared at the audience, and said, "Poem by a fish," then introduced the scene.

Actors also had the opportunity for direct contact with the audience when they took suggestions once or twice during the show for on-the-spot improvs—like getting a first and last line and then having two actors create the scene in between; or an "Option," where one of the performers stands to the side during an improvised scene and stops the action periodically to ask the audience what happens next. One show closed with an opera improvised on an audience suggestion of a Grimm Brothers' fairy tale. Press conferences were also popular, with the audience as the members of the press asking the questions of people like Kennedy and Khruschev (who spoke in Russian gibberish, which was then translated by an "interpreter"). And, of course, suggestions were taken after the show for the improv sets and sometimes during the set for more spot improvs.

Each scene in the improv set was introduced in order to arrange the chairs and to tell the audience which of their suggestions it was based on. Sometimes an intro in the set becomes a stall while the actors backstage are changing hairdos or outer clothing, or are searching for a prop or a pair of just-the-right eyeglasses. These improvised stalls have occasionally ended up in the show, like Tim Kazurinsky's diatribe on the little mailing piece in his *Time* magazine that makes it all the way through the mail only to fall out of the magazine just as he brings it into his living room.

The following intro was for a scene created from an audience suggestion: "And now we'd like to improvise a scene on your suggestion 'beatnik,' so of course we take you to the Art Institute," which became "Museum Piece," with Alan Arkin as a pseudo-beatnik trying unsuccessfully to pick up a very repressed Barbara Harris. And: "Now, on your suggestion *Oedipus Rex*, we take you to a room somewhere," which turned out to be a Great Books class with four ditzy students and their frustrated teacher discussing the play.

The kinds of things many Second City audiences—and much of the American public—want to see gradually have changed over the years, and our shows reflect the interests, concerns, and reference level of our audiences as well as of our writer/performers and directors. Every scene at Second City really comes from how the audience reacts to it from the first time it's improvised in a set

From left to right: Eugene Troobnick, Barbara Harris, Alan Arkin, Paul Sand, Allaudin Mathieu, Mina Kolb, Severn Darden, and Andrew Duncan

I've written dozens of songs for Second City and The Committee. But there were also the ten thousand cues playing the actors on and off, establishing mood, atmosphere, and context, and supplying references— a vast, amorphous opus of fragments. I think these fragments went a long way toward setting the tone of Second City in the early days, of giving it an eclectic aesthetic, and in helping to make a coherent style out of the diversity of theatrical forms that were arising. And I think the modus was passed intact to my successors, who elaborated on it and expanded it in wonderful, creative ways.

—Allaudin Mathieu

● ● ●

You started to hear a new way, a different version of standup comedy at the same time that Second City was forming. It was a style of comedy that you just hadn't seen before. It presumed that the audience was like you. I presumed that, even though there was a big "them," there was also a pretty vocal "us." And Second City [did] comedy with a very strong point of view. And comedy up until that point... was not about a point of view. It was always being neutral and not offending anybody (Johnson, 1999).

—David Steinberg

(where it usually comes out of an audience suggestion) to the time we're trying it out during previews. Recently, the assumption seems to be that the audience should be laughing from the beginning of a scene. That wasn't necessarily important to the actors in the early days, especially when they were trying to find a relationship (people) scene. (Either way, the percentage of improvs that bombed then was about the same as it is now; it's always been somewhere between forty and fifty percent.) "For the most part," said Harold Ramis, "we get an audience that's reasonably well-educated, maybe more patient than the average television audience and more willing to go on that journey with us, which is one nice thing about working at Second City."

When we first opened, our audiences were largely people who read books, newspapers, and magazines, went to foreign films as well as the better American ones, and were experienced theatergoers. Today they're mostly raised on TV and American movies, and often carry cell phones and pagers they forget to turn off during the show. The change in what many audience members expected to see became most apparent after *Saturday Night Live*, *SCTV*, and *Animal House* got going within a year or so of each other in the late 1970s. They were all heavily publicized as having many Second City alumni in them, and Second City became more of a tourist attraction than it had been. It helped business enormously, but quite a number of our customers expected to see the next Belushi or Radner or Candy or Murray doing the same kind of things they were doing on TV, only uncensored. But in 1960, without the help of movies or TV shows, The Second City had become the hot new thing.

● ● ●

No Second City show is complete without scenes about sex: Alan Arkin as a beatnik trying to pick up Barbara Harris as a repressed virgin at the Art Institute; a father (Severn Darden) finding out about his sixteen-year-old daughter's (Barbara) "First Affair"; Eugene Troobnick trying to impress his date, Mina Kolb, with his (nonexistent) ability to order in Chinese in a Chinese restaurant; an entire cast in top hats and tails singing and dancing to the chauvinist, "A Woman Is a Body, Not a Brain"; Chris Farley and Tim Meadows as best friends until Chris has to deal with a black man wanting to date his sister; and on and on.

Of course, sex wasn't restricted to the shows. At one point, for instance, while the first company was rehearsing for a move to L.A. and New York, the second company was rehearsing to replace them, and a musical called *Big Deal* was beginning rehearsals in our new theater next door to Second City (all three directed by Paul Sills), Paul was working with his ex-wife Barbara Harris, who was in the company with and dating Alan Arkin, while Paul's fiancée (now his wife, Carol, sister of Severn Darden's widow, Heather) was waiting tables; Bill Alton was in the second company with his ex-wife Zohra Lampert, while his then-wife Dolores was in *Big Deal*; Roger Bowen was dating his soon-to-be wife Ann Raim, also in *Big Deal*; Avery Schreiber, also in *Big Deal*, was beginning to date waitress Shelley Isaacs, who soon became and still is his wife; and several other less open but equally interesting relationships were also going on (although none of it was ever brought onstage during rehearsals or performances).

On-stage kisses: (above) Sandy Holt and Peter Boyle (below) Mike Nichols and Elaine May

A lot of relationships that led to marriage were formed or cemented at Second City over the years—couples from onstage (Debra McGrath married Dana Anderson, and, when that marriage broke up, married Colin Mochrie), the offices, the bar and kitchen, or mixtures of the above; even actors and audience members. Here are some of them (the list doesn't, of course, include the innumerable short- and long-term liaisons that didn't result in marriage):

Miriam Flynn & Will Aldis
Kimm Culkin & Bob Bainborough
Ann Raim & Roger Bowen
Violet Torre & Jack Burns
Megan Moore & Peter Burns
Nancy Walls & Steve Carell
Mona Burr & Dennis Cunningham
Liz Baird & Bob Derkach
Judy Graubart & Bob Dishy
Judith Dagley & Joe Flaherty
Nia Vardalos & Ian Gomez
Laura Wasserman & Rick Hall
Nancy McCabe-Kelly & Bruce Jarchow
Carol Cassis & Steve Kampman
Anne Libera & Kelly Leonard
Deb Devine & Eugene Levy
Melinda Dillon & Richard Libertini
Julie Libera & Joe Liss
Janet Van DeGraf & Bob Martin
Jill Talley & Michael McCarthy
Jane Morris & Jeff Michalski
Aliza Shalowitz & Peter Murrieta
Aliza Coyle & Joel Murray
Valerie Harper & Richard Schaal
Shelley Isaacs & Avery Schreiber
Lindsey Leese & Tim Sims
Rebecca Weinberg & Rich Sohn
Miriam Tolan & Brian Stack
Pam Roberts & Dave Thomas
Samantha Bennett & Ron West
Bernadette Birkett & George Wendt
Sally Cochrane & Patrick Whitley

And, according to Ann Raim Bowen, "In the year-and-a-half I was at Second City starting in 1961, thirty-six actors and waitresses dated each other. There were eighteen marriages."

Backstage Passes

George Wendt and Bernadette Birkett's romance started when the touring company played the summer Ravinia Festival in Chicago's north suburbs. We used to do late shows after the Chicago Symphony concerts. They were sitting out in back of the theater listening to Beethoven on a beautiful night. That's really when they fell in love. That was a good thing we did there. They're still together. I have a tape from George and Bernadette and their daughter Hillary: "We want to thank you, Joyce, for letting us share a room on the road because Hillary wouldn't be here if it wasn't for you." It's pretty embarrassing.

—Joyce Sloane

• • •

I was living at Emma's boarding house and getting my mail at Second City. One morning I went to collect it but there wasn't any. Wanting to attract the attention of the beautiful Italian actor Richard Libertini, who was sitting nearby, I said, "Nobody loves me." He heard me and said, "Nobody loves me either." We smiled, and I left. Later, we married.

—Melinda Dillon

• • •

Bonnie Hunt met her husband at Second City. He was a banker and a member of our audience. That's how they met. That's an unusual romance to have happened here.

—Joyce Sloane

3 Chapter

The HOT New Thing

A National Phenomenon

In 1960, John F. Kennedy defeated Richard Nixon and became the first Roman Catholic president-elect after clearly winning the first ever televised debates, partly because Nixon was so sweaty and unconvincing on TV. African-Americans began sit-ins at lunch counters in Greensboro, North Carolina, and Congress passed a Civil Rights Act to monitor discrimination against black voters. The Cold War was getting even hotter as the U.S. admitted sending reconnaissance flights over Soviet territory, and Premier Nikita Khruschev threatened to use Soviet rockets to protect Cuba from U.S. military intervention. High-ranking Nazi Adolf Eichmann, hiding in Argentina since the end of World War II, was captured by Israeli Mossad agents

Backstage Pass

To me, the big change between the New York environment and the Chicago environment took place when we did the David Suskind show, which gave us a broad audience for the first time. I felt like we'd been working for college students and professors who understood everything we were talking about, who were on the same wavelength we were. We did the Suskind show and all of a sudden—boom! We became the darlings of New York. The mink coat broads started coming, which infuriated me. I walked off stage one night and said to Severn Darden, "God damn these people! You mention Thomas Mann and you get a laugh here!" That's the kind of laugh I've always hated, where it's just to show us they got our reference, not because the line was funny. My next scene was with Severn. I had to mime putting on a suit of clothes and demonstrate it for him, which I did and said, "How do I look?" Severn said, "Wonderful! You look just like Thomas Mann." The house fell down! I was enraged. That, to me, was the only time I felt any change.

—Alan Arkin

Opening page (left to right): Eugene Troobnick, Mina Kolb, Barbara Harris, Andrew Duncan, and Severn Darden perform Great Books *at the Playboy Club.*

and brought to trial in Jerusalem; the Vietcong organized the National Front for the Liberation of South Vietnam; and the Organization of Petroleum Exporting Countries (OPEC) met for the first time in Baghdad.

The laser was perfected at the Hughes Laboratory; the first communications satellite, Echo I, was launched; the Xerox 914 was the first production-line photocopier; and the Bulova Accutron was the first electronic wristwatch. Tranquilizers and oral contraceptives came on the market, as did the felt-tip pen, and aluminum cans were used commercially for the first time.

Floyd Patterson regained the world heavyweight boxing championship by knocking out Ingemar Johansson. Willem de Koonig, Jasper Johns, René Magritte, and Andy Warhol were among the painters producing new work. Harold Pinter's The Caretaker and Jean Genet's The Balcony had their premieres; the new musicals included Bye Bye Birdie, Camelot, and The Fantasticks; and among the new novels were John Updike's Rabbit, Run and Harper Lee's To Kill a Mockingbird. Controversial and thought-provoking new movies included Alfred Hitchcock's Psycho, Billy Wilder's The Apartment, Stanley Kubrick's Spartacus, and Michelangelo Antonioni's La Notte. In contrast, among the new TV shows were My Three Sons and The Flintstones. It was the year Ray Charles won his first Grammy, Chubby Checker started a dance craze with "The Twist," Roy Orbison sang about "Only the Lonely," and everyone was singing the praises of an "Itsy-Bitsy Teenie-Weenie Yellow Polka Dot Bikini."

An Evening with Mike Nichols and Elaine May opened on Broadway, and Second City started taking off.

Second City Expands

Within a year of Second City's opening, celebrities in town were regularly coming to see us. (In those days we wouldn't dream of asking them to join us onstage in the improv set; now we often do.) When Sir Edmund Hillary and his sherpa came, we put our mountain-climbing scene into the show. Mort Sahl hung around between his own nightclub sets. You could almost hear hearts flutter when people like Anthony Quinn and Cary Grant were in the audience. (In the kitchen you *could* hear the waitresses arguing over who got their table.) Mr. Grant came several times with his then fiancée Dyan Cannon, who was in the touring production of *How to Succeed in Business Without Really Trying* playing in one of the downtown theaters. One night, as I was leading them past the crowd into the theater, a woman whispered very loudly to her husband, "Look, there's Gary Cooper" (who'd been dead a few years). Mr. Grant, a very gracious man, pretended he hadn't heard, and I pretended I wasn't laughing.

By May 1961 we'd opened our fifth Second City show, *Animal Fair or Caviar to the General* (a title with some bearing on the show, since it did have a scene with Alan Arkin as Noah, picking the animals that could join him on the ark and yelling at God to wait a minute until he'd finished). It also had several other scenes considered classics, such as "Football Comes to the University of Chicago," with Andrew Duncan desperately trying to teach football to Alan, Eugene Troobnick, and Severn Darden as three University of Chicago intellectuals; Severn learning about his sixteen-year-old daughter Barbara Harris' "First Affair"; Alan trying to pick up Barbara in "Museum Piece"; "Phono Pal," with Eugene as the off-stage voice of a "How to Win a Friend" record and Paul Sand as its sad-sack purchaser; and Eugene trying to impress Mina Kolb at a "Chinese Restaurant," with Alan and Paul as the politically incorrect, but totally cynical, waiter and busboy, and Severn screaming Chinese gibberish from offstage as the cook.

We'd also made our first unsuccessful record, *Comedy from The Second City*, for Mercury Records (that's when Severn made his, too) and had put together a "best of" show for a Canadian cable company, which taped it live twice in front of audiences jammed into the theater (copies still exist).

Then, in July 1961, we moved the first company to the Ivar Theatre in Los Angeles for eight weeks as a pre-Broadway tryout of *From the Second City*, a revue containing scenes from the first five Chicago shows, with Howard Alk back instead of Alan Arkin, but with Paul Sand still replacing Roger Bowen.

When the company left for L.A., Alan Arkin stayed behind to help create and open the sixth show, *Six of One*, then moved to our new theater next door to create and play the lead in the musical *Big Deal*, and then joined the Second City company in L.A. just before they left for Broadway (that's how valuable he was).

The First City

From the Second City was so successful in L.A. that, instead of closing it as planned when it moved to Broadway, the cast was replaced for a short time by a company that included soon-to-be movie director/writer Paul Mazursky (*Harry and Tonto, Down and Out in Beverly Hills*) and his partner, Larry Tucker.

Paul Sand began studying with Viola Spolin in L.A. when he was eleven. He later studied mime with Marcel Marceau in France. When he first replaced Roger Bowen at Second City, he mostly did pantomimes and played animals, terrified of speaking. Playing the purchaser of the "How to Win a Friend" record in the scene "Phono Pal" finally freed him to

be verbal as well as physical on stage. His characters were often sweet, vulnerable, and socially inept. After Second City, he did shows in New York, including Neil Simon's *The Star Spangled Girl*, *The Mad Show*, and Paul Sills' *Story Theatre*. Then he went to Hollywood, where he made such films as *The Hot Rock*, *The Main Event*, and *Can't Stop the Music*. He starred on the TV series *Friends and Lovers*, played Dr. Michael Ridley on *St. Elsewhere*, and has been seen regularly on many other TV shows.

43

Spotlight on Alan Arkin

Alan Arkin, before doing The Compass in St. Louis, and then The Second City in Chicago, had been part of a singing group called The Tarriers, for whom he cowrote "The Banana Boat Song" ("Day-o, day-ay-ay-o, Daylight come and I wanna go home"), which was later sold to and popularized by Harry Belafonte. Alan eventually quit the group, no longer wanting to be standing in a spotlight wearing silk pants singing made-up folk songs.

Alan remembers his early struggles to make it in acting:

Since I was five, all I ever wanted to do was act, preferably in film. I couldn't get arrested trying to get a career started in New York. I felt total despair. Paul Sills had seen me at The Compass in St. Louis, and Paul and Bernie Sahlins asked me to come and join Second City. I did, and it gave me, for the first time in my life, an opportunity to work all day long. I would come in at nine in the morning, wait for a workshop or rehearsal, do whatever workshop or rehearsal was going on, spend a whole day waiting for someone to talk to and improvise with, do the show, and then talk about the show afterwards. For the first time in my life, I had an opportunity to do what I always wanted to do. I thought it, breathed it, and ate it from the moment I got up in the morning until late every night. Second City saved my life. It literally saved my life. I have a feeling it's true of a lot of other people, too. A lot of mavericks and displaced people end up here. I mean "displaced" in the best sense of the word; displaced because we don't fit into a tightly structured, well-organized society like this country has turned out to be. I'm glad of it. I'm happy about it.

When Alan first arrived at Second City, he could play ten or twelve distinctly different characters, he could play them at any age, and he could do several accents and dialects. He claims Harpo Marx as one of his earliest influences, and you could sometimes see it in the way his face and body would react to something. He could do a great "gooky"—Harpo's signature funny face. Alan could play the guitar, write songs, and sing them. (Many Second City alums hold his song "I Like You Because You Don't Make Me Nervous" among his finest early accomplishments.)

Alan went from Second City to becoming a Broadway star in *Enter Laughing* in 1963, back to Second City briefly, then back to Broadway to star in *Luv*, which was directed by Mike Nichols. After a while, he started having negative physical reactions to being onstage. He blamed a lot of the problem on having to live inside his character for so long at a time. Fortunately, he then began his movie career with *The Russians Are Coming! The Russians Are Coming!* He was nominated for an Academy Award as best actor for that movie and again for *The Heart Is a Lonely Hunter*. Except for a week of trying out a play by Charles Grodin in New Jersey, he didn't return to the stage again until 1999, when he starred with Elaine May; her daughter, Jeannie Berlin; and his son, Anthony, in *Power Plays*, three one-acts he and Elaine wrote between them and which Alan directed.

Among Alan's many other films are *Wait Until Dark*, *Catch-22* (also directed by Mike Nichols), *Little Murders* (which Alan also directed), *Last of the Red Hot Lovers*, *Freebie and the Bean*, *The Seven Percent Solution*, *The In-Laws* (Alan was also executive producer), *Edward Scissorhands*, *Glengarry Glen Ross*, *So I Married an Axe Murderer*, *Mother Night*, *Gross Pointe Blank*, *Gattaca*, *Four Days in September*, *Slums of Beverly Hills*, and *Jakob the Liar*. He's directed on and off Broadway, and is the author of several books, as well as being the father of three talented actors: Adam, Matthew, and Anthony.

Alan and I hit it off well, given our common interests in music and photography. His ear was extraordinarily good, as was his musical memory. The score of *Big Deal* is lost, but at the twenty-fifth anniversary reunion he remembered the melodies better than I did.

—Allaudin Mathieu

Above (left to right): Alan Arkin, Andrew Duncan, Zohra Lampert, Anthony Holland, and Eugene Troobnick • Alan Arkin today

Opposite page (bottom): Arkin (top left) performs the Chinese restaurant scene with Paul Sand (top right), Mina Kolb (bottom left), and Eugene Troobnick (bottom right).

Backstage Pass

The one thing that I think is important is that New York, for us, was always the road. Chicago was the base. Chicago remains the base. Chicago will always be the base. The minute that's not true, it's lost. California's the road, New York's the road, all of that's the road. Chicago is the home.

—Bernie Sahlins

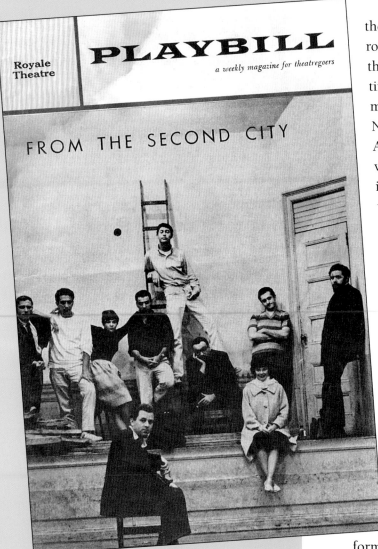

A playbill from the performance of From The Second City *in New York*

The producer of *From the Second City* was Max Liebman, producer of Sid Caesar's TV shows, which had such writers as Neil Simon, Mel Brooks, Woody Allen, and Carl Reiner. We opened at the Royale Theatre on 45th Street between Broadway and 8th Avenue on September 26, 1961, to mixed reviews and not much business—one problem was that Liebman wouldn't let the cast improvise. It closed in under two months; Mercury did, however, put out a cast album. On January 10, 1962, we reopened in more suitable surroundings: Square East, a club in the Village owned by Charles Rubin and Murray Sweig, near Ted Flicker's The Premise. The show flourished there on and off—mostly on—for nearly five years, thanks to an early appearance on David Suskind's TV show *Open End*, which got business rolling.

By the time Square East had been open for a year and the actors there had started getting stage, screen, and TV roles out of it, it had become clear to the actors in Chicago that the next stepping stone in their careers should be getting to Square East. Since the turnover was pretty steady, most of them got there. Still others were recruited for the New York show without first playing Chicago, including Alan Alda, Bob Dishy, and Paul Dooley. Another recruit was Valerie Harper, who never actually got into the show in New York, but did meet and marry Dick Schaal there, took workshops, and was in Second City shows in other cities, as well as in Paul Sills' *Story Theatre*. Of course, she's better known as Rhoda Morgenstern on *The Mary Tyler Moore Show* and *Rhoda*, as well as for her many other TV shows and films.

When Paul Sills tired of directing in New York, he was replaced by former Compass director Larry Arrick, then by Alan Myerson. Myerson, who'd been directing at the Second City in Chicago before directing at Square East, left New York in 1963 for San Francisco with his then-wife Jessica, who'd been in the Chicago Second City company while he was directing there. In San Francisco, they opened The Committee, a far more politically oriented improvisation club, which ran for ten years, including several years in L.A. simultaneously. At one time or another, The Committee employed such former Second City performers as Del Close, Roger Bowen, Ann Elder, Jack Burns, Avery Schreiber, and Allaudin Mathieu, as well as people like Peter Bonerz and Howard Hessman. After The Committee had run its course, Myerson began directing movies and TV, which he still does. He has a son who's now part of an improvisational group in L.A.

In 1964, pianist/musical director Fred Kaz, who'd moved to New York to play Square East, returned to Chicago to replace Allaudin. Fred's replacement for a while in New York was Tom O'Horgan with his harp. Tom had been a nightclub entertainer back in Chicago, singing Irish songs and accompanying himself on the harp. He was also the composer of all the original music we used at the old Playwrights Theatre Club. He later directed the Broadway productions of *Hair*, *Lenny*, and *Jesus Christ Superstar*. Business was a little rocky at that point at Square East, and the show had to close before another was ready. In a week of rehearsals (without improv sets to try out the material since the club was closed) and a week of previews, Alan Arkin and Barbara Dana—who'd met when they were both in *Enter Laughing* and who'd just gotten married—and Severn Darden, with me directing the first and only three-person Second City cast, put together a show of both old Chicago scenes and newly improvised material, and got unanimous rave reviews. (We're all particularly proud of that one, because they said it couldn't be done, including all three members of the cast at one time or another during the rehearsal week. I agreed with them but couldn't let on.) The show was called *A View from under the Bridge* and had a wicked parody in it of Arthur Miller's *After the Fall*, which had recently opened across the street and which we all hated at the time. Miller came to see it after the reviews came out and didn't seem to mind it too much, or at least was polite afterward. With him was Elia Kazan, who directed *After the Fall* and was a fictionalized character both in the play and in our parody—a character who, like Kazan himself, names names to the House Un-American Activities Committee. Kazan didn't laugh, nor did we expect him to; his character in *Under the Bridge*, played by Severn, was called "Fink the Greek."

It was getting impossible to keep a cast together for more than about a minute at a time; the actors were getting hired for plays, movies, and TV faster than we could replace them. (Alan Arkin left soon after the opening of *A View from Under the Bridge* to return to Broadway for *Luv*, and Severn Darden left soon after him.) Square East closed the Second City show for a while in 1965 and ran *The Decline and Fall of the Entire World as Seen Through the Eyes of Cole Porter* for 273 performances. We returned for a short run in 1966 with what was then the entire Chicago cast. In 1969, Bernie again took the current Chicago cast to New York, this time for a brief run at the Eastside Playhouse off-Broadway (72nd Street). Except for college bookings, Second

Spotlight on

Alan Alda

Alan Alda went from Second City New York to the satirical TV show *That Was the Week That Was*, and to such Broadway shows as *The Apple Tree*, costarring Barbara Harris (Robert Klein was in the small chorus), and *The Owl and the Pussycat*, costarring fellow former Compass player Diana Sands. He made a few movies,

then starred in the enormously successful TV series *M*A*S*H* while continuing to make such movies as *California Suite*, *Same Time Next Year*, and *The Seduction of Joe Tynan* (also with Barbara Harris). Since the TV series, he's been in many movies, including *Crimes and Misdemeanors*, *Manhattan Murder Mystery*, and *Flirting with Disaster*. He's also written and directed several films, including *The Four Seasons*, *Sweet Liberty*, and *Betsy's Wedding*.

The front entrance of The Second City:
past (bottom) and present (top)

Opposite page (left to right): A playbill from the production
of Big Deal. • Fred Kaz (left) with Bernie Sahlins

City was seldom as successful in theaters as it was in less formal cabaret spaces. There was another unsuccessful attempt in 1973 in the club on Central Park South called Plaza 9 (which had once been Downstairs at the Upstairs) and a final one in 1984 at the Village Gate. And that's been it for Second City in New York so far, except for the Second City Training Center that opened there in 1998.

A Second Playwrights

On May 9, 1961, after a week of sold-out previews, we opened a 225-seat cabaret theater next door to Second City at 1846 North Wells, and sentimentally called it Playwrights at Second City. The street-level entrance glass doors were surrounded by Louis Sullivan-designed stone arches purchased from the Garrick Theatre just as it was about to be demolished. (We eventually moved Second City into the bigger space, and the Sullivan arches were the only part of the building we took when we moved again in 1967.) Across the top of the arches are bas-relief heads of four composers—we're not quite sure who.

There was an open ticket booth on your right when you entered; and again tickets were sold from a small, open metal cashbox. Then you went down a flight of stairs to a bar and waiting room where we served drinks and showed silent movies in the winter when the beer garden was closed. Behind this room was the actors' dressing room, from which the sounds of disagreement would occasionally waft through the bar.

Halfway down the flight of stairs to the bar was a landing which, if you turned right, led to the back kitchen/bar, the back entrance to the theater for the wait staff (who had to climb up a short flight of stairs with full trays in order to get to their customers), the washrooms, and a door leading to the beer garden. The main entrance to the beer garden was off the sidewalk through two large gates in a filigreed iron fence.

To get from the waiting room to the theater, you had to go back up the stairs, past the ticket booth, through the lobby, through a doorway, and up a short flight of stairs where a hostess was waiting to seat you. The stage was wider and deeper than the Second City stage next door, and had a red velvet draw curtain you could close during set changes and intermissions.

We opened the new Playwrights with Jules Feiffer's first ever theater piece, a revue called *The Explainers* adapted by him from

Big Deal

☆ an opera for politicians

his cartoons. The cast had several future Second Citizens in it, including Del Close. Paul Sand took a break from the Second City show next door to be in it, too. The show was directed by Paul Sills, with music by Allaudin Mathieu played by Fred Kaz, who'd been Allaudin's vacation replacement at Second City.

Our second show at Playwrights, *Big Deal*, which opened in August, was a three-act, jazz musical rewrite of *The Beggars' Opera* and *The Threepenny Opera* set among Chicago's ward politicians. It was improvised from a scenario by David Shepherd and again directed by Paul Sills, composed by Allaudin Mathieu, and played by Fred Kaz. The cast, along with Alan Arkin as Macheath, included soon-to-be Second City performers Del Close, Avery Schreiber, and Dick Schaal, as well as Roger Bowen's future wife, Ann Raim, and Bill Alton's then-wife Dolores.

Business wasn't great, so in November 1961, we moved Second City into the larger space at 1846 and Playwrights into the smaller one at 1842. We reopened Playwrights with the political satire *The Conscience of a Liberal*, a two-man revue written and performed by Roger Bowen and Bob Coughlan (a former Compass performer). Then we did really excellent productions of several important new plays, all in their Chicago premieres: Jean Genet's *The Maids*, and Edward Albee's *The Zoo Story* and *The Death of Bessie Smith*, all directed by soon-to-be New York Second City director Larry Arrick. We also put on Samuel Beckett's *Krapp's Last Tape* with Severn Darden in the title role, and Harold Pinter's *The Caretaker*, which was my first solo effort as a director.

All the plays were huge hits, but how long can you run an Equity theater in a 125-seat house, even serving drinks, burgers, and Viennese pastries before the show and during intermission? We found out when we had our first less-than-successful show in 1963, a promising new play by Bernie Sahlins called *The Puppet*. We had to close down, even though Claudia Cassidy in the *Tribune* liked it. (We brought Joseph Chaikin in from New York to be in it. During the time he was there, he studied with Viola Spolin and learned her transformation games, which he later used to help develop the Open Theatre in New York.)

Spotlight on

Fred Kaz

Fred Kaz became pianist/musical director of Second City Chicago in 1964 and stayed at the job until 1987, the longest run so far of any performer at Second City—he'd been doing it in New York since 1962, and went from Chicago in 1987 to do it for a while in Santa Monica. He's a great improviser, a wonderful composer, a lyricist of meaningfully satiric songs, and a fine jazz pianist, even though he lost a couple of fingers on his left hand in a factory accident when he was very young. Fred also played the show at our first place in Toronto and even directed one show at our former suburban outpost in Rolling Meadows, Illinois. His wisdom and astuteness have saved many a Second City scene over the years. Fred is living in his boat now, docked in Southern California, and seems to have really retired (although you never know).

Spotlight on
Joyce Sloane

During the late winter of 1961, a woman appeared in our lobby asking if she could do group sales for us by selling out shows to benefit organizations. Since we were then building Playwrights at Second City in the south half of the beer garden next door, Bernie told her that if she could sell out a week of previews, she had the job. She did it, and that's how Joyce Sloane started at Second City.

Joyce recalls her first season at Playwrights and Second City:

Bernie and I crawled in and out of that theater as it was being built. He asked me to sell out the first week. I was so young and so stupid, I guess, I didn't know theaters don't open with the first week sold out, so I did it. But I had two groups that wanted the opening night. One was the University of Chicago Cancer Research Foundation and the other was the Junior Board of the Travelers' Aid Society. Sheldon said, "That's easy. We'll make one the first preview." I didn't even know what a preview was. That first night, the carpet people were still tacking down the carpeting. The University of Chicago people arrived, and it was spring, so ladies were in their lovely dresses. They forgot to connect the flue in the kitchen, so all the smoke backed up into the lobby! Even before the show started, we had the fire department over, and everybody was out on the street.

Joyce Sloane eventually began booking the touring company's gigs as well as being "the benefit lady"; then she became associate producer, then producer, then producer emeritus, and always the universally acknowledged "mother" of Second City, as well as of the Chicago theater community in general.

Second City alum Rose Abdoo tells this story about Joyce:

More than teaching me about this career and giving me a chance, putting me on this path, I've learned so much about having a sense of humor about myself. Joyce has the best sense of humor about herself. So much so, I quote her, I do her in my act. We had dinner at the Italian restaurant across from Second City. It's great to go out to dinner with Joyce because you get free stuff! The chef was very excited that she was there and sent out a free dessert. Joyce said to me, "Look, Rose. It's crème brulée!"

I said, "Joyce, I can't have any of that. I'm trying to diet."

"Have some."

"Joyce, you know, I really can't."

"Have some!"

"Joyce, you know, I really can't! I'm trying to diet! Why don't you have some?"

"It's too rich."

"Joyce, you know what? I can't eat that! I'm trying to diet!"

"Rose, it was free! Have some crème brulée."

I said, "I can't. Joyce, it's your dessert. Why don't you eat the crème brulée?"

"Rose, you know I have a heart condition. Either you eat it and spend an extra forty-five minutes on the treadmill, or I eat it and die. It's your choice."

I ate the crème brulée. Of course, I put that bit in my show and told her that I would do it in New York. She would call me and say, "How did I go over tonight? Did I get a big laugh?" Always the best laugh in the show.

When I was living out in Los Angeles, there was an obituary printed in the *New York Times*. It was my name and my credits, but another actor. They confused things. An old-time fan of Second City called and asked, "Is Mike Hagerty dead?" Joyce simply said, "No, no. If Mike Hagerty was dead, he would've called me."

—Mike Hagerty

● ● ○

Joyce knows everyone in the entertainment industry; the people she doesn't know are her cousins. From Joyce I learned that a producer should be fluent in the New and Old Testaments and that the Irish are just Northern Jews.

—Joe Keefe

● ● ○

To many, the heart of Second City is Joyce. Like a proud mother, she keeps us all connected through updates on other cast members and extended family —even ones you don't know, because, like the wife of a third cousin, you're still related. It is her refusal to say "good-bye," but rather, "until you return to the circle" which keeps Second City a very special family.

—Judy Belushi Pisano

Joyce with Dave Miner

51

In 1966, Jo Forsberg started a children's theater on Saturday and Sunday afternoons where we did slightly cut-down versions of *A Midsummer Night's Dream*, *The Mikado*, *The Tempest*, and *Charley's Aunt*. Jo later turned it into a Sunday afternoon improv show, often asking children in the audience to participate onstage. It soon began being announced to Second City audiences during the "outros" (announcements after the show but before the improv set) as, "Sunday, Sunday, the little bastards' fun day."

The Actors as Actors

In April 1959, Mike Nichols and Elaine May did an evening at Town Hall in New York as a sort of trial run for what became their phenomenally successful two-person Broadway revue. Most of the show's scenes had been developed at The Compass, including the first-act closer. Mike introduced it as a piece in the style of the Italian dramatist Luigi Pirandello, whose plays are filled with shifting realities in his quest for an understanding of what is truth. They began the twenty-minute scene as a young brother and sister playing a game of house in which they pretend they are their parents having a fight. After a while the audience realized that they were no longer the kids playing the parents having the fight, but had gradually become the parents having the fight. Then little side comments began to creep in that eventually turned into Mike and Elaine themselves having a fight, which got so serious and intense that Byrne Piven, who was in the audience, started toward the stage to break it up before they hurt each other. At that moment, a man the audience had never seen before—the stage manager—came onstage, stopped the fight and worriedly asked Mike and Elaine what they were doing. They said they were doing Pirandello, bowed, and it was intermission time. Byrne was left stranded in the aisle, deeply embarrassed; he still laughs at himself about it. Mike and Elaine were not just comic geniuses, they were also wonderful actors, and that's part of the secret of the success of The Compass and of The Second City.

Alan Arkin (left), Paul Sills (middle), and Anthony Holland (right) discuss the direction of a performance.

Here's how Bernie Sahlins, Alan Arkin, and Harold Ramis view the Second City method of acting:

Bernie Sahlins: It's probably unique in theater history that a group of people from the classical theater applied classical techniques to popular art forms. We were Shakespeare actors, we were Brecht directors, we were people who'd grown up in the theater. We took these techniques—solid acting, rigorous structure, high reference level—and put them to work. I think that's why Second City has survived. It's not television. It does not come from television. It's not film. It does not come from film. It comes from the theater. As long as it holds on to that, it's going to do well.

Alan Arkin: I've done a lot of directing over the years and whenever somebody from Second City would come in and read a part, they would know exactly what their function was in the entirety of the script, unlike almost any other actor I've ever worked with. Most of the actors I know who haven't worked this way come in and they're myopic. They know what they want to do, and it may have nothing to do with what anybody else is doing in the play. Second City actors will immediately save a week's time because they know what their function is in the play. They have their antennae up for what the other actors are doing and need—almost invariably.

Harold Ramis: Every actor speaks a different language. I was directing Robin Williams once in a film. I said, "Robin, can you do that faster?" He said, "Faster is not a direction!" I said, "Okay, I think your character would be feeling an urgency at this point.

I watched the unfolding of events from a vantage point no one else had: the piano bench. These actors have a heightened way of seeing people, a specialized empathy that requires great receptive capacities. What might come out onstage as aggressive satire, went in offstage through a porous observer. "Doing" character is a marvelous talent, and I never had the knack for it, and still don't, but because of all those thousands of hours watching dozens of actors work in scene after scene, doing character after character, I see people differently. People are somehow more accessible. They're funnier. And I enjoy them more.

—Allaudin Mathieu

Frames 1–3: Hamilton Camp (left) and Dick Schaal • 4 and 5: Camp (left), Avery Schreiber (middle), and Mina Kolb (right)

He's desperate, he's going out of his mind." Every way I could say it. "Okay, fine. Great." In the same movie, Eugene Levy had a little improvised piece. I said, "Eugene, that was a minute-twenty. Can you do it in a minute?" He said, "Sure."

Alan Arkin: I remember looking at written transcripts of scenes we did at Second City that were considered minor masterpieces. When they were written down on paper, they looked like hash! It looked like nonsense! I realize the incredible investment of persona, or acting technique, that went into a lot of the scenes when nothing was there. It gave me a sense of how much more important the actors were in terms of their nuances than what was necessarily in a script.

Spotlight on **Failure**

Above (from left to right): Bob Coughlan and Del Close in Big Deal.

Opposite page (from left to right): Hamilton Camp, Avery Schreiber, and Mina Kolb in My Friend Art is Dead.

Unlike most actors just starting out, when you're at Second City, you have the unequalled experience of performing in front of audiences six nights a week, fifty weeks a year, honing your comedic performance skills while playing anywhere from six to ten characters a night for whom you've usually created your own dialogue and behavior or are creating it on the spot. All this while getting paid Equity salaries that at least let you eat regularly and have a decent roof over your head, without having to hold down a "straight" job at the same time. You learn quickly what works for you and what doesn't and, hopefully, why some scenes work and others don't. Furthermore, since you do some of your improvising in front of audiences who know you're improvising, allowances are made for failure in public, permitting you to try things you might not have dared otherwise.

To Second City veterans, failure is understood as an integral part of the finished product:

Mick Napier: The model actor-improviser at Second City is someone who will have the attitude of, "Sure, I'll try it," and, if it falls on its ass, will say, "Sure, I'll try it again." Someone who will boldly and fearlessly go into the unknown and see what happens.

Tom Gianas: At the beginning, when they first start improvising, many actors fear failing up there. But then slowly, as they're there for a little while, they start to not fear it as much. Then, eventually, they begin to look forward to it. Rick Thomas was a great director and performer at Second City. He used to say, "If you're on the Titanic and it's going down, start drinking water!"

Tim Kazurinsky: You must fail for the audience to trust that you're truly creating. When you do an improv set, you're dying about a third to half of the time. In a weird way, the audience loves to see that. They don't want to see the tightrope walker go right across the canyon. The good ones, they'll pretend that they're going to trip and fall. That's what makes you more like a wizard. If you just did it well all the time, people wouldn't be impressed.

Bernie Sahlins: I think that if any material is to work, the actor has to be using his top intelligence. I think you have to think of the audience as being at least as smart as you are, if not smarter. There's no substitute—it's not a Second City rule, I think it's a dynamic of the form—that if you're playing down to an audience, they smell it; and no matter how brutish an audience is, the one thing they understand immediately is when you're talking down to them, and they hate you for it (Showtime, 1988).

A standing argument persists as to whether improvisation is a means of creating set material or an end in itself—suitable for an evening's entertainment. As a means, which is how Second City uses it, the chance of failure is usually restricted to the improv set after the regular show. As an end, failure can come any time. Del Close and Bernie Sahlins were in a never-ending disagreement on the subject. To put it simply, Del, who called improv "theater of the heart," believed it could be both, though his preference was for straight improv; Bernie, on the other hand, believes it's a way to create material, not an entertainment in and of itself:

Bernie Sahlins: We did not think of improvisation as a presentational form. Improvisation was a way to avoid having writers, a way to do public rehearsal, a way for each actor to find his own maximum strengths that he brought to the role. When we presented a show, it was complete. It was rehearsed. It was a work. We improvised because we needed material for the next show. I think that if we only did improvisation, we'd lose the audiences. It's a technique, like fencing or mime or anything else, which you use to arrive at an idea. The game part—playing the game—is fun for a while, but I think as a pure presentational form, it doesn't work.

Del Close: When material is being developed in the sets, the audience loves to watch the growth process before their very eyes. And that is really the Second City approach to improvisation. It's not free improvisation. The audience likes being part of the creative process. But the kind of improvisation that I am particularly addicted to is that kind that does not aim at creating material, that aims at creating a momentary, fragmentary experience that has some kind of a totality to it. It's kind of like fireworks, the most ephemeral of art forms. Once it's gone, it's gone, baby. There's the afterimage for a few seconds, but nobody will ever see anything like it again (Showtime, 1988).

Second City is an arena in which the audience comes recognizing that part of what you do is going to fail. There's no place in the country where you can do that. Anywhere! There's no arena anywhere in the country where failure isn't looked on as a moral issue. But that's the only way you learn. You learn by your failures. This place encourages it and doesn't treat you like you're a moral leper.

—Alan Arkin

Not all improvisations turn into scenes and make it into a show. Some of them just don't have it. And there are those rare nights onstage—and I mean they're rare—when the magic isn't there. It never really happened to me, of course. I think the magic was always there when I was on stage. At least that's what my family keeps telling me.

—John Candy

One snowy night an audience suggestion was "shaggy dog." So Tony Holland and I ran out into the freezing snow (without coats or boots) several blocks to his apartment, grabbed his shaggy dog, and the three of us ran back to Second City. I announced, "And now on your suggestion, 'Shaggy Dog'…" Lights out. Tony put his dog on a chair and whispered, "Stay." Lights up. There sat a real shaggy dog…. I don't remember *anyone* laughing.

—Paul Sand

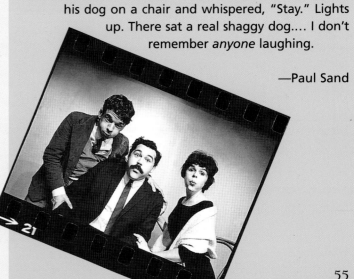

55

Chapter 4

The 1960s

Changing the Approach

The tumultuous 1960s both provided rich soil for cultural and political satire and discouraged it, as the changes and events that took place ran the spectrum from inspiring to ridiculous to tragic.

The assassinations of John and Robert Kennedy, Dr. Martin Luther King Jr., Medgar Evers, and Malcolm X didn't leave much to laugh about. Yet, somehow the escalation of the war in Vietnam and the splitting of the country into angry factions proved good targets for satire. The anti-war protests, bloody riots, and police brutality of the 1968 Democratic Convention in Chicago and the continuing Cold War also fed Second City. The society that Second City satirized and reflected was changing fundamentally—and, of course, it ended up

Disc 1
Tracks 4–8

Spotlight on
Melinda Dillon

Melinda Dillon was the first coat-check girl at Second City before joining the cast. After Second City, she went on to play Honey in the original Broadway production of *Who's Afraid of Virginia Woolf?* Among Melinda's film credits are *A Christmas Story*, *Absence of Malice*, *The Prince of Tides*, *Magnolia*, and, most famously, the mother of the little boy in *Close Encounters of the Third Kind*.

Melinda recalls her "big break":

It was soon after the opening of the club. When I got to work I found our three producers in a panicked and heated discussion as to whether the show could go on or not without Barbara—Barbara Harris was ill! They were still at it when the patrons began to arrive. I already had twelve hats. So, knowing what I had to do, I interrupted them.

"What do you want?!" Bernie Sahlins yelled.

"Sorry, sorry," I said. "I know the show. I can do it."

They looked at each other, then Bernie said "No! She's not smart enough to wait tables, you gonna let her ruin the show?"

They looked at each other some more. Then Howard Alk said he had a "feeling" about me. Then Paul Sills smiled and, always the one to welcome a jump into the great unknown, said, "Let's do it. You're on." So we did! And it was grand. I adored Barbara and had followed her every move and nuance, and being the monkey I am, I knew the show. (Bernie was right about the tables.)

changing the approach of the actors themselves, as they alternately faced reality with scathing satire and ran from it to more pure comedy.

Race riots erupted in the inner cities all over the nation. Chicago cops murdered Black Panther leader Fred Hampton in his bed. Richard Nixon was elected President in 1968. And these were just a few of the low points.

But the decade also offered hope. John F. Kennedy created the Peace Corps, and Lyndon Johnson signed the Civil Rights Bill into law. In 1962, more than one hundred thousand people marched on Washington in support of civil rights, and Dr. King delivered his "I have a dream" speech. In 1969, Neil Armstrong was the first man to walk on the moon.

Muhammad Ali gained the world heavyweight title in 1964, defeating Sonny Liston, but was stripped of the title in 1967 for refusing induction into the army. The Green Bay Packers won the first Super Bowl in 1967.

Rolling Stone *began publication. Among the new books were such inflammatory works as Eldridge Cleaver's* Soul on Ice, *Betty Friedan's* The Feminine Mystique, *Marshall McLuhan's* Understanding Media, *and Ralph Nader's* Unsafe at Any Speed. *American literature was both enhanced and shaken up by such books as Truman Capote's* In Cold Blood, *Joseph Heller's* Catch-22, *Ken Kesey's* One Flew Over the Cuckoo's Nest, *and Kurt Vonnegut's* Slaughterhouse-Five.

Important new plays included Who's Afraid of Virginia Woolf? *and* The Odd Couple. *New musicals included the first rock musical on Broadway,* Hair. *Otherwise, the decade saw the last of the golden age of the Broadway musical, with such shows as* Fiddler on the Roof, Funny Girl, and Hello, Dolly. Lenny Bruce died of an overdose in his bathroom in 1966.

The movies went through a sea change in adult subject matter, in experimentation, and in violence, all reflecting the times much more than Hollywood had usually been known for. Among them were Bonnie and Clyde, Dr. Strangelove, Easy Rider,

Barbara Harris and Eugene Troobnick perform on stage.

The Graduate, A Hard Day's Night, Midnight Cowboy, The Wild Bunch, *and at least two important foreign films:* 8½ *and* Jules and Jim.

By 1964, 90 percent of U.S. homes had at least one television set. Among the new and highly rated TV shows of the decade were The Andy Griffith Show, Bonanza, *and* The Fugitive, *and three trend-setters:* Laugh-In, 60 Minutes, *and* Sesame Street.

The counterculture was gaining steam in the pop music business. Berry Gordy began his Motown sound, and in 1964, the Beatles achieved international popularity. In 1967, the first large rock music gathering, the Monterey International Pop Festival, featured such stars as Otis Redding (who died in a plane crash soon after), The Grateful Dead, Janis Joplin, Jefferson Airplane, The Mamas and the Papas, Jimi Hendrix, Sly and the Family Stone, and The Who. The Woodstock three-day festival of "peace, love, and rock" was held in 1969, the year John Lennon married Yoko Ono.

At Home and in London

The second Chicago company began with Alan Arkin, Roger Bowen, and three former Playwrights actors: Bill Alton (succeeding Andrew Duncan as straight man), Zohra Lampert (Bill's former wife), and Tony Holland. They were joined by Melinda Dillon and, from Feiffer's *The Explainers,* folk-singer/actor Hamilton Camp. Del Close and Avery Schreiber would eventually replace Alan Arkin and Roger Bowen. As you can tell, whenever choices were equal or better, we've always preferred working with people we know—regardless of the occasionally complex interpersonal relationships.

The title of the seventh show, the first after we switched spaces with Playwrights, was *Alarums and Excursions,* another Shakespeare stage direction. Zohra Lampert left for the New York company at Square East late in 1961, just before the switch, and from there went to Broadway, the first Lincoln Center acting company, movies like *Splendor in the Grass,* and lots of other film and TV work. She was replaced by Joan Rivers before *Alarums and Excursions* opened.

In 1962, Second City opened another Shakespeare stage direction, *A Knocking Within,* directed by Alan Myerson, with Mina Kolb back from New York replacing Joan Rivers, who'd gone to Square East, and Dick Schaal from *Big Deal* replacing Hamilton Camp. That year we also did our first "scenario" show, *My Friend Art Is Dead,* directed by Paul Sills, for which each member of the

Backstage Pass

I was once doing a scene with Barbara Harris—she played everything except me, practically—and we needed a fur coat. So we took it from Melinda Dillon in the coat-check room. We walked out to do the scene and from the audience came the scream, "My coat!" There was general embarrassment onstage and a terrific laugh from the audience.

—Severn Darden

In 1962, Second City played the Establishment Club in London. The cast (from left to right): John Bird, Elanor Bron, Jerry Geidt, John Fortune, Cardle Simpson, Allaudin Mathieu, Bill Alton, Del Close, Avery Schreiber, and Dick Schaal (Mina Kolb not pictured)

Spotlight on
Joan Rivers

Joan Rivers (born Molinsky) was never really happy at Second City. Her style was different enough from the others' so that she wasn't easily able to blend into the ensemble—she was a born stand-up. She often felt frustrated and disliked, and living at Emma's depressing boarding house didn't help. She was, however, able to create some excellent two-person "people" scenes with Tony Holland and Bill Alton, and, of course, audiences liked her a lot. Oddly enough, given her stand-up persona, several of Joan's most successful characters at Second City were insecure and shy—like the model who finds love with Tony as the equally shy and insecure tailor fitting a dress on her, or the dental assistant with Bill as her married boss, sharing an after-hours drink out of the rinse cups as they talk about their artistic aspirations and share a single kiss. Those characters were the closest to the real Joan of the time, although she was also quite capable of turning on the "Can we talk?" persona when she wanted to, both onstage and off.

Joan replaced Zohra Lampert at Square East for a short time, and became the first (though hardly the last) former Compass or Second Citizen since Shelley Berman to have a successful and long-running solo act. She's also had her own talk show, written and directed movies, published a couple of books, and, with her daughter Melissa, made a brave TV movie about dealing with the suicide of Joan's husband Edgar. Joan and Melissa host a notorious pre-Academy Awards show.

Joan created a blackout—"Our Children" 🆑 —that's still in the Second City repertoire: a man (Bill Alton) and a woman (Joan) are saying goodbye to some unseen departing guests. As they close the door, the wife goes into a rant against the guests, how boring they are, how disgusting their eating habits are, and on and on, ending with, "I don't ever want them here again," to which her husband reasonably responds, "But honey, they're our children!"

audience got a button that said, "Art Is Dead." At the end of the show we raised Art, played by Avery Schreiber, up to heaven on a pulley that eventually seriously hurt his back. It was our first "special effect."

BERNARD SAHLINS,
PAUL SILLS AND HOWALD ALK

PRESENT

"MY FRIEND ART IS DEAD"

STAFF FOR SECOND CITY

		WITH	BILL ALTON
GENERAL MANAGER	SHELDON PATINKIN		DEL CLOSE
STAGE MANAGER	GEORGE RICHIE		SEVERN DARDEN
PRESS REPRESENTATIVE	IRVING SEIDNER		MINA KOLB
	DANIEL J. EDELMAN & ASSOCIATES		DICK SCHAAL
			AVERY SCHREIBER
PHOTOGRAPHY / MORTON SHAPIRO			also Dennis Cunningham
ARTISTIC REPRESENTATION / WILLIAM MORRIS AGENCY			
ELECTRICAL ENGINEERING / CHARLES E. THOMPSON			

DIALOGUE IMPROVISED BY THE COMPANY
SCENARIO AND DIRECTION BY PAUL SILLS

A weird little blackout came from that show. Avery, portly and with a big black mustache, was onstage wearing an apron, humming "O Sole Mio," and miming turning a barbecue stake. Mina called out from backstage, asking when the barbecue would be ready (so the audience would know what Avery was miming). He called back that it would be soon, then resumed turning and humming. Red-bearded Dennis Cunningham, dressed as a beatnik with a guitar on his back, walked on, stopped, stared at Avery, and said, "Hey, man, nice tune. But your monkey's on fire."

Later in 1962 we did a "best of" revue with Mina Kolb, Bill Alton, Del Close, Avery Schreiber, and Dick Schaal. It was called *The London Show* because it was put together in order to then trade places with Peter Cook and Dudley Moore's London group called "The Establishment." (Cook and Moore, famous at the time for *Beyond the Fringe*, weren't in it; they just produced it.) So, while the London company played Chicago, Second City played at the Establishment Club in Soho beginning in October, just in time to catch a lot of flak about the Cuban missile crisis from the very rowdy English audiences, both in the club and on the streets.

An alumni cast played London again in 1963, this time in a theater instead of a club, and that same year Bernie Sahlins produced a TV series in Manchester called *Second City Reports* for Granada TV, where he met his wife Jane, who was a production assistant. Our third and last London show so far was in 1965.

Backstage Pass

I knew Joan Rivers from 1959, when she was auditioning up and down the boardwalk in Atlantic City for cabaret gigs with a friend of mine—the same friend, Johnny Meyer, who took me to audition for The Compass years before. When she showed up at Second City, I was glad to see her, and I wrote one of my best songs for her, "East Side, West Side (of Berlin)." She was terrified of singing it, but she put it over well. Her model and tailor scene with Tony Holland was truly one of the fine early scenes, right up there with Alan Arkin and Barbara Harris' "Museum Piece." I never got tired of watching those scenes, which is rare for me, who had to watch an awful lot of scenes.

—Allaudin Mathieu

Upper left: Playbill from the 1962 production My Friend Art is Dead
Above: Left to right: Avery Schreiber, Joan Rivers, Bill Alton, and Del Close

Back in the states, Second City created a blackout called "Lenny Bruce" CD that debuted the use of the word "shit." It was put into the show right after Bruce was arrested in New York in 1963. All but one member of the cast was discovered hanging around on stage when the lights came up. The missing cast member came hurriedly onstage carrying a newspaper and said, "Hey, did you hear? Lenny Bruce was arrested for obscenity." The rest of the cast said, "No shit!" and the lights blacked out. It was actually the first use of any profanity that strong on the Second City stage, although the word had been mouthed in "Ahab," an earlier blackout:

The lights come up on two men standing on opposite sides of the stage, each miming a boat's steering wheel.
Man 1: "Ahoy there."
Man 2: "Ahoy there. Who be ye?"
Man 1: "I be Captain Ahab of the good ship *Pequod*. Have ya seen anything of a great white whale?"
Man 2: "Aye. About three days back. We killed it."
Ahab snaps his fingers while mouthing "shit," and the lights go out.

In the early-to-mid 1960s, profanity wasn't as regular a part of the show as it would later become. Although, the first use of the f-word, that mother of all obscenities, happened the night after the JFK assassination—appropriately, it was improvised. Second City was closed the night of the assassination, the only Friday night it's ever been closed. The next night, the audiences clearly wanted to laugh for a while as a break from weeping in front of their TVs; and laugh they did, perhaps even harder than the show warranted. During the suggestion-taking for the improv set that night, under the category "current events," someone called out, "the assassination." The entire audience gasped; Del Close turned angrily to the man and asked, "Just what the fuck did you want to see, sir?" and everyone burst into applause.

After that November weekend, no one wanted to do or see much in the way of political satire for a couple of years, though Lyndon Johnson, Barry Goldwater, Vietnam, and the civil rights movement finally fed the country enough fodder for us to be able to resume.

Above, left to right: Del Close, Dennis Cunningham, Bill Alton, and Avery Schreiber • Below: The Royal Alexandra Theatre in Toronto

The Royal Alex in Toronto

In spring 1963, we did the first of several very successful yearly bookings—the others all at Christmastime—at the Royal Alexandra Theatre in Toronto, most of them cast with alumni. These shows consisted of two or three acts of "best of" material, including an occasional on-the-spot improv.

Ed Mirvish had just bought the Royal Alex in 1963 when we played there. The first opening night, there'd been a snowstorm, and the planes couldn't come in. Bernie Sahlins chartered a plane and put the cast on it, but they couldn't land because it was an American plane and didn't have permission to land. Ed Mirvish pulled all sorts of strings to get that plane down. Joyce Sloane and I waited at the theater, ready to do a poetry reading if necessary. The cast finally arrived, and it was impossible not to notice Severn Darden wearing a full-length fur coat for his trip to the Great White North. We developed a wonderful audience in Toronto through the Royal Alex bookings; even the actors from Stratford would come in and see us.

Toronto critic Nathan Cohen had fallen in love with Second City after seeing it in Chicago. In fact, he's the one who gave us the idea of opening a theater there after writing in his newspaper column: "What a wonderful gift it would be to have a permanent Second City here."

The audiences in Toronto were wonderful. The bookings at the Royal Alex—with casts that included Valerie Harper and Dick Schaal (who later got married), Linda Lavin, Bob Dishy, Omar Shapli, David Steinberg, Jack Burns, Avery Schreiber, and Penny White—started Bernie Sahlins thinking seriously about opening a permanent Second City in Toronto. As a step toward that possibility, he produced a series of *Second City Reports* for the CBC in Toronto in 1964, using the Chicago company.

Back Home

During the early 1960s we tried Sunday-brunch/Monday-night screenings of classic movies for a while; this was before the days of revival houses or VCRs. Alan Arkin and I picked the movies each week; we stopped the series when the Clark movie theater downtown became a revival house for both classic American and foreign films, open all night and with a new double feature every day.

We booked local musicians for chamber concerts on Monday nights for a couple of years, and one summer we tried a teenage weekend nightclub in the deserted 1842 space called, for reasons no one can remember, "Fred." High-school kids did old Second

Spotlight on
Avery Schreiber and Jack Burns

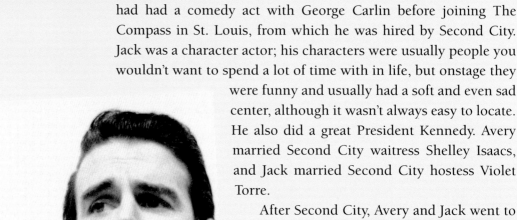

Left to right: Avery Schreiber • Jack Burns

Avery Schreiber and Jack Burns met at Second City. Avery was a fat, mustachioed clown and a good character actor as well. Jack had had a comedy act with George Carlin before joining The Compass in St. Louis, from which he was hired by Second City. Jack was a character actor; his characters were usually people you wouldn't want to spend a lot of time with in life, but onstage they were funny and usually had a soft and even sad center, although it wasn't always easy to locate. He also did a great President Kennedy. Avery married Second City waitress Shelley Isaacs, and Jack married Second City hostess Violet Torre.

After Second City, Avery and Jack went to The Committee in San Francisco, then formed a very successful comedy team, popular in nightclubs, on records, and TV; they even had their own summer TV show. Their most famous routine "Cab Stand," CD was about a cab driver (Avery) and a very talkative and lonely conventioneer (Jack), which had been created at Second City with Dennis Cunningham as the cabbie. Avery's TV and film work includes the sitcom *My Mother the Car*, roles in such films as *Don't Drink the Water*, *Airport 79: Concorde*, *Robin Hood: Men in Tights*, and *Dracula: Dead and Loving It*, as well as a very famous series of commercials for Doritos. Jack was also very active in commercials, including being the voice of the crash test dummy in a lot of auto-safety spots. He wrote *The Muppet Movie*, and has been a voice on both *Animaniacs* and *The Simpsons*. Both men are now semi-retired, Jack much more so than Avery, who still appears occasionally on TV and has become one of the country's best improv teachers. He even returns to Chicago periodically to teach master classes.

City scenes, and a teenage garage band played a repertoire of mostly early Beatles songs. Attended almost exclusively by friends and relatives, and even by them with less and less frequency, it didn't last long.

Paul Sills returned to Chicago in 1963 to direct the eleventh show, *To the Water Tower*, which included a one-scene second act called "The Peep Show" about two conventioneers, looking for some "action," who are steered instead by a cab driver to a house where the men's fantasies are turned into seeming reality. Richard

Libertini, MacIntyre Dixon, and Jack Burns were added to the company for that show.

Richard Libertini and MacIntyre Dixon had had an act called The Stewed Prunes before coming to Second City. They were asked to join after a group of us went to see them work and nearly fell on the floor laughing, especially at the parody of us taking suggestions.

Del Close directed the twelfth show, *20,000 Frozen Grenadiers or There's Been a Terrible Accident at the Factory.* Then it was decided that he was needed back onstage, and I was handed the

Backstage Pass

I'd just graduated from the Goodman Theatre School with my master's in directing. I put together a group to do what I was seeing happen at Second City. We opened up a club called The Blind Pig. The Blind Pig was the owner, who was one-eyed. Paul Sills came, I think Bernie and Sheldon came, and Howard Alk came and asked me to join their company when finished. A few months later, after a fight in the basement during which the Blind Pig took off his eye patch and tried to put out *my* eye—he didn't want to pay us—we closed the place and left. I came to Second City in 1961. First I was in *Big Deal* at Playwrights at Second City, then I was put into the Second City company. The way you got into Second City in those days was you hung out at the bar. I hung out at the bar, and one of the waitresses there—who I'm now married to thirty-seven years—was giving me a hamburger every time I came in to hang out. That's how I was eating! I lived around the corner at a place called Emma's. I got everybody a room there.

—Avery Schreiber

Above left: Del Close (left) and Avery Schreiber (right) • Above: Avery Schreiber and Floyd Muturx in Big Deal

Spotlight on
David Steinberg...

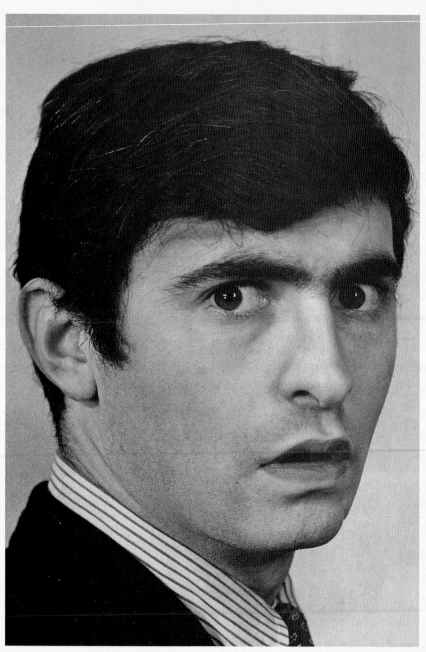

David Steinberg is from Winnipeg, Canada. Growing up, he was called "Duddy," a Yiddish diminutive form of David. He sort of studied to be a rabbi; he was able to improvise a sermon on any Old Testament character, most famously Moses. And he sort of went to the University of Chicago, for a while. But mostly he wanted to be a comedian. His fondest memory of his U of C days was being in a production of the old Broadway musical *Good News*. From the moment David was hired, he was adored by the Second City audiences, though not necessarily by his fellow actors. David himself says he was selfish. Like future stand-ups Shelley Berman and Joan Rivers before him, he almost always knew what was working for him, whether it allowed focus for the other actors onstage or not.

On David's first night at Second City, he joined the improv set. Afterwards, he witnessed a backstage fistfight between one of the actors and the stage manager. The cast had decided to end the set that night with an improvised opera based on an audience suggestion of a fairy tale. The suggestion was "Rumpelstiltskin," and David found himself without a role to play. He put on a costume hat backstage anyway and listened very carefully to what was happening onstage. Very early in the scene, just as the Queen had agreed to give up her baby to Rumpelstiltskin if she couldn't guess his name, David crossed the stage, stopped, waved, and said, "Hi, Rumpelstiltskin, how're you doing?" He then continued across the stage and exited as the cast and audience roared with laughter and the lights went out. One of the actors didn't think the stage manager should have taken the lights out and ended the scene on that joke, and let him know it. David had definitely arrived. (The next time we got "Rumpelstiltskin," he waited until nearer the end of the story before doing his crossover.)

True to the pattern of soon-to-be stand-ups established by Shelley Berman and Joan Rivers, most of David's best scenes at Second City were either alone or with one other person, who usually ended up playing the straight man or woman. Among his best were a "people" scene with Judy Graubart (later of Upstairs at the Downstairs and *The Electric Company*) about two shy war protesters gradually warming up to each other after a rally by talking about how bees court; another "people" scene as a cynical old Jewish shopkeeper finding a genie (Richard Libertini) in a bottle; and the Groucho Marx–like psychiatrist (based on a character first created by Severn Darden) he took with him to TV. His sermon on Moses became a staple of his stand-up act and was the piece that got the Smothers Brothers kicked off CBS when he did it on their show in 1969.

David left Second City to pursue an acting and stand-up career in New York. The acting didn't work out too well, but the stand-up act took off. He was a host of his own TV shows, a frequent replacement for Johnny Carson on *The Tonight Show*, and eventually began directing and writing movies, all the while continuing to take his act on the road. He eventually tired of traveling so much, and has devoted himself to directing TV sitcoms, including many episodes of *Mad about You*.

David had his own Canadian sitcom in the mid-1970s called *The David Steinberg Show*. It had a weekly guest star and a supporting cast that included John Candy, Joe Flaherty, Dave Thomas, and Martin Short. The format of the show was an acknowledged debt to Jack Benny. David played himself as the host of a variety show. Sometimes the TV audience would see the variety show, sometimes they would see backstage, and sometimes they'd follow David to the Hello Deli across the street. Although David's persona at Second City and in his act usually had been brash and aggressive, on the sitcom, he played the Benny-type role of the one who was being put upon by the for-the-most-part pretty dumb characters who surrounded him, both at work and at the deli. The kinder, gentler, older David Steinberg, developing a new image, worked very hard to get most of the laughs for other people.

Steinberg plays the straight man as Ann Elder tries to get close.

Backstage Passes

In St. Louis, during the Theatre Guild tour of the U.S. (well, part of the U.S.), one Saturday night, people were barely trickling into the huge old legit theater. Catching sight, from backstage, of hardly a dozen theatergoers in the orchestra, I conveyed this information to Severn, who was taking the air just outside the open stage door, chewing on his tortured white handkerchief. It was already eight o'clock, and I said to Severn, "Where is everybody?" He answered, "Judy, it's Saturday night...people go places."

—Judy Graubart

• • •

There was one person who defied all the tides of Second City and continually playwrote: Fred Willard. He'd make up hilarious things, and they had nothing to do with what was in front of him. He drove Paul Sills crazy because it worked. It was electric.

—Robert Klein

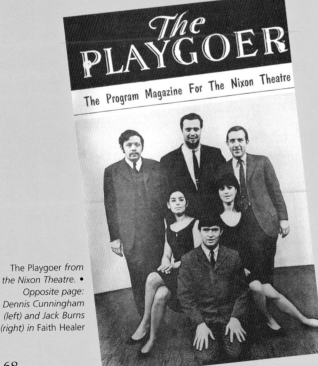

The Playgoer *from the Nixon Theatre. • Opposite page: Dennis Cunningham (left) and Jack Burns (right) in* Faith Healer

job in August 1963 and remained artistic director until 1968. My first show was *Thirteen Minotaurs or Slouching Toward Bethlehem*, with Jack Burns, Avery Schreiber, Del Close, John Brent, Ann Elder, Dick Schaal, Omar Shapli, and Melissa Hart (still a student at Northwestern University, who had to get difficult-to-acquire permission to be in shows outside of school, and later played Sally Bowles in *Cabaret* on Broadway).

When Dick Schaal, an accomplished improviser of mime props and physical transformations, who often played rather thick-headed, though kindly, people, left for Square East in early 1964, David Steinberg joined the Chicago company with his then comedy partner Gene Kadish. Del Close had seen them working in a small club in Old Town and suggested we check them out. Although we only had room in the budget at the time for one actor and decided it should be David, he refused to come unless we also hired Gene, so we stretched the budget a little further. Gene soon quit and became a lawyer.

Richard Libertini and Melinda Dillon returned to Chicago for one show in 1964, *Inside the Outsiders or Rainwater for Everyone*. By then, Jack Burns and Avery Schreiber were in the Square East company.

In 1965, we agreed to do a ten-week, eight-city tour as part of the Theatre Guild subscription season, which Bill Alton and I co-directed. While we were on the road, a show Bernie Sahlins put together in England called *The Oxford-Cambridge Revue* played the club in Chicago. Our tour opened in Detroit with a cast of Bill Alton, Severn Darden, David Steinberg, Judy Graubart, Melissa Hart, and Robert Benedetti. The subscribers' average age was about sixty, and they were expecting their usual fare—road companies of shows like *My Fair Lady* or the latest Broadway comedy. Our brand of satire so infuriated some of them that we lost the Guild several hundred subscribers during the ten weeks.

As Joyce Sloane later put it, "I think we single-handedly destroyed the Theatre Guild with our show."

Most offensive was "Faith Healer," a scene about a clearly fake, opportunistic, and bigoted TV evangelist named the Reverend Moly ("Holy Moly!")—a character created by John Brent—and three people who hoped to be cured by his laying on of hands. The scene took off on both Cubans and Jews living in Miami and ended with Moly unable to cope with what appears to be a real miracle. "You bullshittin' me?" he asks the man who's been cured. "No." "Jesus Christ, it's a miracle." Blackout. Intermission. Exit a chunk of the audience who don't return for the second act. (Jack Burns and Avery Schreiber used the piece in their act, with Jack playing Moly and Avery playing all three of the would-be healed, a Cuban, a Jew, and the totally-contorted and crippled Southerner who's miraculously healed.)

After the tour, David Steinberg and Judy Graubart returned to Chicago, where they were joined by Joan Bassie, Alex Canaan (who had a role on *Another World* for a while), Robert Klein, and Fred Willard.

David Steinberg could be very generous, as when he wouldn't take the job unless we also hired his comedy partner. He could also be generous onstage, as when, in rehearsal, Fred Willard wanted to try playing the host of an amateur hour with everyone playing really terrible amateurs while Fred did his deadpan best to cover up how bad it all was (Fred was into parody, not satire). We decided to rehearse it once before trying it that night in the improv set. Alex Canaan played a Texan who did impersonations of Bogart and Cagney, both sounding like they came from Texas. Judy Graubart played a frightened young woman who did finger tricks and got her hands stuck together. Robert Klein came out as Herbie Shaloo, a total nerd who sang "I Can't Give You Anything But Love, Baby," accompanying himself on the broom. Then David came out as a very old man who did "impersonations of insane people," beginning with a catatonic fit. He then went into the fit, which Fred, as the host, couldn't get him out of no matter how hard he tried. We were all laughing really hard except Joan Bassie, who hadn't come up with anything yet and didn't think she could follow David's fit, so David gave it to her and said, "I'll come out after it and see what I can do."

That night in the set Joan was Mrs. Rebecca Hubbard, "Eighty-four wonderful years young," as Fred put it. For her "first trick" she did the catatonic fit, remaining standing frozen no matter what Fred did to try and revive her verbally—"And for your second trick?" "Moving right along, dear," "Quality instead of quantity, eh, Mrs. Hubbard?"—or even physically—stamping his foot to scare her, hitting her on the back as if being friendly but actually much too hard, and finally shaking her—all the while keeping up a patter of pretending everything was all right. By now the audience was howling with laughter. Fred gave up on Mrs. Hubbard and called out the next contestant. David entered as a ventriloquist, carrying a long pole with a hat on it as his dummy, and froze when he saw the frozen Mrs. Hubbard. The audience laughed even harder. After a well-timed pause, David said, "Looks like a catatonic fit." The audience howled. David's big trick was smoking a cigarette and drinking water while talking for his dummy, but he choked on the cigarette with a mouthful of water,

Spotlight on
Robert Klein

Robert Klein joined the Second City company when he was twenty-three years old. He'd been trying to be in show business, but wasn't having much success. Unlike other future stand-ups, Bob never did stand-up material at Second City or went onstage alone except to do occasional introductions. He excelled at helping to create ensemble scenes. After Second City, he became a successful stand-up and recording artist. He's been in such movies as *The Owl and the Pussycat*, *The Bell Jar*, *Hooper*, *Primary Colors*, and *Mixed Nuts*, a regular on the TV drama *Sisters*, and the host of several shows. On Broadway, he's done everything from being in the small chorus of *The Apple Tree*, starring Barbara Harris and Alan Alda and directed by Mike Nichols, to the male lead in *They're Playing Our Song* and *The Sisters Rosensweig*.

As Robert tells it:

I'd gone to college to be a doctor, but a few things got in my way: calculus, physics, biology, zoology, reading, spelling, comprehension, inclination, aptitude, attitude, and talent. So I went into history and political science, the proper preparation for comedy. I had the good fortune in this small, western New York college, Alfred University, that there were two classy men, a two-man theater department. Starting my sophomore year, I got interested. They then told my father that I should go to the Yale drama school. They could get me in. My father said, "Yale? To be an actor? Did Eddie Cantor go to Yale?" He had a point. After one year, I left graduate school. I started substitute teaching to make a couple of bucks and get a little apartment. Then James Burrows, my old friend from Yale (now the well-known TV producer/director/writer), had this little revue going on in New Haven. Two guys with tuxes. An agent came and said, "Second City is coming to New York, they're looking for people." I was a little radicalized, I was a little political, my friends were kind of left-wing City College guys. That's where I wanted to be.

There were maybe thirty-five auditioners in this conference room at William Morris. I was paired with Fred Willard; we were total strangers at the time. We got suggestions from the other auditioners; they wanted the job, so they gave you hard ones! Fred and I were given the suggestion that he was a clubowner and I was a performer. I had a crude improvisational talent. I was creative. We got the job! [Second City also tried to hire Billy Dee Williams out of that audition, but he decided he didn't want to come to Chicago.]

Having a show and then an improvisation session was the best of all possible worlds for me and, I think, everyone else as an actor. I've applied this technique in the thirty-odd years I've been doing stand-up comedy. Instead of another actor being my improvising partner, it's the audience, the room, the smell, the feel. That's how I write my material. The lesson I learned from Viola Spolin and her son Paul Sills—it's as simple as pie and there's no greater substitute for it—it's that if I'm going to improvise with you, it's what you present right that second in front of me. Those glasses, your lovely nose, your sweater. It isn't playwriting. I loved putting my time in at Second City. It was much more important than the Yale Drama School.

Backstage Pass

Bob would stand in the dressing room and do bits for me. Every night I'd request favorites. One night I told him, "Bob, you've got to put together a stand-up act."

—Fred Willard

Left to right: Robert Klein today • Klein receives odd medical treatment from Fred Willard in a Second City publicity photo.

Spotlight on
Fred Willard

Fred Willard could be a clown (a rather vacant-headed one) or a straight man (but a dryly sarcastic one, as in the "Original Amateur Hour" he hosted). Nothing ever seemed to upset Fred. He was so laid-back you sometimes thought he wasn't present at all. But he heard everything, he saw everything, and he understood everything.

When he and Robert Klein were hired in 1965 and found themselves in a company with David Steinberg, Robert was intimidated and frustrated by Steinberg's domineering ways, but not Fred; he just didn't take him seriously, and David loved him for it. After Second City, Fred joined the Ace Trucking Company improv comedy group. He played the lead in Alan Arkin's production of *Little Murders* off-Broadway, then went on to do many commercials and lots of TV, most famously *Fernwood 2Night* as Martin Mull's sidekick, co-host of *Real People*, and a semi-regular on *Roseanne*. His movies include *This Is Spinal Tap*, *First Family*, *Waiting for Guffman*, and *Austin Powers: The Spy Who Shagged Me*.

One of Fred's favorite characters was a truly stupid and clumsy vampire whose fangs were two cigarettes hanging out of the sides of his mouth. Fred was also a constant source of ideas for silly blackouts. Here's one: the lights come up on a woman sitting on a chair. Fred enters and says, "Miss Jones, take a letter." As he begins dictating a business letter, Miss Jones, while taking shorthand, starts blinking, her eyes becoming severely irritated. Fred finally notices and asks her what's wrong. When she says it's her contact lenses, he responds with, "Here, let me help you." He leans over, plucks out her contact lenses, then steps back in awe as the piano plays a harp-like glissando. "Why, Miss Jones," he says, "you're beautiful!" Blackout.

Another one: a man and woman are standing onstage when the lights come up. Fred says, "And now Mary Smith will sing 'The Star Spangled Banner.'" As Mary opens her mouth, from the rear of the auditorium a male voice yells out, "Mary Smith is a whore!" After a stunned silence—and a lot of laughter from the audience—Fred says, "Nevertheless, Mary Smith will now sing…" By then the lights have faded out. **CD**

Both blackouts are still in Second City's active repertoire.

spit the water into Fred's face, and got kicked offstage. Then Fred quickly signed off the show, picked Joan's stiff body up under his arm, and carried her off as the lights faded. The scene, which was put into the next new show, got some of the biggest and longest laughs in the history of Second City. It was hardly the most meaningful scene ever done there, but it was one of the funniest; even people who only wanted satire at Second City couldn't help laughing. And David had supplied someone else with some of the biggest laughs in the scene. His real concern was that the scene be good, that the show be good. It's just that he was often sure he was the only one who knew how that could best happen.

In 1966, when Bernie took the entire Canaan-Graubart-Klein-Steinberg-Willard Chicago company to New York to reopen Square East, and no alumni were available, a replacement company—Bob Curry (the first African-American Second Citizen), Sid Grossfeld, Sandy Holt (who later joined the Ace Trucking Company improv group and is now teaching in L.A.), Jon Shank, David Walsh, and Penny White (who later moved to New York, worked with Paul Sills on Broadway in his Story Theatre shows, and is co-creator of "Stories, Ink")—had to be put together hurriedly and with great difficulty out of the workshops. From this we learned that the workshops weren't enough for preparing people for being in the Second City show; experience was needed. This led to the formation in 1967 of the first Touring Company. They learned material from old shows, and Joyce began booking them. (Today there are three national touring companies working out of Chicago, one out of Detroit, and one out of Toronto.)

Paul Sills came back to Chicago in 1966 to give me much needed relief for the twenty-first show, *Through the Eyes of the Inmates or God Is Only Sleeping*, when even *Time* magazine was asking whether God was dead. Paul came in again in 1967 for the twenty-fourth show, *The Return of the Viper*, which had a one-scene second act of an LSD trip through time and space guided by David Walsh as Timothy Leary. By then, with Vietnam escalating and the antiwar and civil rights demonstrations getting more heated, political satire was once again becoming an important part of our shows.

Dennis Cunningham, one of the cast members from the 1960s, has a unique perspective on the period:

I've long had the feeling that the last few shows Paul Sills put on in the 60s—My Friend Art Is Dead, The Peep Show, The Return of the Viper, and also Big Deal, were really cogent, adroit, and right-eously prophetic works of political theater in the best tradition, com-

Spotlight on
Peter Boyle

Peter Boyle had spent two years in Chicago in the touring company of *The Odd Couple* when he was hired by Second City. He found himself in a company with a group who mostly knew nothing about politics or tough satire and didn't care to learn. Peter was just the opposite and found the experience almost constantly frustrating. Although no real fights broke out, it got to a point where either Peter or most of the rest of the company had to go, so

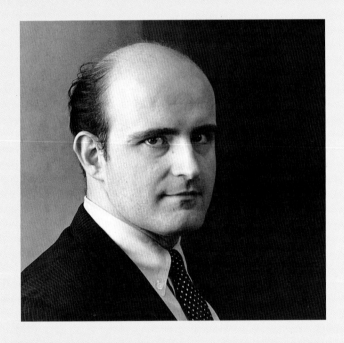

Peter went. It was a loss, both because we needed his deep concern with what was going on in the world and because he was good onstage, a talented character actor then as now. Since then, of course, after his big success playing a bigoted construction worker (the title character) in *Joe*, he's been in many movies, including *Taxi Driver*, *The Dream Team*, *Malcolm X*, *Honeymoon in Vegas*, Eddie Murphy's version of *Dr. Doolittle*, and perhaps most famously as the Monster who could sing and dance (sort of) to "Puttin' on the Ritz" in *Young Frankenstein*. He's Ray's father on the TV series *Everybody Loves Raymond*.

bining good, up-to-the-minute information and insight about what was happening in the country with top-notch humor and impeccable mise-en-scène. I'm biased, for sure, because I was in Art Is Dead and Peep Show (and I even wrote a couple of the songs in Big Deal), but it wasn't until a long time later that I realized how deep a lot of that stuff was in reflecting political and social realities that were otherwise imperfectly perceived back then, to say the least. I mean, there was a whole scene in The Peep Show about a CIA plot to assassinate Castro—in 1962! It was really a joke to us then, except it was really happening. And there was a lot more of what the 60s would go on to be about—at least for white people—in those shows. So I think they represented a real high point, and I remain very glad I was in on it.

By 1967, Wells Street had become a major place for going out in Chicago, with stores, head shops, restaurants, and bars opening everywhere over a three- or four-block area; there was even a Ripley's Believe It Or Not Museum. On August 1, we and the Sullivan arches moved two-and-a-half blocks south to our current 350-seat space in Piper's Alley at 1616 North Wells, a block west of the original Playwrights Theatre Club. David Steinberg came back to be in the twenty-seventh show, the first in the new space, a "best of." Again, Joyce Sloane sold out a week of previews; this time there was still wet paint on the walls the first night. Peter Boyle was in that show, along with J.J. Barry, Martin Harvey Friedberg, Sid Grossfeld, Burt Heyman, Sandy Holt, and Lynne Lipton.

We also franchised a Second City show to a Bourbon Street nightclub in New Orleans in 1967, cast locally but retaining artistic control from Chicago—our first such attempt since Square East. It was the wrong show in the wrong place and lasted a very short time; the customers, usually drunk even before they arrived, were expecting to see strippers and cheap comics and were sorely and audibly disappointed. When the owner saw our rehearsal of the mimed "Strip to Bach," he asked if the woman doing it could actually strip. We all immediately said no in chorus, but it was already clear what we were in for when the show opened (and that doesn't include the intense August heat and humidity or the baseball-sized flying cockroaches).

In 1968, Bell & Howell co-produced with us the only Second City movie to date, *The Monitors*, a low-budget, ultra-low special effects, science-fiction comedy/adventure starring Guy Stockwell,

Top to bottom: Sandy Holt, Peter Boyle, Lynne Lipton, and Martin Harvey Friedberg • Martin Harvey Friedberg

74

Susan Oliver, Larry Storch, and Avery Schreiber, with many Second Citizens in supporting roles and with cameos by such people as Alan Arkin, his sons Adam and Matthew, comic Jackie Vernon, and Senator Everett Dirkson. About twelve people not connected with Second City saw it during its run in movie theaters; it can still sometimes be seen on TV late at night. It isn't all that bad.

Avery came to Chicago in 1968 to co-direct the twenty-ninth show with me, *Showdown at Credibility Gap or What We've Got Here Is a Failure to Communicate*, a comment on a quote of Lyndon Johnson's, not an attempt to make the audience think we were doing *Cool Hand Luke*. As the country was getting more and more divided, Peter Boyle in particular was seeing to it that political satire was well represented in the show, including Peter's scathing running commentary on all the Presidential candidates, presented as if the candidates, played by the rest of the cast, were walking the runway in a fashion show.

By then I, like pretty much every Second City director (and performer) before and after me, felt that I'd done enough Second City shows—at least for the time being, if not forever. Mike Miller (who went from Second City to The Committee in San Francisco, and then on to Hollywood) took over as artistic director in 1968, after we'd co-directed the thirtieth show, *A Plague on Both Your Houses*, which opened just before Mayor Daley's notorious "shoot to kill" Democratic Convention, and which probably had the most political content of any show ever done at Second City. It was also the angriest show in memory.

Earlier in the year we, along with all the other businesses on Wells Street, had been ordered to close for a couple of days and nights during the riots following the assassination of Dr. Martin Luther King, while the National Guard patrolled the streets in open vehicles, carrying heavy weapons. During the Democratic Convention there were no such orders; the police could "handle it." Second City is very near Lincoln Park, and shortly after eleven o'clock each night during the whole week, we could hear the kids being chased out of the park, could smell the tear gas, and could see the police pushing people up against the wall of the drug store across the street from us and occasionally hitting them. Paul Sills and some others set up a hostel for the kids in the by-now-deserted beer garden and former Second City at 1846 Wells.

In 1969, Bernie Sahlins took the entire Chicago cast to New York, and a whole new generation of Second City performers brought a different style and attitude to the show. They called themselves "The Next Generation."

● ● ● ○

Backstage Passes

Paul Sills came in and began to work with our company in 1967, which included J.J. Barry, Martin Harvey Friedberg, Bert Heyman, David Walsh, and Sandy Holt. He created a full-act psychedelic piece called "The Trip." For me, this whole experience was, appropriately enough, mind-blowing. Paul introduced me to a gutsy and intuitive realm of "playing." It was a great learning experience. This piece rode the waves of what was happening in the late 60s: psychedelics, Timothy Leary, The Tibetan Book of the Dead, headphones, The Beatles, The Rolling Stones, Bob Dylan, Vietnam, the whole transformation of family and culture and what was "going down." I loved this show—not only because it was my first experience with Paul as a director, but because it was so "hip." This was what was happening. And we were (as Viola Spolin's theater games call it) "exploring and heightening" onstage what was to be an amazing shift in consciousness throughout the country.

—Penny White

● ●

During the '68 Lincoln Park riot/free-for-all, a policeman threw me up against the wall and put an automatic weapon to my neck. It was on the steps of Second City at 1616 North Wells. I can't say it was my favorite Second City memory, but it was my most memorable.

—Murphy Dunne

Spotlight on
Familiar Faces
and Some You Haven't Seen • • •

Some Familiar Faces & Voices:

Paul Dooley (1962–63 Square East)—Mike Nichols saw him and hired him for *The Odd Couple* on Broadway. Paul then made a few TV appearances and had his first major film role as Dennis Christopher's blue-collar father in *Breaking Away*. Since then he's been seen in *Popeye*, *Sixteen Candles*, *Waiting for Guffman*, *Angels in the Endzone*, *Runaway Bride*, and *Happy Texas*, among many other movies and TV shows.

Linda Kash, who started out as a classically trained actress, went from The Old Firehall to such films as *Waiting for Guffman*, *Urban Safari*, and *Ernest Goes to Africa* and has been on numerous TV shows, including *The Newsroom*, *Seinfeld*, *Ellen*, *Minor Adjustments*, and *The Bookfair Murders*.

Tony Rosato was cast in Toronto's touring company with John Candy as his director, went from there to mainstage, then to *SCTV*, and then *SNL*. Since then he's been in such TV shows and feature films as *Kissinger & Nixon*, *Rent a Kid*, *Mystery Date*, and *Switching Channels*. He's now a regular on the campy Canadian action drama *Relic Hunter*.

Robin Duke started taking classes at Second City Toronto at Catherine O'Hara's insistence. A character actor who specialized in talkative, often gauche characters, she replaced Catherine on *SCTV* and then moved on to *Saturday Night Live* from 1981 to 1984, where she received an Emmy nomination for her work. She's also been in other TV shows such as *Degas*, *North of 60*, and *Boston Common*. She's appeared in many films, including *Club Paradise*, *Multiplicity*, *Stuart Saves His Family*, *Groundhog Day*, *I Love Trouble*, and *Only You*.

Danny Breen is probably most familiar for his Cheerios commercials. He was a regular on *Not Necessarily the News* and is now a producer for *Whose Line Is It Anyway?*

Top to bottom: Paul Dooley (left) with Jane Alexander (right) • Tony Rosato • Robin Duke • Danny Breen

Mike Hagerty was the quintessential Second City "working guy" character. He's been in many movies, including *Wayne's World*, *Speed 2: Cruise Control*, *Stuart Saves His Family*, *One Good Cop*, *Dick Tracy*, *Inspector Gadget*, and *Austin Powers: The Spy Who Shagged Me*. Mike's TV credits include *Ally McBeal*, *Friends*, *The Drew Carey Show*, and *Seinfeld*.

Miriam Flynn is a Second City favorite who has starred as Cousin Catherine in each of the *National Lampoon Vacation* movies. She was also the voice of "Maa" in the film *Babe*. Additional film credits include *Waiting for Guffman*, *For Keeps*, and *Mr. Mom*. Miriam is also a regular on TV with appearances on *Dharma & Greg*, *Buffy the Vampire Slayer*, *Ally McBeal*, and *The Practice*.

John Kapelos was another local favorite who began his film career while still at Second City. He has been in films like *Thief* (with Jim Belushi), *Doctor Detroit* (with Dan Aykroyd), *Class*, *Sixteen Candles*, *The Breakfast Club*, *Nothing in Common*, *Roxanne*, *Internal Affairs*, *The Shadow*, *The Relic*, and *Deep End of the Ocean*. John played detective Donald Schanke on the first two seasons of *Forever Knight*. Other TV credits include *The West Wing*, *The Practice*, *Seinfeld*, *Home Improvement*, and the HBO movie *The Late Shift*.

Isabella Hoffman had already established herself as a talented (and beautiful) actress when she joined Second City. She went on to costar in *Dear John* with Judd Hirsch, and as "Megan Russert" on *Homicide: Life on the Streets*, where she met her husband, Daniel Baldwin. Isabella is now a regular on Showtime's *Beggars and Choosers*.

Steve Carell was one of the best character actors ever at Second City. He and his wife, **Nancy Walls**, who was discovered while waiting tables at a restaurant across the street from Second City, moved to New York, where he did *The Dana Carvey Show* and she went on to *Saturday Night Live*. Steve and Nancy are now regulars on *The Daily Show* with Jon Stewart.

Joel Murray followed his brothers Brian and Bill to Second City in 1989's *The Gods Must Be Lazy*. He's been in such movies as *The Cable Guy*, *Shakes the Clown*, *Scrooged* (with Bill), and the cult hit *One Lazy Afternoon*. Joel was a regular on *Love & War* and *Grand* and is now a regular on *Dharma & Greg*.

Top to bottom: Mike Hagerty • John Kapelos • Nancy Walls • Joel Murray

Suzy Nakamura plays Toby Ziegler's assistant on *The West Wing* and was in the HBO special *Larry David: Curb Your Enthusiasm*.

Ron West always had a prop gun in his pocket when he walked onstage, just in case it was the only way out of a scene. He was the tall guy with the beard and glasses who got charred to a crisp in his only scene in *Backdraft*. He's been on *Whose Line Is It Anyway?* in Britain and has a recurring role on *Third Rock from the Sun*.

David Pasquesi does multitudes of voice-overs on radio and TV, including many for McDonalds. He's also been in an occasional movie, including *Father of the Bride* as Martin Short's sidekick and the schoolteacher in *Groundhog Day*.

Patrick McKenna started as a theater manager at Toronto Second City. He honed his comic skills with The Second City Expo in Vancouver. He then came to Toronto Second City mainstage and, after that, performed his stand-up comedy throughout Canada and the United States. McKenna won a 1998 Gemini Award for his work in *Traders* and another one for his role as the lovable and naïve Harold Green in *The Red Green Show*. McKenna has made guest appearances on numerous series, including *Made in Canada*, *Blackfly*, *Street Legal*, and *Due South*, as well as roles in the feature films *Joe's Wedding* and *Writer's Block*, starring Kelsey Grammer.

JoBe Cerny is the voice of the Pillsbury Dough Boy.

Some Who Chose Different Paths:

Bob Clemens, **Kevin Doyle**, and **Pat Andrews** all joined Chicago's finest, despite the amount of grief we've given the police department onstage over the years.

Joe Doyle ran for Chicago Alderman. He didn't win, so he went into TV and film production.

Barbara Hall (waitress at Second City Toronto) became the Mayor of Toronto.

Mary Charlotte Wilcox performed on Toronto's mainstage and was a featured player on *SCTV* before becoming ordained as a priest in the Anglican Church. She lives and works in Edmonton.

There are hundreds of other stories: **Dennis Cunningham** and **Eugene Kadish** became lawyers; **Alex Canaan, Harv (now Grant) Robbin**, and **Peter Burns** became advertising executives; **Robert Benedetti** and **Omar Shapli** became highly respected university educators. There have been TV, record, and commercial producers, agents, film editors, novelists, playwrights, and literary managers.

Some interesting examples of people who never made it to a Second City mainstage, but who certainly found major performing careers anyway, include: **Julia Louis-Dreyfus** (of *Seinfeld*), **Andy Dick** (*Newsradio*), and **Jeremy Piven** (*The Larry Sanders Show*), who were in touring companies but left before ever getting to mainstage.

There are some who never even made it onstage at all:

Greg Cohen, a host at Second City, was a writer for Conan O'Brien and *MadTV*.

Jon Favreau, also a host, wrote and starred in *Swingers*.

Jeff Garlin, box office (and occasionally onstage at Chicago e.t.c. between firings and quittings, though he never opened a show), has a stand-up act and wrote for and costarred in HBO's *Larry David: Curb Your Enthusiasm*.

W in O RD. . . .
by George Wendt

Like a lot of people, I first saw Second City as a patron. I was brought by my older sister when I was in college. This would be like 1968. I thought it was great, a fantastic evening. And I laughed hard. At that time the company included Peter Boyle, J.J. Barry, Burt Heyman, Martin Harvey Friedberg, and Ira Miller.

I came back to Second City shortly after that, and those guys were replaced by a bunch of real rookies. They were real raw, unprepared types: Joe Flaherty, Harold Ramis, Brian Doyle-Murray. All of a sudden, it was like *whoa!* These guys seem more like my age. Where those other guys seemed more like jaded old actors, these guys were cool.

I was really intrigued.

Then I graduated college, and I was off doing what I was going to do. You know: What are you going to do with your (echo) *life, life, life, life, life, life?*

I was traveling around Europe the way young men do when they get out of college, and want to avoid working and find out what they want to do with their *life, life, life, life, life, life.* So I started by a process of elimination: what wouldn't I want to do? I was literally listing them—teacher, fireman, doctor. And it turned out, the only thing I wouldn't hate doing was being in the cast of Second City.

Second City looked for all the world like a bunch of people goofing off onstage. I was pretty sure they got paid for it.

I knew you could take workshops to learn what they did at Second City, so when I got back to Chicago in the summer of 1973, I called the Second City box office, and they told me the workshops started in September. They sent me a flyer. I paid my tuition for the workshop with Josephine Forsberg, and I went. I really liked it. Eventually, I signed up for two workshops a week.

One day Josephine said to me, "You might be ready for the children's show."

"Really?" I said.

"Yeah. Tell you what. Show up at the theater at eleven-thirty."

I said, "Isn't the show at two-thirty?"

She said, "Yeah, but be there at eleven-thirty."

So I showed up dutifully at eleven-thirty, and the door to the theater was locked. I rang the bell and waited—and waited and waited. I rang the bell again. Finally, Josephine Forsberg came down and let me in.

You know, back in the old days they used to smoke cigarettes at the show. And the porter didn't work on Sundays, so the floor was covered with all these cigarette butts. Josephine handed me a broom and dustpan. I kind of looked at them and said, like, "What's this?"

She said, "Welcome to the theater."

Eventually, I understudied the kids show. And then I did the kids show. In the course of a year, I had two auditions for the touring company.

The night before the first audition I went to a White Sox game with some friends. We decided after the game to have a drink at a local bar and wait for the traffic to clear. We got jumped in the bar. It was a tough neighborhood. So I showed up at the audition with a black eye and gashes everywhere. Bernie Sahlins says, "Do five characters coming through the door." Five characters with a real shiner and a puffy face. I didn't get in the first time.

But the second time I did, and I spent about a year in the touring company. And that is where I really began to learn. There were two touring companies back then. One touring company did an Equity gig at a club in Kansas City, and one performed at colleges. In the touring company I met Jim Sherman, Miriam Flynn, and Will Aldis.

After a year in the touring company, Bernie opened a company in Pasadena, and everyone in the resident company went out there. So those left in town who weren't in the resident company were put on the mainstage, including me.

I first went on October 1975 and performed on the mainstage until that summer when I was fired. Actually, I was sent back to the touring company. It was the first of many firings and hirings for me.

What was I fired for? For not being funny, for flagrantly sucking onstage.

But eventually I learned what was funny and what wasn't. That's the thing about Second City, they teach you, or you learn, what works and what doesn't, what's funny and what isn't.

That's what I learned.

5
chapter

The 1970s

New Blood and New Directions

The end of the 1960s was signaled by, as much as anything else, the antithesis of Woodstock, the Stones' debacle at Altamont. The 1970s were ushered in by the Ohio National Guard opening fire on a group of demonstrators at Kent State, killing four students, one of whom was simply on her way to class.

America had lost its innocence in the 1960s. It had awakened to the realities of race, sex, war, money, and politics. Hundreds of thousands of people had mobilized to change society for the better. And, although they made great strides, the problems they faced weren't going to go away that easily. By the 1970s, and especially after Watergate, many had lost their idealism, had become cynical, and

Backstage Pass

We became known as the "Next Generation" when we took over Second City because the level of cultural reference for us was different. The original companies of the late '50s and early '60s had been Freudian, alienated, post-war, beatnik, bohemian in their philosophy and outlook. We were political in a different way. We were radical, born out of the 1968 Chicago convention. We looked like the guys who were in the streets getting clubbed by the police, but we weren't really in the streets. The language changed. John Belushi introduced a whole new language to the stage with the classic line, "Eat a bowl of fuck." I still don't know what it means.

—Harold Ramis

Opening page: (left to Right) Eugenie Ross-Leming, John Belushi, Jim Fisher, and Judy Morgan

Harold Ramis (left) and David Blum (right) in The Next Generation

turned to improving their own lot. It was the beginning of the so-called "me" decade, which would, of course, be eclipsed by the overt greed of the 1980s.

The Vietnam War had ended. Ford pardoned Nixon. The voting age was lowered to eighteen, and abortion was legalized in the Supreme Court's ruling on Roe v. Wade. The first test-tube baby was born. Muhammad Ali regained the heavyweight title, and Dock Ellis pitched a no-hitter for the Pittsburgh Pirates while tripping on LSD.

As much as any time in memory, Americans wanted to laugh. Popular comedies of the 1970s included TV shows like The Mary Tyler Moore Show, The Bob Newhart Show, Happy Days, and Soap and movies like Young Frankenstein, Monty Python and the Holy Grail, and Animal House. At the same time, TV shows like All in the Family, Good Times, and Sanford and Son and movies like M*A*S*H (as well as the TV series), Blazing Saddles, Monty Python's Life of Brian, and Network sharply satirized such issues as race, religion, war, class, mass media, and corporate greed.

Among the powerful, trend-setting, and envelope-pushing new films were Five Easy Pieces, Last Tango in Paris, A Clockwork Orange, Carnal Knowledge, Cabaret, Annie Hall, and Apocalypse Now.

Ms., High Times, and People hit the newsstands. Influential new books included Bob Woodward and Carl Bernstein's All the President's Men, Kate Millet's Sexual Politics, Alexandr Solzhenitsyn's The Gulag Archipelago, Alex Comfort's The Joy of Sex, and such novels as Erica Jong's Fear of Flying, John Irving's The World According to Garp, and William Styron's Sophie's Choice. More traditional bestsellers were Erich Segal's Love Story, William Peter Blatty's The Exorcist, and Stephen King's first novel, Carrie (all turned into hit movies).

Off-Broadway you could see National Lampoon's Lemmings, American Buffalo, and Buried Child; on Broadway, Amadeus and The Sunshine Boys. Important new musicals included the form-breaking concept musicals Company, Chicago, and A Chorus Line. In addition, a few rock musicals found success, including Godspell, Jesus Christ Superstar, Grease, and The Wiz. The Who's Tommy, the first rock opera, was performed at the Metropolitan Opera House.

Jimi Hendrix, Jim Morrison, and Janis Joplin died of alcohol and drug abuse, and the Beatles split up. The last half of the decade was dominated by disco.

The Next Generation of Satire

George S. Kaufman said that satire is what closes on Saturday night. Bernie Sahlins says satire is reactionary, that it's saying, "Look, this is the status quo, society's rules and ethical principles, and this is how you're breaking them." Another kind says, "These are the rules, and they need changing." Believing that only one of those ways of thinking is possible is what much of the conflict and violence in America was about in the late 1960s and early '70s.

Ever since Second City's third or fourth show, people have been complaining that we don't do political satire anymore. Second City has always done political satire of one kind or another, sometimes more, sometimes less, depending on the times, and rarely as much as people seem to remember. The 1968 show *A Plague on Both Your Houses* proved, however, if proof were needed, that it's very difficult to find the humor in what makes you that angry or scared. It wasn't until the withdrawal from Vietnam and after the disclosures of Watergate that things even started to calm down in America, and people could comfortably begin the return to examining their own navels.

The 1970s also proved to be a pivotal decade for Second City. There were some lean times during those years when Bernie had to scrimp and save to keep the theater afloat, all the while taking a chance on a whole new kind of Second City performer. Our audiences were growing older and less loyal, and even though the new company was starting to bring in younger audiences, Bernie had to borrow money from his father to pay the bills. In retrospect, he thinks the ticket prices were probably too low: "We were afraid to raise them, thinking we might lose our audience." Tickets in 1971 cost $3.95 on weekends and $2.95 on weeknights. Sometimes things got really bad.

"We took our touring group on the road to California," recalls Joyce Sloane. "Our promoter—the man who set up the dates and was risking all the money—was Stan Seiden. We were in the middle of California when Stan realized that the actors and I had no money. 'How will you eat?' he asked. I shrugged my shoulders. Bernie had sent us on the road with no cash at all—we didn't have any—but he knew that through sheer personality and charm I could get Stan to give us some money. It worked."

When we opened our Second City in Toronto in 1973, it gave us another channel of incredible talent, but the money still wasn't exactly rolling in, and many questioned whether or not we could survive. However, with the debut of *Saturday Night Live* in 1975—with our alumni making up nearly half the cast—the tide began to turn. By the end of the decade, with *Animal House* and our own *SCTV* further spreading the name, business finally turned around.

Back in 1969, when Bernie took the entire Chicago cast to New York, he may have had a hidden agenda, since it really was

Spotlight on
Brian Doyle-Murray

Brian Doyle-Murray, Bill's older brother, was one of the "Next Generation" cast members. After leaving Second City, he stayed busy as a writer and comic character actor. He cowrote *Groundhog Day* and wrote for both *SCTV* and *Saturday Night Live*, and also made periodic appearances on both shows. He's been seen on many TV shows, and was a regular on the sitcoms *Good Sports* and Chris Elliot's *Get a Life*. Brian's been in such movies as *Modern Problems*, *Club Paradise*, *National Lampoon's Vacation*, *Multiplicity*, *Waiting for Guffman*, and *Wayne's World*.

Joe Flaherty is a major sports fan. When Pittsburgh Pirates star Roberto Clemente died in 1972, Joe, who was still in the Chicago Second City cast at the time, disappeared for a few days, and no one knew where he was, not even his wife, Judith, who was in the touring company. He'd gone to Puerto Rico to mourn in the airport there.

—S.P.

• • •

When I was first hired, I met Joe Flaherty and he looked at me and said, "What are you, twelve?"

—Nia Vardalos

• • •

I always loved the laugh. You know, just going for the laugh. If it were something setting up something abstractly, with a lot of references, I would much rather just go for the belly laugh. And I guess the trick is trying to keep some sort of line. I'm not the worst, but I opened some of the floodgates for the low references you'll find now (Showtime, 1988).

—Joe Flaherty

• • •

Joe Flaherty showed me the difference between shtick and entertainment. At first, in a cocktail party scene, for example, I'd roam around the stage shooting up or swearing to get a laugh. Flaherty taught me subtlety (Rosenthal.1972).

—John Belushi

time to move Second City in new directions and find new audiences. A much cooler, more laid back, and less psychological, angst-ridden approach to satire seemed necessary. And this time we had a touring company ready to take over—David Blume, Brian Doyle-Murray, Jim Fisher, Joe Flaherty, Roberta Maguire, Judy Morgan, and Harold Ramis. They had long hair, wore blue jeans onstage, and swore. Although Bernie would later contend that they weren't really "hippies" at all, the new cast was indeed a reflection of the youth culture of the 1970s. And they had a show ready, one they'd been working on forever out on the road. It was called *The Next Generation*.

The shows took on a different look and feel. Everything loosened up. Second City always has been a mirror for the audience, and this time was no different. The counterculture of the late 1960s and early '70s took over much of Old Town in Chicago, and we were in the center of it. Head shops, candle stores, and record shops lined the streets. Across the street at The Earl of Old Town, folk singers like Steve Goodman, Bonnie Koloc, and John Prine made regular visits to the theater, and vice versa. Jerry Rubin and Abbie Hoffman dropped by to improvise with the cast while they were part of the "Chicago Seven" trial, sometimes having to sneak in and out using the company's props as disguises. The scenes onstage started being more direct in their criticism of politicians, corporations, and organized religion.

As they were remaking Second City in the image of the day's youth, the company created many classic scenes in such shows as *Justice Is Done or Oh, Calcoolidge*; *Picasso's Mustache*; *Cum Grano Salis*; and *Premises, Premises*, most of them directed by Bernie Sahlins. The subjects of the scenes from these shows included a V.D. clinic run by a very strict and judgmental nun (CD), people unable to contain their laughter at the funeral of the man who got his head caught in a gallon can of Van Camp's beans, a PTA meeting about whether or not the school should offer sex education, a taxidermist who brings his girlfriend home to meet his dead and stuffed parents, and a ballet about Chicago police brutality called "Swine Lake."

In 1972, Del Close returned to Chicago and directed *43rd Parallel or McCabre & Mrs. Miller*. The timing was perfect. He found a group of performers eager and excited to learn from him.

Harold Ramis said of Del:

Del Close, though older, was of our generation. He had always been possibly a century ahead of his time. There was no hope of catching up with Del, but he took us to new places spiritually and in

Spotlight on
Joe Flaherty

Joe Flaherty worked with Michael Miller in Pittsburgh. When Mike became the director in Chicago in 1968, he brought Joe in as stage manager and to work out with the touring company. When it was time to move the company up to mainstage, he moved up with them. In 1972, he joined the *National Lampoon* show on tour, and in 1973, he moved to Toronto to be in and direct several Second City shows there. He was one of the original members of the *SCTV* cast in 1976—the only one to do the whole run of the show—as well as one of its writers and associate producers. Joe's been in such movies as *1941*, *Used Cars*, *Stripes*, *Club Paradise*, *Innerspace*, *Back to the Future II*, and *Happy Gilmore*. Among his many TV appearances, probably most notable was as the father in the excellent and sadly underrated series *Freaks and Geeks*.

Joe is so solid a character actor that many *SCTV* fans were unaware for a long time that he played both station owner Guy Caballero and newscaster Floyd Robertson or that Floyd did double duty as Count Floyd, the host of "Monster Horror Chiller Theater," who lived in an upright coffin and introduced bad horror movies usually starring Dr. Tongue (John Candy).

Joe was notorious for bailing out of improvs that weren't going well, usually by finding a quick and silly way to make an exit. One night Dave Thomas, Ben Gordon, and several other people were auditioning for Second City in Toronto by working out in the improv set. A few of them did a scene with Joe set in a rowboat on the water. It was going really badly and Joe tried, several times, to dive off the mimed boat and "swim" off stage. Each time he tried, Dave, fully aware of Joe's reputation, was ready for him. He grabbed him by the ankles and prevented him from leaving. The scene bombed, but Dave got the job.

Joe also frequently liked to "pimp" the other improvisers (setting them up for a fall) by doing such things as miming picking up a book, realizing it's in Latin, and handing it off to someone to read out loud, or answering a mime phone and handing it off to anyone onstage, saying, "It's for you." He loved to catch people off-guard. Such behavior is, of course, absolutely against the rules of improv, but it was really funny.

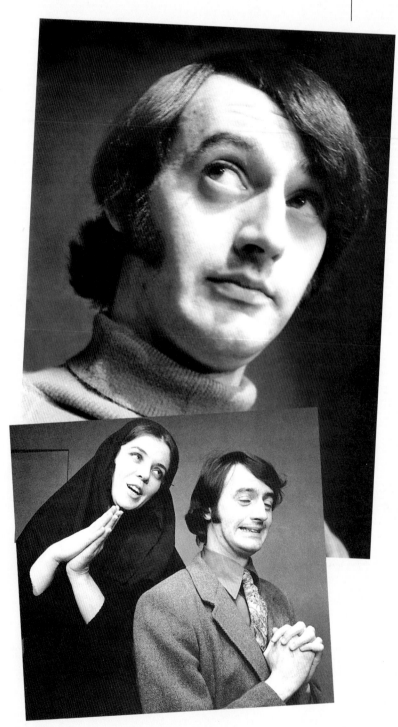

Above: Flaherty and Roberta Maguire in Picasso's Mustache

Spotlight on Harold Ramis

Harold Ramis had been "Party Jokes" editor of *Playboy* magazine before joining the Second City cast in 1969, after taking improv workshops and being in the touring company for a year. (His audition was doing an improv set to a full house on a Saturday night.) Even in his early days in the show, he was already showing his instincts as a writer and director, and he was good at coming up with endings for scenes—not an easy accomplishment. Harold went from Second City to the *Lampoon* show, was head writer, associate producer, and a cast member of the early *SCTV* shows, and had his first Hollywood hit as cowriter of *Animal House*. His career went from there to directing, writing, and/or acting in such movies as *Meatballs*, *Stripes*, *Caddyshack*, both *Ghostbusters* movies, *Baby Boom*, *Club Paradise*, *Groundhog Day*, and *Analyze This*, many of which are among the highest-grossing comedies of all time.

Harold and his family live in the Chicago area. He sees almost every new Second City show and, afterwards, gives notes and encouragement to every new generation of performers, writers, and directors.

Right: Joe Flaherty and Ann Ryerson look on as David Rasche (middle) and Harold Ramis (right) begin improvising an audience suggestion in Premises, Premises.

consciousness that none of us had been before. Part of it was you didn't understand a word he was saying, but he was somehow communicating something subliminal to us about taking chances, about really listening, about breaking out of any predictable structures, letting go of structure. On a personal level, Del said something to me. I used to kind of stand upstage of everyone, make funny faces, and lob in funny lines—I would kind of score with the audience. Del pulled me aside after a show and said, "Someday you're going to look in the mirror and you're going to say, 'I'm so cute and I'm only forty-five years old.'"

Harold Ramis (left) and Joe Flaherty (right) perform in a scene from Cooler by the Lake.

The Road to Mainstage

"The Next Generation" was the first mainstage company to be cast completely out of the touring company. Now, with Second City Training Centers in Chicago, Toronto, Detroit, New York, L.A., and Cleveland; and touring and mainstage companies in Chicago, Toronto, and Detroit; the hope of would-be Second Citizens is that they'll go from a training center to a touring company to a mainstage. However, that isn't an automatic process. There are auditions: auditions for getting into a training center, auditions between some levels in the training centers, and auditions and callbacks for getting into a touring company (although you don't have to have gone to a training center to qualify). When it comes to getting to a mainstage, the actor's work in the touring company is usually his audition. But, occasionally, someone gets hired straight into a resident company through auditions, which causes shock waves that often take months to settle.

Every time we'd be improvising, the directors would say, "Stop writing, just go with what's happening." I couldn't resist it, because you'd be improvising and the person you might be improvising with would go off on some idiotic tangent that you couldn't imagine. You knew what you wanted them to say. It was almost like the Password game where you say, "You're the..." and want them to say "doctor," but they're going to turn out to be a Martian. I couldn't psychically influence what was happening onstage. I love the process of improv, but as soon as I had the opportunity, I started writing what everyone else was going to say. Del Close once said, "If you concentrate on making everyone else on stage look good, then you will look good. Even if the scene bombs, even if it totally sucks, at least the audience will get the message that cooperation and respect for each other is possible. If nothing else, you could maintain your dignity with that awareness of each other." To this day I believe that.

—Harold Ramis

We did a road show once at a Toronto hotel. After not getting one laugh during the entire first act, we were relieved to discover that none of the doctors we were playing to spoke English!

—Maggie Butterfield

Spotlight on
John Belushi

John Belushi went to a Wisconsin state college his freshman year, then transferred to the College of DuPage near Wheaton, Illinois, his hometown. In order to help himself through school, he and his friends Tino Insana and Steve Beshakes started a restaurant cleaning service. When that didn't take off, they formed an improv group instead and played nearby schools, coffeehouses, and churches. All three transferred to the University of Illinois-Chicago in 1970 and did their improvs in a nearby coffeehouse for a few months, where they began developing a respectable amount of usable material.

When John joined Second City in 1971, he was twenty-one years old and hadn't even done any time in the touring company. He was one of the ones audiences immediately singled out for future stardom. After he left Second City, John did *The National Lampoon Radio Hour* and *National Lampoon's Lemmings*. Then came *Saturday Night Live*, *Animal House*, and from there on a rocket to the moon, including such movies as *1941*, *The Blues Brothers*, *Neighbors*, and *Continental Divide*. John died of an overdose at the Chateau Marmont in Los Angeles in 1982. Many of his friends and peers took the warning and quit substance abuse cold. A few didn't. For those who did, John didn't die in vain, though that doesn't lessen the loss. The John Belushi Scholarship Fund, created to help aspiring young Chicago performers, was established in his name during Second City's twenty-fifth anniversary celebration.

Judy Belushi Pisano (John's widow) describes a typical day for them, back in the early 1970s:

Basic day: Sleep late. Judy to school (University of Illinois) and John to Lum's, a restaurant on the corner of Wells and North. There he would encounter other cast members. Hours of poring over the

Top: Belushi as Mayor Richard J. Daley • Bottom: Belushi plays a hippie. • Right: A get-well poster made for Belushi by Gilda Radner when he was hospitalized for a bad knee. The poster now hangs in the offices of Second City.

newspaper gave the cast the opportunity to share what was going on in the world, each reading aloud interesting or funny stories. This usually lasted right up to rehearsal. I returned to the apartment in the late afternoon, as would John. Just enough time for a light meal, perhaps a nap, a shower, and off to the show for John, homework for me. After the show we usually hung out at one of our apartments, smoked grass, and had a late meal while we watched old movies on TV. If a good B movie came on, the phone lines buzzed as the guys called to make certain each was watching. The next night, a parody of the movie was inevitable. These were some of the silliest sketches, always a bit "inside" and very funny. The Second City days are warm memories, filled with love and laughter, days I will treasure always.

Among his characters at Second City were Mayor Daley, Marlon Brando, Truman Capote, and Joe Cocker. One of his characters was an inept tax man who asked a client, "About how many children do you have?"

Once John became famous, he lived in a kind of bubble when he was in public, always surrounded by friends, some of them also his bodyguards. There was no other way to keep his fans from swarming him. Jim Belushi remembers his brother's impact on a room at the height of his fame:

Harold Ramis (left), Eugenie Ross Leming (middle), and John Belushi (right) stage a mimed western.

Will Aldis and I were doing our Whitehorse Tavern scene 🅲🅳 *when John walked onto the stage. I could feel the rush of air from the audience. He sucked the wind right out of the theater. I was so humbled by the magnitude of his presence and the response from the audience, I wanted to urinate on myself. The audience didn't stop cheering for five minutes. John just paced back and forth miming ordering a drink and then playing the jukebox. The audience would not stop; Will and I just stared at him. Finally over the roar he said, "Oh, this is a gay bar," and left. We tried to continue the scene and it was impossible. We were stuck, so a minute later John popped his head through the door and said, "Come on. There's a better bar down the street," and we ran offstage with him.*

I went out to the College of DuPage to sell a series of short experimental films called the Arts and Entertainment Series to the head of student activities. As long as I was there I thought I'd try to sell them Second City. He said, "We don't need Second City. We've got a student who goes to see your shows and comes back and does the whole thing for us." I said, "Oh yeah? Well, I'd like to meet him!" He said, "Well, he's right over there playing foosball." He took me over, and this student looks up, raises one eyebrow, and, of course, it was John Belushi. I told him to come and see us. Soon after that he transferred to the University of Illinois' Chicago Campus. He would run up the Second City stairs all the time giving me a flyer for a show he was doing at some church over there. When Second City was looking for replacements in 1971, I called John in, and he came to audition. He blew Bernie away. He'd been a football player at DuPage. He always said, "Attack the stage like a bull!" That was John's thing. John had some bad habits, but he was always very serious about the work.

—Joyce Sloane

● ● ●

John was a rare blend of characteristics. He had a classical beauty, and he was funny-looking. He could be impishly sweet or outrageously funny. He could frighten you or melt your heart with a smile. His eyes told all. He had the power to make people think, to shake things up and say, "Don't get so uptight," to mess things up and say, "It's OK!" He had the energy to make things exciting. He had the spirit to make things fun. His reward was to hear people laugh.

—Judith Belushi Pisano

Danny Aykroyd was eighteen when I first met him. When you watched television with him, he knew every car, every truck, every gun, what year it was, what model it was. I would be going up to Toronto for the show at the Royal Alex, and Danny had Valri Bromfield as his partner. They'd wait at the Royal York Hotel for me to get off the bus from the airport. Dan would carry my suitcase with one arm to show me how strong he was. Valri would rip off flowers some place and bring them up to my room. They arranged a performance at the Variety Club in Toronto so I could get a look at them, which I did, and brought them down to Chicago. They slept on the floor of our manager's house. They were wonderful. When we opened our own place in Toronto, of course we called Dan and Valri. That's how they came to us.

—Joyce Sloane

● ● ●

The concept of *Ghostbusters* came from Dan, whose family has a psychical history. Dan subscribes to the *Journal of Psychical Phenomenon*, and there were transmediums in his family. There were ghosts and all that, so he's into it. I'm a skeptic, I came from the completely other place. That was a happy marriage because that's what the *Ghostbusters* were. We envisioned them as "ghost janitors." You have these paranormal phenomena and guys who treat it in a very mundane way. That was the comic edge of the film. I think something that people respond to in that movie—I always heard it a lot about *Stripes*, too—people say, "It looked like you guys had a lot of fun making those movies." Which is true, we did. Twice in my life—when we did *Animal House* and when we did *Ghostbusters*—we actually were saying to ourselves as we did it that these were going to be the biggest comedies ever. Of course, we were stoned.

—Harold Ramis

The preliminary audition used to be "five through the door": two people at a time are told they're at the information counter of a store that has everything someone could ask for. One of them will play the information clerk, the other will play five different characters. Each of those characters has to come through the stage door, go to the information desk, ask where to find something, receive the information, exit through the door, and return immediately as the next character. After the first actor has done five characters, the two actors switch roles and go through the whole process again. Actors were judged on whether or not they followed the rules; whether each character was distinct from the other five; whether they played characters or "joke" characters; whether the character's request fit the character; and whether you wanted to see the actor come back the fourth and fifth time (or even the third). This very difficult exercise is no longer used in Chicago. When I asked Joyce Sloane why, she pointed out that there are no longer any doors onstage.

These days, the auditions are mostly two people at a time improvising a scene after being given the "first and last line" by the people holding the audition—usually all the producers, directors, and teachers available. It's an imposing lineup to anyone auditioning, but the reason isn't to intimidate; it's so that no one person can be blamed by someone who didn't get in. You never know who's crazy.

The best advice about auditioning for Second City is: don't try to be funny, and, for heaven's sake, don't go for jokes. Just be present to your fellow actors and work honestly off what you're getting from them; the old saying "acting is reacting" is maybe even more true of improvising. And, as we're constantly saying at Second City, always work off the top of your intelligence. That means reference level and point of view, of course; but it also means "calling it like it is"—because what you see and hear is also what the audience sees and hears, and they also see how you are reacting to it. If you're dishonest in your reaction and go for a laugh instead, the audience will know it—especially if they're producers, directors, and teachers. You'd know it too, if you were in the audience.

If you've auditioned successfully, you may get a chance to perform in one of the numerous touring companies. Touring companies do old scenes and create some original material. In Chicago, the number of companies gradually increased from one to three as more and more bookings came in. The Canadian touring company was formed soon after we became established in our own place in Toronto, as were classes, taught by John Candy and me

Spotlight on
Dan Aykroyd

Dan Aykroyd was with Second City Toronto from 1973 to 1975. Before that, he'd studied criminology and deviant psychology. Dan left Second City to become a member of the first cast of *Saturday Night Live*, where, among many other memorable characters, he and his friend John Belushi created the Blues Brothers, leading to the feature film based on the characters. He's also been in such movies as *Neighbors*, *Trading Places*, *Driving Miss Daisy* (for which he received an Academy Award nomination), *My Girl*, *Gross Pointe Blank*, and the *Ghostbusters* movies.

Dan's friends from his days in Toronto—Marcus O'Hara, "X-Ray" McRae, Richard Kruk (an ex-cop who came in and did the improvs on his last night still in uniform as a Toronto policeman)—are still his friends. He always looked out for everyone—staff, cast, whomever. It was his duty, as he saw it, to take any injustice he saw in the theater and find the means to correct it. That meant management had to keep a "heads up" for Danny.

Dan was serious enough about fighting injustice that, when he joined Second City, he also had an application in to join the Royal Canadian Mounted Police. Dan's sense of loyalty not only included everyone at Second City, it also included, and still includes, Second City itself. He sees every one of our shows whenever he's in a town where one's playing and frequently talks about how important his time with us was and is to him. Dan was in the cast when I moved up to Toronto to direct. Dan called Andrew Alexander one day around lunch time and told him he was very angry and on the way over to kill the both of us. It had something to do with his feeling I was being too tough on Catherine O'Hara when directing her in some material she was learning for a touring company gig. Andrew told Dan he was leaving for lunch, called and told me, and left for lunch. Dan never followed through, and he showed up for the show that night. I sort of didn't manage to make it to the theater. Neither did Andrew.

Above: The first Toronto cast, left to right: Gilda Radner, Brian Doyle-Murray, Gerry Salsberg, Dan Aykroyd, Joe Flaherty, Jayne Eastwood, and Valri Bromfield

Spotlight on
Gilda Radner

Left: The Second City cast at the Firehall: (top, left to right) John Candy and Dan Aykroyd (bottom, left to right) Rosemary Radcliffe, Eugene Levy, Gilda Radner

Gilda Radner, though born in Detroit, was a member of the original Second City Toronto cast starting in 1973. She went from Second City to *Lampoon's* radio and stage shows, and from there to the first cast of *Saturday Night Live*, where she created such characters as Roseanne Roseanna Dana and Baba WaWa, then on to do her own one-woman Broadway show, *Gilda Live*, directed by Mike Nichols, and such movies as *The Rutles*, *First Family*, and *Haunted Honeymoon* and *The Woman in Red*, both costarring her husband, Gene Wilder. She published her book, *It's Always Something*, shortly before she died of ovarian cancer in 1989.

Joyce Sloane remembers Gilda:

Gilda saw us perform at Ann Arbor. She was going to school there. We flew the resident company up to Ann Arbor for the night, and everybody went to Carmen's for dinner. Gilda said she had her nose pressed up against the door, she wanted to be with us so bad. We didn't know her. When we went to Toronto to audition for our first show in our own place there, she was in Godspell. Gilda was a terrific girl. Really girly-girly. When my daughter Cheryl left to go to school in Switzerland, she stopped off in New York. She'd broken her nose sledding and had a big bandage on her nose. She went to see Gilda in Lunch Hour *with David Rasche on Broadway. I'd already seen it on opening night, so I met them at Sardi's afterward. Gilda—who loved clothes, she loved to shop and to buy clothes—was wearing an army jacket and a baseball hat so that she wouldn't be recognized. I walk in and there's Gilda with her arm around Cheryl with a clown nose on to match Cheryl's bandage. She was that kind of warm, vulnerable, affectionate person. Everybody loved her. She was such a girlfriend! I remember sitting in her kitchen in Greenwich Village and Judy Belushi came in through the back door—she was working on a book called* Titters. *John was still alive at the time. Gilda was baking cookies, we were sitting and yakking and just having the best time. That's the way Gilda was; she was a real good girlfriend that you would want to go shopping with or have lunch with or split a dessert with because you knew it was bad for you. She always wanted to split a dessert. She worked at being thin, she really did.*

When Gilda left Toronto, she sold me her car for two hundred dollars, but forgot to clean it out before turning it over to me. She'd clearly used it as a large annex to her purse; there were packets of Kleenex, safety and straight pins, a bit of makeup, a sewing kit, combs and brushes, some birthday cards, a bra, and a few other odds and ends. She never missed any of it, and when I mentioned it to her she said, "Oh, give it all to somebody who needs it."

Rachel Dratch, one of the most recent Second Citizens to go from Chicago mainstage to *Saturday Night Live*, said, "Watching Gilda Radner, you never thought, 'There's the token woman.' She held her own with all the guys."

Gilda Radner lights up the stage.

I remember when Gilda would drive me home at night after the show to her little house on a quiet street in Toronto. She had a cat with three legs and a dog called Snuffy. She loved the Scottish nanny who had brought her up and cared for her. When she came to town to see the show, Gilda proudly introduced her from the stage. I also remember that she would jump into the arms of Joe Flaherty while we were working on a new show and say, "They'll miss me, Joe. They'll miss me if I don't have anything to do!" And Joe would think of some way to get Gilda out onto the stage. Everyone loved her.

—Rosemary Radcliffe

Gilda had a tremendous impact on all of us because she was so good, so human, so much herself, and so loved by the audiences and her colleagues. She had this innate ability to be sweet and vulnerable, but at the same time there was a side to her that wasn't afraid to go for the jugular.

She is still very much with us today. I'm on the worldwide Chicago and Toronto boards of Gilda's Club, an organization that provides meeting places where people with cancer and their families and friends join with others to build social and emotional support as a supplement to medical care. Gilda would be amazed at the effect she's had on people—not simply because of her comedy, but because of the legacy of her fight with cancer and the philosophy that emanated from that battle. In fact, The Old Firehall, Second City's home for its first twenty-five years in Toronto—where Gilda worked—is being renovated to house a Gilda's Club.

—Andrew Alexander

Top: Jim Fisher holds up John Belushi. • Bottom: (from left to right) Don DePollo, Ann Ryerson, and Jim Sherman enact a scene from East of Edens.

to begin with, which eventually became a training center. The Detroit touring company and training center came to life shortly after we opened a Second City there.

Lance Kinsey recalled a memorable episode from his touring company days in the late 1970s:

I was in the touring company that played The Cellar Door in Georgetown just outside Washington, D.C., during the Carter administration. We noticed as we were rehearsing that there were more people in the theater than usual. They were milling around, checking under seats, and most of them had little things in their ear. Upon investigation, we discovered that they were Secret Service agents, and President Carter's sons, Jeff and Chip, would be attending the show. Needless to say, we were all very excited. So excited that it never occurred to us to go over the content of the show with the Secret Service. We had a blackout in the show called "Freeze!" where a cop pursuing a suspect shoots him six times, with a few more clicks of the gun for good measure, then yells, "Freeze!" as the suspect lies dead in a heap on the ground in front of him. The audience always loves this blackout, and they did again that night. The Secret Service agents, on the other hand, did not, and we later found out that John Kapelos almost got shot by one of the agents as he was gunning me down onstage because we never allowed them to check our prop gun.

The touring companies do their shows on the Second City mainstages on Monday nights. In Chicago, the three touring companies alternate Mondays; they charge next to nothing and usually sell out to an audience with an average age of about twenty-three. They're known as RedCo, BlueCo, and GreenCo. Naming the first two with colors was an idea taken, appropriately enough, from the circus. When we needed a third company, Joyce Sloane just picked another color.

Toronto

In Spring 1973 Bernie Sahlins, Joyce Sloane, and Del Close held auditions in Toronto for a permanent Second City there. Ten years after our first show at the Royal Alex, our name seemed secure enough to give it a try. Among the many talented auditioners was nineteen-year-old John Candy; Del decided he needed him in Chicago, so John moved there while the cast for Toronto was assembled.

John Candy and Dan Aykroyd, in separate interviews, remembered their first audition:

Dan Aykroyd: We were all kind of scared because the audition was five characters. You had to walk out as one character and then, a minute later, come back as another character. I think what we did was say, "Oh, John, please come down and watch us. Please come down and offer us some support."

John Candy: I was invited by Dan and Valri Bromfield to join them for lunch. And they'd put my name on the list to audition, unbeknownst to me. And while I was standing around waiting for Dan and Val to finish their work there, my name was called. They pushed me into a room.

Dan: I said, "What do you got to lose?" And he went up.

John: I said, "Aw, I'll kill you. I'll kill you for doing this to me." And I went into this theater, and I was scared. They said, "Go up on stage there. This is a department store exercise. You have to do this game. That's all we want from you." Sweat was all over me.

Dan: As soon as they saw Candy onstage, you know, it didn't matter what he did. It was just a presence. I think they were really more thrilled about getting Candy that day than they were about getting Valri or me.

John: Two days later they called and said, "Would you move to Chicago?" It took me about five seconds to get my mouth open. They said, "You'll be there for a couple weeks." I ended up living there for about a year and a half.

Bernie and Joyce opened their 250-seat Second City cabaret theater on Adelaide Street in Toronto in association with Sam Shopsowitz, owner of one of the most successful delis in town. The cast—a mixture of locals and imports from Chicago—was Dan Aykroyd, Valri Bromfield, Brian Doyle-Murray, Jayne Eastwood, Joe Flaherty, Gilda Radner, and Gerry Salsberg, with Fred Kaz as pianist/musical director. (At the time of the auditions,

Backstage Passes

Things weren't going well financially on Adelaide Street. I do remember coming up to work one night with Gilda, getting to the door, and finding a padlock on it. We were hugging each other and crying. We felt like the gypsy theater group that had been shut down by the mean old sheriff.

—Dan Aykroyd

Toronto theater in those days was just exploding, and a lot of it—Theatre Passe Muraille, Factory Theatre Lab—was in places like The Firehall, old converted industrial spaces, painted black. There was a real passion for self-discovery among young Canadians. "The Canadian identity" was being endlessly debated. Many Canadian plays and movies were trying to discover essential "Canadian-ness," and they proved ripe for satirizing. The audience knew the references. The cast threw themselves into the spoofs.

—Andrew Alexander

There's so much going on in the United States, it's hard to parody. In Canada, because things are taken seriously, there is something to rebel against. Canada is a good straight man (McCrohan, 1987).

—Catherine O'Hara

97

Jayne, Gilda, and Gerry were all in the local cast of *Godspell*, as were future Toronto Second Citizens Eugene Levy, Andrea Martin, Derek McGrath, Martin Short, and Dave Thomas.)

With an excellent cast—the first to have three women—some material of their own, and some brought up from Chicago, the Adelaide Street show was vintage Second City. However, the media weren't paying the show much attention. Add to that the complaints about a lack of Canadian content, and that we opened in the summer with no air conditioning, and couldn't get a liquor license, and business was not good.

"We needed to have food to justify a liquor license in Toronto," recalls Joyce Sloane, "but we really didn't have the ability at that time to provide food service. So we used to sneak across the alley to the creperie next door any time a customer ordered a food item. We would then run back across the alley with the pastries or whatever and serve them to the customers. Things got so bad, I remember, that Gilda came in with a roll of our toilet paper—the cheapest you could buy—and said, 'I know that money is tight, but can't we please get a better brand of toilet paper?'"

Above: (from left to right) Eugene Levy, Dan Aykroyd, Gilda Radner, Rosemary Radcliffe, and John Candy hang out in the trunk of a car. • Below: John Candy and Andrew Alexander pose with their Emmy award.

Although Adelaide Street had to close, Bernie and Joyce didn't give up. Instead they found a partner in a young Canadian entrepreneur. Andrew Alexander took over the Second City Toronto franchise in 1974 and reopened the show at The Old Firehall. In 1985, when Bernie sold the whole thing to Andrew and his partner Len Stuart, Andrew became the executive producer of Second Cities everywhere. According to him, the early days in Toronto were shaky at best:

I happened to meet Bernie and Joyce because they were looking for a place to rehearse before they opened on Adelaide Street. I was working at the St. Lawrence Centre in publicity and marketing, and I found them a place. Then I moved to Chicago while they opened in Toronto. I had a job at a theater there called the Ivanhoe, but I hung out at Second City. Bernie and Joyce told me about the problems they were having in Toronto. They had an incredible cast, but they had to close after six months. Joyce was looking for investors, just trying to keep the doors open. She and Bernie asked if I'd be interested in trying to run it. I knew a guy from the meatpacking business named Jim Patry who'd actually invested in the last four weeks on Adelaide Street. I asked if he'd be interested in investing some more. He put up seven thousand bucks, I think. I worked out a deal with Bernie to pay him a royalty and cleared up some of the debts. We

acquired the rights, formed a company called Moongold Productions, and opened at The Firehall in February 1974.

Toronto's changed a lot, but in our early days it really was impossible to get a liquor license there unless you served food. Every few weeks, the Liquor Control Board would check your receipts, and if you were selling more booze than food, you'd lose your license. So Andrew created a dinner and show package for The Old Firehall that he could market for groups. The people who'd bought the package—many just bought tickets to the show—would have their meal in the upstairs dining room, then move downstairs for the show. It was very successful, but some of the package deals could be pretty tough on the cast.

The worst audience I remember is one night when the whole show was sold out to the employees of a condom factory. They'd all had dinner and about six drinks each upstairs before the show started. By halfway through the first act they were throwing the contents of their drinks at each other and at the stage. John Candy even got hit by a flying ice cube. He got very angry and yelled at them, but they just yelled back. Their voices were getting louder and their language fouler as the show went on. The first act closed with the "PTA" scene developed in Chicago, a meeting with the PTA chairman on stage and the rest of the actors out in the audience as parents and teachers. Although it was never a problem before, this did, unfortunately, mean that the audience was meant to feel like they too were PTA members. Worse still, the subject of the meeting, whether or not sex education should be taught in the school, proved especially provocative to them. Normally about ten minutes long, the scene took forty. They were standing on their tables, they were arguing with the actors about sex and anything else they thought might be funny, they were trying to jump the actors and jump on the actresses, and they were throwing their drink glasses along with their drinks. The actors ploughed through somehow, ducking and weaving all the way, and then refused to return for the second act. The audience never knew the difference.

Part of the charm of Second City Toronto came from the building itself. The Old Firehall was a reconverted fire station built in 1886 and deserted in 1968. The brass pole the firemen slid down was just on your right as you entered the lobby; after a couple of drinks, many customers would try it.

Top to bottom: *The Old Firehall theater in Toronto* • *Clockwise from bottom left: Andrea Martin, Eugene Levy, Dan Aykroyd, Catherine O'Hara, and John Candy*

I think the people who came out of Second City in Toronto were personalities; and I think because we were friends, there was a very comfortable, familiar, joyous feeling of celebration when we performed, and I think it was much more that contagious feeling than an intellectual feeling (Showtime, 1988).

—Andrea Martin

Top to bottom: Martin Short and Steve Kampmann • Toronto cast: (top, left to right) Joe Flaherty, Eugene Levy, John Candy, and Allan Guttman (bottom, left to right) Gilda Radner and Rosemary Radcliffe • John Candy and Joe Flaherty

The Old Firehall had a discotheque on the first floor and a restaurant on the second when we moved in. Previews for our first show were performed between the rock bands' sets in front of a beer-swilling, uncomprehending audience. By the time the show actually opened, Second City was the only entertainment. In a May 1976 review in the *Toronto Star*, critic Gina Mallet wrote, "The Old Firehall is ideal. It is hot, sweaty, overcrowded. It is also redolent of adventure and daring."

Joe Flaherty and Bernie Sahlins codirected the first Firehall show, *Hello Dali*. Joe was also in the cast, along with John Candy (who moved back from Chicago to do it), Eugene Levy, Rosemary Radcliffe, Gilda Radner, and pianist/musical director Allan Guttman. Joe soon was replaced by Dan Aykroyd, Gilda by Catherine O'Hara. The show got excellent reviews, and audiences began showing up in decent numbers. With good food and liquor now legal to serve and supplementing a truly funny show, Second City Toronto was on its way to becoming as big a part of the Second City legacy as Chicago. And it's the only Second City outside Chicago to last, although the one in Detroit is well on its way.

From the very beginning of Second City's tenure under Andrew's watchful eye, the show at The Old Firehall began developing its own Canadian voice.

Among the scenes in the show was an all-purpose Canadian play called "I'm Gonna Be All Right, You Creep, Leaving Home and All, Eh?" (or simply "Canadian Play" 🅲🅳), which joined together the titles of several recent, successful, and basically depressing Canadian plays and movies about people trying to find themselves. The scene depicted a family dinner, with a mean and boring father (Joe Flaherty, later replaced by Dan Aykroyd), a submissive mother (Rosemary Radcliffe), a bad poet and flamingly gay son (Eugene Levy), an unhappy-at-being-a-hockey-player son (John Candy), and a brain-damaged daughter (Gilda Radner, later replaced by Catherine O'Hara) at the table.

The audiences also loved anti-American scenes. The perception American tourists have of Canadians was the subject of a scene in which would-be American spies were being trained to dress and behave like stereotypical Canadians—a scene which managed to satirize preconceptions on both sides of the forty-ninth parallel.

Also in the show were a musical about the massage parlors that had blossomed up and down Yonge Street, Eugene Levy's act with a trained amoeba jumping between chairs, and Eugene doing an interview with Gilda playing a character who later became Emily Litella on *Saturday Night Live*.

The Next "Next Generation"

In 1973, Bernie Sahlins took the "Next Generation" cast to New York. Another whole new cast was in Chicago, and Del Close was working to find a new way of doing Second City shows. Someone sat through a rehearsal one afternoon in 1973 and wrote—anonymously, I'm afraid—what she saw and heard. (Although Joyce Sloane doesn't remember who wrote it, she kept it. She throws nothing away, as you can easily tell if you walk into her office.) The company was John Candy, Tino Insana, Bill Murray, David Rasche, Ann Ryerson, Dick Staahl, and Betty Thomas. They were all at least six feet tall and gentile; they were called "The Tall Goyim." The following is what she saw and heard that day:

2:00 P.M.: The Second City actors straggle in for rehearsal. Sucking on cigarettes or armed with cups of coffee, sandwiches, yogurt, and newspapers, they drift into the empty theater to wait for the full cast to arrive.

2:15 P.M.: A breathless actor runs into the room, apologizing for being late. The others look up in acknowledgment from their papers or food.

2:20 P.M.: An actress runs in with music in her fist, exuding apology. Her excuse—accepted. Raúl Moncada [the stage manager] turns the stage lights up, revealing napkins, butts, more of similar ilk. Three hundred–odd empty bentwood chairs face the stage.

It's time to start work on material for the next revue. Clearing his throat, director Del Close calls the meeting to order.

Del: Before we decide on an angle or approach, maybe we should ask ourselves again what we'd like Second City to be—I mean, we've been in existence for fourteen years now, and we should keep asking ourselves what it is we're trying to say.

Tino Insana: Why do people say that we don't do political satire at Second City anymore? Our show has political satire in it.

Jim Staahl: People aren't as shocked by satire as they used to be. Everybody's doing political satire. Look at Watergate. Newspaper writers, performers, everybody's doing it. We're better off going for less obvious targets, like Kissinger, Carey, Congress members, hitting local politicians…

Pictured faces (from left to right): John Candy, Betty Thomas, David Rasche, Jim Staahl, Tino Insana, Ann Ryerson, and Bill Murray

David Rasche: Did you read that article on Dick Gregory? He says there's always that thing about the purpose of satire. If two guys are in a hole, and I make one guy laugh, it's not going to get him out of the hole. But it may make it a little more bearable in the hole, until the guy gets enough energy to get out of the hole. In a way, I think that's about as far as you can go. Nothing terribly earth-shaking. I mean, people in our audience don't walk out of Second City a new person.

Ann Ryerson: Some people seem to think satire isn't satire unless the audience is squirming in discomfort because their personal values are being attacked—like Don Rickles humor. We don't attack people as much as show them how they're acting, and let them draw their own conclusions. I think there's so much negativism around these days that people get defensive and stubborn if you attack them directly. And nobody learns anything once they've withdrawn into a shell. We lure them.

John Candy: I think we're vicious at times, too, though "vicious" doesn't mean we hate the person. It just means everyone's ass is up for grabs, and we should expose as much as we know.

David: I see Second City as a platform for saying something. I think we as a company have found that there is a correlation between the directness of the attack and the results of the attack.

Jim: Right. You just can't walk out onstage and say, "I hate war." You have to show how war affects the average or the unusual person, how his life is affected.

Bill Murray: I think too often we get into an extension of the absurd. It appears to be increasing recently. Are we developing tunnel vision? Granted, it's a technique in itself, and a difficult one to master, but I wonder if it's good for us as a group.

Betty Thomas: I don't think we have tunnel vision. I feel that this company is leaning again toward a game feeling in the scenes we're doing. And that's how Second City was started—with an element of game within a scene. I look at this type of humor as art, like painting. You take one element of character, or essence of being, and expand it.

Tino: We're never satisfied with what we do, which is positive, because we always strive to improve our minds and our work. You know, you find yourself constantly looking for comedy

Top: John Candy (left) ponders Bill Murray's comments during a scene.
• Below (clockwise from bottom): David Rasche, Jim Staahl, Ann Ryerson, John Candy, Bill Murray, Betty Thomas, and Tino Insana

situations. You find yourself at a party saying, this would be a good bit.

Jim: I don't think people realize how much homework we do. It's not one of those jobs that you leave at the office. We go to movies, pour over books and magazines, and, of course, subscribe to *Psychology Today*. You have to know what's in today's news.

Ann: It's not easy trying to stay one step ahead of the audience with the wealth of information pouring out daily.

Jim: We could just do improvs, and they would be good improvs. But, when we work on a new show, we put extra thought into it. Things aren't there just by accident. I feel that when we go backstage and mull over the nightly improvs, we can make the proverbial statement and add a comment.

David: There are two abilities at Second City. One is the ability to improvise and grab the moment. The other is the ability to recreate that moment. In putting together a show, you have to use that second ability, which is to be able to recapture what you did the first time. And it can be difficult to duplicate spontaneity...

Tino: Do you ever see Second City as a sort of college? When you leave this theater, you're out in the world with your "degree." But it certainly is an end in itself.

David: I don't know why people in Chicago ask us, what do you do after this? The answer is nothing. Second City is an end in itself. It is something to be mastered.

John: Sure. And we should keep ourselves open to all forms of satirical comedy—blackouts, short scenes, songs, choral pieces, interviews. I'd like to try a long major piece for the new show—perhaps a one-act scenario.

Bill: Yeah, maybe like a Sherlock Holmes investigation into the nation's affairs, where the action switches to different settings, and the cutting from setting to setting becomes more and more complex and confusing....

Top (left to right): Betty Thomas, David Rasche, Jim Staahl, and Cassandra Danz in Et Tu Kohotek *• Below (left to right): Betty Thomas, Bill Murray, Mert Rich, Paul Zegler, and Ann Ryerson*

The show they'd started working on ended up being called *Phase 46 or Watergate Tomorrow, Comedy Tonight*. The same

Spotlight on Bill Murray

Above: Bill Murray and Tino Insana (left) dress for the part.

Bill Murray grew up in Wilmette, Illinois, in Chicago's north suburbs, with eight brothers and sisters. (His older brother, Brian, and younger brother, Joel, also played Second City Chicago's mainstage.) Bill joined the Second City company in Chicago in 1973, the same week as John Candy. For a while, he lived in Bernie and Jane Sahlins' basement until a fire down there made it clear he'd better move elsewhere. After Second City, he joined his brother Brian and John Belushi on *The National Lampoon Radio Hour*, then went into the *Lampoon* show in New York. He was also a regular on the short-lived variety show *Saturday Night Live with Howard Cosell* on ABC. In 1976, he replaced Chevy Chase on NBC's *Saturday Night Live*, then went on to such movies as *Meatballs*, *Caddyshack*, *Stripes*, the *Ghostbusters* movies, *Tootsie*, *Little Shop of Horrors*, *Scrooged*, *Quick Change*, *What About Bob?*, *Groundhog Day*, *Ed Wood*, *Rushmore* (for which he received a Golden Globe nomination), and *Cradle Will Rock*, many of which are among the highest-grossing comedies of all time.

Joyce Sloane recalls some of Bill's misspent youth: "Bill was in the touring company with Betty Thomas back in 1972. We were playing Notre Dame, and St. Mary's College is right there, which is a girls' school. We lost him for a couple of days. I heard that he did the whole 'Trouble in River City' from *The Music Man* on top of a table in a restaurant and got thrown out. He was a handful."

You couldn't keep your eyes off Bill onstage because there was so much going on inside the guy that you knew something would come popping out sooner rather than later. He emitted a true sense of danger. Bill developed several characters at Second City that he later used to good advantage on TV, most especially his lounge-lizard singer/emcee. When the company did "The Watergate Symphony" on various instruments they'd mastered, Bill was the only one without anything to play. He ended up getting a lot of laughs by breaking balloons in time to the music.

In 1974, in order to keep Second City's name in front of the Toronto press, Andrew Alexander persuaded Bernie Sahlins to switch Toronto and Chicago casts for two weeks. That meant Gilda Radner (replaced while in Chicago by Catherine O'Hara), Rosemary Radcliffe, John Candy, Eugene Levy, and Dan Aykroyd went to Chicago, and Betty Thomas, Debbie Harmon, Paul Ziegler, Mert Rich, and Bill went up to Toronto.

"I wasn't there, but this is how I heard it," recalls Second City alum Robin McCulloch. "One night at The Firehall, a guy kept heckling Bill all night. Finally, during the suggestion taking for the improv set, Bill lost it, screamed, 'Fuck you and your date too!' jumped off the stage, grabbed the guy, pulled him out back, and reinvented the angle at which his arm should bend. I think we all, deep in our hearts, had a time when we had the same thought cross our minds. Bill just stood in for all of us."

Clockwise from left: Bill Murray introduces himself to Tino Insana and Cassandra Danz at the start of a scene. • Murray reads to the audience from a newspaper. • Murray, with Jim Staahl, as a chef with an interesting approach to handling food.

Disc 1
Tracks 1 & 14

Backstage Passes

Bill Murray is a great stand-in for all the people I knew and admired growing up: very brave comedian, very down-to-earth, very honest in his work, and extremely creative.

—Harold Ramis

●　●　●

Being the shortest cast member, I had to ask Betty—then a very tall waitress—to not serve drinks in the center aisle while I was doing my monologue. It blocked the audience's view.

—Jim Fisher

●　●　●

After I made *About Last Night...* I got a big, black Mercedes. I'm driving it from the dealer's, and John Candy pulls up right next to me—in a big, black Mercedes. He says, "America, it's a good country, yeah?" We'd worked together in Second City for nothing.

—Jim Belushi

anonymous someone also sat through the planning of an improv set, probably that same night:

Betty Thomas streaks onstage, still wearing a black choir robe from the final scene in the show. Balancing a large manila sketchpad on her knees, she records audience suggestions for the improvisational part of the show. "Come on now," she coaxes, "what's really important to you?"

Backstage, actors strip off layers of costuming and gravitate toward the backstage "green room"—a cozy place of green-painted cinder blocks, a faded pink couch, and a blue plastic chair.

When she's finished, Betty joins the others and hangs the suggestion pad on the wall. Everyone silently scans the list, looking for an image or word that will trigger a scenic idea.

"Let's see," Tino Insana mumbles. "Suggestions for places. 'Nixon's office,' 'bathroom,' 'on top of a bald man's head,' 'zoo,' 'bordello'..."

David Rasche grabs Jim Staahl by the arm. "OK. How about this, Jim? Nixon and a man from the general accounting office are going over a list of Nixon's expenditures, and—"

Jim jumps in, "—and Nixon says everything's for defense purposes, like his swimming pool and—"

David interrupts excitedly, "—and Nixon keeps trying to distract him and in the end offers him a bribe—for defense purposes. Okay, Raúl, write up 'Nixon-Accountant' on the board."

Raúl Moncada writes "Nixon-Accountant" and looks at his watch. "Fifteen minutes, and we only have one scene and one blackout up."

The tension expands. So does the collective volume in the room.

"Hey, who's in charge of thinking up the group scene tonight?"

They all look at Ann Ryerson and Bill Murray, who look at each other.

John Candy says, "I had an idea for a scene this afternoon after rehearsal. A couple comes to look for an apartment in a 'changing neighborhood' and..."

"Do you want to try that scene on football we did last night again? But this time, let's cut the cheap jokes."

"Tino, telephone."

"I'm hardly doing anything tonight!"

"Five minutes, gang."

"Will everyone please be quiet and listen to John explain the group scene? Bill? Bill! Listen!"

Raúl runs off to print the running order for the night's set, to be posted at every entrance. He hands one to Fred Kaz [the pianist].

Spotlight on
Betty Thomas

Betty Thomas studied art and art history, was a public school substitute teacher, and worked as a waitress at the Chicago Second City before joining the cast in 1973. She went from there to *Hill Street Blues*, thinking she was only going to be used for one episode. She became an integral part of the cast, and her portrayal of officer Lucy Bates on the highly-acclaimed series won her an Emmy. Betty also acted in some movies, including *Used Cars*.

After testing her wings directing a few episodes of *Hill Street Blues*, she came back to Chicago to direct *Kuwait Until Dark* at Second City. She then started directing movies—most of them big hits—including *The Brady Bunch* films, *Private Parts*, *Dr. Doolittle* (the funny one with Eddie Murphy, not that terrible musical with Rex Harrison and Anthony Newley), and *28 Days*. She won an Emmy for directing the HBO sitcom *Dream On*, and also directed the HBO movie *The Late Shift*, about the show business war between Jay Leno and David Letterman.

"We used to call her 'Broadway Betty,'" recalls Joyce Sloane. "She drove a truck—when women didn't drive trucks. We challenged her, we dared her to take Del's classes. She took the classes and became a great student of Del's." Betty says of her first experience with improv: "The first time I did a group improvisation like that, like a 'Harold,' where everything was sort of created and you were creating a movie, basically, but onstage in the midst of the moment, when I had that experience I said, 'Oh, wait a minute, this is too good.' It was just better than life. It seemed like improvisation was just sort of heightened life" (Johnson, 1999).

Betty was a little tomboyish. She had very little modesty and didn't wear underclothes, not even backstage when changing from street wear to show wear, even if there were visitors backstage. She used to travel around L.A. in a helicopter—she had her own license. It really wasn't a stretch for her to play a cop on *Hill Street Blues*. When Andrew Alexander heard that Betty was directing the occasional *Hill Street Blues* episode, he and Joyce agreed it would be a great idea to have Betty direct the next show. She was terrified, but she did it, and it was great. Years later, when Betty was promoting *Private Parts*, she would always mention her directing at Second City and how important it was for her.

Above: Thomas (right) collars a criminal in a scene with Ann Ryerson (left) and Eugenie Ross-Leming.

Don DePollo

Don DePollo joined the Second City Chicago cast in 1974. He was one of Second City's favorite performers and best-loved teachers after retiring from the stage show. He was a little, odd-looking guy, and he played little, odd-looking characters, including feisty old men and, most famously, a raven. Donny died on September 18, 1995.

Two floors above Chicago's Second City is Donny's Skybox, a small cabaret theater named in his memory.

Lee Ryan remembers a moment of quintessential Don DePollo:

"While subbing for someone during a mainstage show," he said, "I walked by Don DePollo backstage. He looked a little down. I whispered, 'How are you, Don?' He said, 'I don't know, Lee. I'm feeling old, tired. Here I am doing goofy bird characters, and I'm not sure I care anymore.' Before I could respond, Donny's whole energy changed to a ferocious bolt of passion. He almost hit me waving his arms. 'Out of my way! Out of my way!' He then charged through the center door, making his entrance to the scene as the raven."

"Endings," says Fred, "does anyone have any endings?" Fred often signals the man on lights when to end a scene. "Does 'Bijou' have an ending?"

"No, Fred, it's open." That means Fred will have to "feel out" the scene's conclusion, using his discretion.

"Who stole the white chef's apron?!" someone yells as he searches frantically through the approximately hundred various coats, sweaters, and costumes along the prop wall. "I need it for the opening blackout."

Bill Murray rifles through the prop box for a rubber chicken, grabs a rifle, and stands ready to enter stage. The lights dim. Fred swings into up-tempo intro music. Whispers and prop-hunting backstage.

Bill slips onstage as the stage lights come up. "Hi there, welcome to our improv set…"

North by North Wells

The local Chicago theater scene began to grow in the 1970s. Paul Sills was in at the beginning, creating the first of his Story Theatre shows at a storefront theater he started with several other directors. One of the reasons writers and directors like David Mamet and Stewart Gordon (writer-director of *The Re-Animator*) started their first theaters in Chicago was because they'd studied with Paul, and he was there. This, plus a little storefront musical called *Grease*, was a big part of the beginning of today's nationally and internationally recognized community of more than 125 Chicago theaters. Of course, Second City was there first.

When Chicago's Steppenwolf Theatre doubled the size of its ensemble in preparation for its move into the city from the far suburbs, they asked me to help them form the larger ensemble by teaching them Viola Spolin's games. At the time, the group included Joan Allen, Terry Kinney, John Mahoney, John Malkovich, Laurie Metcalf, Jeff Perry, and Gary Sinise. I did the same thing with the then–newly formed Remains ensemble, which included Gary Cole, D.W. Moffat, Amy Morton, and William Peterson.

Many of the multiplicity of other theaters and comedy clubs in Chicago were started by, acted in, and directed by people who'd studied the games in school, at Second City, Players Workshop, ImprovOlympic, or Annoyance Theater. And many of those people have also moved on to fame and even fortune in L.A. and New York. As I've said, few areas of comedy or acting in general in America haven't been at least partly influenced by the work of Viola Spolin, Paul Sills, David Shepherd, The Compass, or Second

Spotlight on
James Belushi

James Belushi, known to everyone as Jim, joined the 1978 Second City Chicago cast in *Sexual Perversity Among the Buffalo* after spending thirteen months in the touring company. He went from there to *Saturday Night Live*. He's been on Broadway in *The Pirates of Penzance* and *Conversations with My Father*. His movies include *Salvador*, *Little Shop of Horrors*, *Red Heat*, *K-9*, *Only the Lonely* (starring John Candy), *The Principal*, *Curly Sue*, and *Return to Me*, directed by Second Citizen Bonnie Hunt. Jim's also into music with his group, The Sacred Hearts Band.

Agnes Belushi, Jim's mother, made a deal with Joyce Sloane that she could hire Jim to work at Second City only after he graduated from college. He was talented enough to join a touring company right out of high school, but Agnes was determined that college was the right thing for Jim, and Joyce agreed. Once Jim was hired for a touring company, another deal was made. His brother John told Joyce that he didn't want Jim performing any of his old scenes. Again, Joyce agreed. It was hard enough for Jim to develop his own voice when everyone was comparing him to his famous older brother, which Jim found frustrating for a while.

"I was out with the touring company at Southern Illinois University," remembers Joyce. "The actors were doing a workshop and I just spoke a little bit. I told the students that 'there are some people who can play against the rules, and it still works for them. One of those people was John Belushi.' There was a tittering in the audience, but I didn't know why. Jim was sitting in the back row being properly embarrassed."

Jim's first show after leaving Second City was a Chicago production I directed of David Mamet's *Sexual Perversity in Chicago*, in which Jim played Bernie Litgo. He was very nervous about doing a play after so many years at Second City, and he worked very hard during rehearsals. It was a big hit, ran for months, and got Jim the role in the movie version, *About Last Night*....

Above: Belushi belts out a tune, with Meagan Fay by his side.

I almost got mugged one time, but the guy recognized me from the *Police Academy* movies. I had to sign an autograph instead of giving him my wallet.

—Tim Kazurinsky

• ● •

The first time one sees a show on the mainstage is usually one's favorite memory there, and it is mine. The revue I saw included the song "Cowboys," with George Wendt, Tim Kazurinsky, and Bruce Jarchow, with Fred Kaz on the piano. When what seemed like an unbelievably drawn-out (but hilarious) vamp finally transformed into a side-splittingly funny song, I thought the gods themselves had come down to earth for my amusement. I came back to watch the improv set every night for the next two years and never changed my mind—they were comedy gods.

—Mark Belden

• ● •

Probably the one time I remember most at Second City was when George Wendt did Leonid Brezhnev and I played Deng Xiao-Ping in *Issues and Alibis.* **CD** George would do Russian gibberish, I would do Chinese gibberish, and we each had a "translator." We took questions from the audience, and a fellow stood up who was with the Chinese Council General and tried to nail me by asking his question in Chinese! I was thrown for a loop. I just stood up and started speaking to him in Chinese gibberish, pretending he was an old friend. We did this shtick for about a minute. He played along. I did gibberish, he did real Chinese, and it was hilarious. Our conversation continued through the lights fading out.

—Tim Kazurinsky

City. As noted drama critic Richard Christiansen said in the *Chicago Tribune* in 1994:

> All dates of recent Chicago theater history can be traced from the birth of Second City…because it was Second City that thumpingly proved that a resident company, bred in Chicago and an essential part of the local scene, could be a unique, sleek, highly skilled, and commercially viable form of living theater. Before Second City, the tradition of Chicago theater had been shadowy; after Second City, the possibilities became limitless.

Second City, though a strong name locally, wasn't the kind of nationally recognized institution it became starting in October 1975 with the premiere of *Saturday Night Live*. The oldest baby boomers were hitting thirty, and the youngest were teenagers; they were the first TV and rock-and-roll generation, exactly the audience for *SNL*. The buzz surrounding the show was soon so intense that the media and the public wanted to know where this hip, cutting-edge program came from, and the actors always credited their time at Second City as paving the way for their current success. Our name started appearing more frequently in national publications like *Rolling Stone*, *Time*, and *Newsweek*. Soon many more people, both native and tourist, wanted to see "the place where Belushi got his start." And they weren't disappointed with the casts they saw in Chicago or Toronto. By the late 1970s, more and more people also started moving to Chicago to try and get hired by Second City, often instead of finishing or even going to college.

Del Close took directing credit for most of the shows in Chicago during the rest of the 1970s, but he and Bernie Sahlins basically worked on them together. It was during this time that the ide-

Top to bottom: Bernie Sahlins • Del Close

Spotlight on
Tim Kazurinsky

Tim Kazurinsky is both a writer and a short, dour clown. He was born in Australia. Within a year of moving to Chicago and with a lot of hard work, he'd lost his accent. He was an advertising executive until he joined the Second City cast in 1978 for *Sexual Perversity Among the Buffalo*. Many of his characters were either old men or hyperactive kids, and they rarely seemed to have necks. He also played the naughty dummy to George Wendt's ventriloquist, sitting on George's knee. Tim went from Second City to *Saturday Night Live* from 1980 to 1984. Then he started writing scripts and acting in some movies, including *Neighbors*, *Continental Divide*, and the *Police Academy* series. Now he's mostly a screenwriter, beginning with *About Last Night…*, which he and cowriter Denise DeClue adapted from David Mamet's *Sexual Perversity in Chicago*. Among his other writing credits are *For Keeps*, *The Cherokee Kid*, and *Three Men and a Little Lady*.

Tim took an organized approach to improvisation:

We videotaped the sets at Second City, but the quality was so bad that it was like six figures of death moving around the stage. They were too cheap to pop for a new camera, so I started audiotaping the sets. That was my contribution—that, and the little bins where you put your props. OK, I'm a little anal. By audiotaping the sets, I had a better idea of the scene. They would improvise a scene and then my cast was always like, "No, no, don't write it, don't write it, we'll just improvise it some more." They would improvise way beyond where they should've gone. The editing process, they didn't know it. I remember I would go back and listen to the eight times that scene was done. I would go, "About right there, about the third time…" and I would type that up. After it was kicked out of the show because it wasn't working anymore, I'd pull out the script and say, "It worked when it was like this." What you learn at Second City as a writer— besides timing and when the jokes work and all that—is the editing process.

Tim and his family live near Chicago, and he comes to Second City fairly often to help, encourage, and berate the newest company members.

Kazurinsky (left) and Bruce Jarchow (right) in Issues and Alibis

Spotlight on George Wendt

George Wendt joined the Second City mainstage in 1975 for the show *Once More with Fooling*, having served time in the touring company. After a year, he was sent back to the touring company for a while for further "seasoning," then brought back to mainstage in 1978 for *Freud Slipped Here*. After leaving Second City in 1980, he had small roles in a couple of movies, then played Norm on *Cheers*. He's also been in many other TV shows and movies, including *Fletch*, *Gung Ho*, *The Little Rascals*, *Spice World*, and the TV movie of *Bye Bye Birdie*. He also starred in *Art* in London and on Broadway.

George was a brilliant slow and grumpy clown. Even when he played high-energy characters, a languid side would show through. Among his many unlikely creations at Second City along with Mayor Daley and a hip priest, were the "Test-Tube Baby" in a musical number for which he wore a very large infant's sunsuit and bonnet; a politician in a taped campaign ad (George did it live) whose speech was being played backwards and forwards while Tim Kazurinsky as a PR guy made edits; and George, Tim, and Bruce Jarchow as cowboys (Tim carrying a blow-dryer as his gun) riding the range, bored and silent for minutes on end, and finally breaking into a silly barbershop quartet for three singers.

George also likes to barbecue, even when it means doing it outdoors in the dead of winter.

Right: Larry Coven (left) checks out Wendt's unibrow in "Issues and Alibis." 🔊 • *Above: Wendt as a larger-than-normal baby*

ological split between them about the use of improvisation became apparent, but it was also a key ingredient in the success of the shows. Since Del loved process, the improv elements of the work were more interesting to him than rehearsing and setting the scenes that came out of them. Since Bernie came out of a theater tradition, he demanded that the shows be well balanced, well thought out, and polished. As the decade rolled on, more often than not, Del would start the process of building a show, and Bernie would come in and finish it. It didn't always break down that clearly, but close enough.

Left to right: Shelley Long, Will Aldis, Steven Kampmann, and Miriam Flynn

Among those in Second City Chicago and Toronto casts in the mid- to late-1970s were Jim Belushi, Brenda Donahue, Miriam Flynn, Mary Gross, Tim Kazurinsky, Eugene Levy, Shelley Long, Andrea Martin, Catherine O'Hara, Martin Short, Dave Thomas, George Wendt, and eventual directors and Training Center teachers Don DePollo and Michael Gellman.

In 1975, a Second City company made up of both Chicago and Toronto alums opened in a dinner theater in Pasadena, California, for what was hoped to be a new permanent Second City. But with an audience with an average age a little older than the Theatre Guild's, it was, like New Orleans, in the wrong place at the wrong time and only ran nine months.

Although Pasadena was a big disappointment, *Saturday Night Live* premiered that year, and Bernie Sahlins and Andrew Alexander started talking about another kind of project: assuming that *SNL* would continue looking to us for talent, if we could supply the talent to make a TV show like that work, why couldn't we do our own show? We could and did. By the twentieth anniversary party in Chicago in December 1979, *Animal House* and *Meatballs* had been released, *Saturday Night Live* was as popular as ever, and we had put *SCTV* on the air. We'd truly become a nationally known institution, and business was booming. ● ● ●

Shelley Long came from Fort Wayne, Indiana, and, after a couple of years at Northwestern University, started writing for Encyclopædia Britannica children's films. She became a local celebrity co-hosting the TV show, *Sorting Out*. After taking workshops with Jo Forsberg, Shelley joined Second City Chicago in 1976 in *North by North Wells*. She left Chicago for Hollywood, where she attracted major attention with her role in *Night Shift*. She then starred in the first several years of *Cheers*, followed by such movies as *Irreconcilable Differences*, *The Money Pit*, *Outrageous Fortune*, *Troop Beverly Hills*, and *The Brady Bunch* movies.

Shelley played lunatics and lovers, spinsters and smarmy talk-show hosts equally well. In one scene she created, she got picked up by Steve Kampmann at a class reunion, only to reveal to him later that she was a transsexual who was one of his buddies when they were in school. In another, she was Miriam Flynn and Eric Boardman's daughter telling them she was moving in with her boyfriend when such things weren't done much yet.

Spotlight on
Saturday Night Live
The Second City Connection ● ● ●

In October 1975, when NBC put *Saturday Night Live* on the air, it was taking a big chance. TV comedy was Mary Tyler Moore; Carol Burnett; Bob Newhart; *Welcome Back, Kotter*; and *Happy Days*. But NBC decided they wanted to try an edgier kind of comedy, granted not in prime time, but right after the late news on Saturday night when lots of younger people were still watching the tube. After all, they were doing well with the *Tonight Show* on weeknights, why not try network programming at that hour on the weekend as well? So they agreed to let Lorne Michaels—a Canadian, a former performer, and a sometime student at the Toronto Second City workshops—put together a group of "Not Ready for Prime Time Players." Joyce Sloane remembers having breakfast with Michaels when he told her about a show he was pitching to NBC—a late-night sketch show that would have a rock 'n' roll attitude, separating it from TV variety shows of the past. He used writers and performers from several different places, including *The National Lampoon Radio Hour*, *National Lampoon's Lemmings*, and the Second Cities in Chicago and Toronto. Of course, the show has now celebrated its twenty-fifth anniversary and spawned a whole host of stars.

For years, *SNL* writers and producers have checked out the talent at the various Second Cities at least once a year. The ones they think might be what they're looking for are asked to audition. Kelly Leonard, Second City's current producer, talks about why Second City's actors have found such success at *Saturday Night Live*:

Album cover from the Blues Brothers album,
Briefcase Full of Blues

What is it that makes a Second City actor such a good prospect for SNL? First and foremost, it is the improvisational training. Second City actors have to think quick on their feet, and a live TV show demands quick thinking. Also, at Second City, our actors write and perform their material. Nothing prepares you better for the

114

harshly competitive world of Saturday Night Live *than the ability to create your own opportunities as writer/performer. Another benefit is the experience one gets at Second City from working in an ensemble. Learning to be successful within the group dynamic is no minor feat.*

Here's a list of the Second City alums who've gone on to be in the cast of *Saturday Night Live* so far:

1975:	Dan Aykroyd, John Belushi, Gilda Radner
1976:	Bill Murray
1981:	Robin Duke, Tim Kazurinsky, Tony Rosato, Mary Gross, Brian Doyle-Murray
1983:	Jim Belushi
1984:	Martin Short
1988:	Mike Myers
1990:	Chris Farley, Tim Meadows
1995:	Dave Koechner, Nancy Walls
1998:	Horatio Sanz
1999:	Rachel Dratch

And there are even more Second City alums who've become writers on *Saturday Night Live*:

Peter Aykroyd

Dick Blasucci

Paul Flaherty

Brian Doyle-Murray

Rob Riley

Nate Herman

Michael McCarthy

Bob Odenkirk

Cindy Caponera

Lori Nasso

Tom Gianas

Ali Farahnakian

Jerry Minor

Adam McKay (writing supervisor)

Tina Fey (first female writing supervisor)

Del Close (who acted as a sort of director/advisor for a while)

Backstage Passes

Saturday Night Live basically gets written in one night, and you can often tell. We come in on Tuesdays—Tuesdays are our writing nights. You come in kind of whenever you want in the afternoon. Sketches are due the following morning by ten. You write all night and turn them in sometime in the morning. There's a read-through on Wednesday, and if your sketch goes, you become a producer of sorts of your sketch and are responsible for the look of the sketch and even the performances to a certain extent. I think having been at Second City gives you credibility there. There's Harvard people there, people from the Groundlings, and people from Second City and stand-up. Very few people are outside of those four groups. You take a lot on because you come from Second City and know how to fix things quickly. If you're improvising, you have to fix things on your feet, so the luxury of having three or four days to fix a sketch is delightful. You're used to helping other people figure out how to get their characters on and the best setting for characters. You take on a lot.

—Tina Fey

I went to Second City, where you learned to make the other actor look good so you looked good, and *National Lampoon*, where you had to create everything out of nothing, and *Saturday Night Live*, where you couldn't make any mistakes, and you learned what collaboration was (*Parade*, 1999).

—Bill Murray

6 Chapter

SCTV

Second City on the Air

Jimmy Carter, who wore sweaters, quoted Bob Dylan, and had felt lust in his heart, was elected President in 1976. Chicago's first Mayor Daley died. Seventy percent of U.S. manufacturing was controlled by 451 companies earning 72 percent of the profits, up from 59 percent in 1960. The Concorde began regularly scheduled flights. Bill Gates had just started Microsoft the year before, and Steve Jobs and Steve Wozniak founded Apple Computer. Word processors and fax machines started taking hold. Shere Hite's The Hite Report: A Nationwide Study of Female Sexuality *and Alex Haley's* Roots *(with the mini-series in 1977) were published. New movies included* Taxi Driver, Rocky, *and Alfred Hitchcock's final film,* Family Plot *(with Barbara Harris and Bruce*

Disc 2
Track 1

Backstage Passes

Before I got into Second City, I was an ad man; I was working for McCann-Erickson. Worked there for about a year and a half, wrote some commercials for Coca-Cola, and my creative director came to me, put his arm around me, and said, "In three years, you'll be a creative director," and I thought, "Well, that's it. I'm out of here," and I quit (Showtime, 1988).

—Dave Thomas

● ▪ ●

As far as a transition from Second City, we had this wonderful opportunity with *SCTV* to take all the things we'd learned onstage and directly translate them into television without any network sponsors or producers in authority. We were the authorities. We got to do what we wanted and operate the same way we did onstage, just in a different medium.

—Harold Ramis

Opening page: Rick Moranis and Dave Thomas as Bob and Doug MacKenzie

Above: John Candy, Joe Flaherty, Eugene Levy, Dave Thomas, and Rick Moranis

Lower Left: John Candy

Dern); and new TV shows included Mary Hartman, Mary Hartman; Laverne & Shirley; Charlie's Angels; *and* The Muppet Show.

In 1976, Second City unveiled, on Canada's Global TV Network, its answer to *Saturday Night Live: SCTV.* (For an exhaustive, funny, and impressively fair recounting of the making of the show, pick up a copy of Dave Thomas's book *SCTV: Behind the Scenes.*) The original writer-performers, all Second City Chicago or Toronto alumni, were John Candy, Joe Flaherty, Eugene Levy, Andrea Martin, Catherine O'Hara, Harold Ramis (also head writer), and Dave Thomas ("as the Beaver" in the opening credits the first season, which he grew to hate intensely, even though he's the one who decided to do it in the first place). Catherine and Dave continued doing the stage show while shooting the TV show until exhaustion set in and Dave finally and justifiably blew up on the set one day. Andrew Alexander immediately replaced him onstage with Dave's good friend Martin Short, and Catherine with her friend Robin Duke. Bernie, Andrew, and Milad Bessada of Global TV were the producers of the first season of *SCTV*, with Harold Ramis, Joe Flaherty, and me as the associate producers. Harold left for a while after the first thirteen shows to write *Animal House*, and Brian Doyle-Murray joined the writing staff. Among the other former Second City performers during the run of the show were Tony Rosato, Robin Duke, Brenda Donahue, John Hemphill, Mary Charlotte Wilcox, and Martin Short.

SCTV came at an extremely fortunate time in the financial history of Second City. Although business was picking up some in Chicago, there were still some difficult times—and even more so in Toronto.

Andrew Alexander was having trouble paying the bills at The Firehall because the owners weren't paying their bills. Andrew remembers his initial reaction to doing a TV show:

Bernie Sahlins had been bugging us to do TV, and I didn't want to. But then Lorne Michaels came out with Saturday Night Live, *and we decided we wanted to do our own show. In a meeting with Allan Slaight, Global TV's owner, he said, "I can give you a studio and crew if you can come up with the rest of the money." My partner Len Stuart put up thirty-five grand, a lot of money in those days. Those were our above-the-line costs for the first seven shows. If Len hadn't come along, there would definitely not have been a television show. And I don't know how much longer I could have kept going at The Firehall. The doctor, lawyers, and judge who owned it weren't business guys at all, and I needed that. Instead, there was a lot of high emotion.*

Len Stuart describes how he helped Andrew get Second City Toronto on solid footing: "I knew Andrew had paid a dollar for Second City in Canada. So I said, 'Look, for fifty cents, I'll buy half of Second City and work with you to sort out these problems with the Firehall.' I didn't know much about the theater business, but it looked like it could be fun. I handled the conversation with the Firehall owners. By this time, we had *SCTV* and they knew they had something going in their building. We had already found another location. So I got a meeting with the owners and told them unless they let me take over their bank loans in exchange for the building, we would leave. I showed them the lease on the other place, and they took the deal."

The premise of *SCTV* was a day's programming on the very bad high-frequency TV channel SCTV (which, of course, stood for Second City Television) located in the fictional small town of Melonville. "We thought," says Harold Ramis, "'well, we're doing it at a really cheesy Canadian television station—let's *be* a cheesy television station!' That was the group consensus. We'd do station characters, and then we'd do what had become our stock and trade at Second City, which was sketch comedy and parodies."

Along with seeing the day's programming—parodies of shows, movies, promos, and commercials you might see on a real TV station—the audience also learned bits and pieces about the lives of the usually inept people who worked at the station. The first episode, for instance, followed the gradual nervous breakdown of *SCTV* star Johnny LaRue (John Candy), tracking him from his exercise show (largely consisting of such things as opening and closing the refrigerator door, leaving his heart "beating

Spotlight on Eugene Levy

Eugene Levy was in the first Firehall cast in 1974 after playing Jesus in the Toronto production of *Godspell* that had so many future Second Citizens in the cast. Eugene's pitch-perfect comic timing is probably the slowest since Jack Benny's. He's a character actor who's also an excellent straight man. After *SCTV*, he's been in such movies as *National Lampoon's Vacation, Splash, Father of the Bride, Club Paradise, Armed and Dangerous, Waiting for Guffman,* and *American Pie*. He starred in and directed *Partners 'n Love* and *Once upon a Crime*.

Eugene was part of a cluster of talent that came from Hamilton, Ontario, and McMaster University: Eugene, Martin Short, Dave Thomas, and Paul Shaffer (David Letterman's band leader, who was also in that production of *Godspell*). One of Eugene's best-loved scenes was a solo piece he did at The Firehall. He played a circus trainer for an amoeba circus and really made the audience see that amoeba as it jumped from chair to chair, while all he did was hum. It was a brilliant piece of physical comedy.

Bottom: Candy and Joe Flaherty take center stage on SCTV.

Opposite page, top to bottom: A young John Candy • Candy works his way through a hockey skit with Joe Flaherty (left) and Dave Thomas (middle).

John Candy was a clown, the kind of clown who tried to hide his vulnerability behind a mask of clearly fake bravado and arrogance—a blowhard. In the early days in Toronto, he was in *The Clown Murders,* a slasher movie, and *Silent Partner,* a suspense film starring Elliot Gould and Christopher Plummer. Then came *SCTV.* After that, he went into the movies, including roles in *The Blues Brothers* and *Stripes.* Getting hit in the head by that ball in *Splash* got him particularly noticed. For a while, he was sure his career was going to be the comic sidekick, which would have been all right with him. He turned in memorable supporting roles in movies like *Volunteers, Little Shop of Horrors, Home Alone, Spaceballs,* and *JFK.* However, he went on to star (or costar) in such movies as *Summer Rental; Armed and Dangerous; The Great Outdoors; Planes, Trains & Automobiles; Only the Lonely; Uncle Buck;* and *Cool Runnings.* He became a part owner of the Toronto Argonauts football team with his friend Wayne Gretzky and was working with Andrew Alexander and Len Stuart to create an all-comedy TV network in Canada when he had a heart attack and died while shooting *Wagons East* in Mexico in 1994.

John was well over six feet tall and big even when he wasn't overweight. He was first hired in Toronto for the Chicago Second City in 1973, a nineteen-year-old, scared novice. The Chicago company dubbed him Johnny Toronto. In those days, he would occasionally disappear onstage—not exit, disappear. He'd go inside himself, maybe trying to think of what to do, maybe afraid of failing, maybe intimidated by what Bill Murray, Betty Thomas, and the others were doing onstage, and, despite his size, you'd just forget he was there, as if he'd turned invisible. It took three or four new shows and a lot of confidence-building before the problem disappeared.

John was even nicer than you probably thought he was from seeing his work. Even when he played sleazy, egomaniacs like Johnny LaRue, you couldn't help loving him, especially since he often ended up a loser.

During brainstorming sessions for ideas for *SCTV* scenes, John would come up with twenty in a row. Maybe only two would be good, but they'd be really good.

John loved kids' movies. He loved *Sesame Street* long before he got to be in *Follow That Bird.* One of his happiest assignments was voicing a character in Disney's *The Rescuers Down Under,* since he particularly loved Disney movies.

His favorite practical joke was to point his finger at your chest and say, "Ooh, what's that?" and when you looked down, he'd flip his finger up into your face and say, "Gotcha." His favorite response, when he had no response, was: "I know you are, but what am I?"

He was a good cook. Although Canadian, he understood America's Thanksgiving and, especially, what that meant in terms of food. During the first year of *SCTV,* he invited some of us Americans for dinner on Thanksgiving. We were to arrive at around 6:00 P.M. At 6:15 he was still dressing the twenty-two-pound turkey. At around seven, he got it into the oven. We ate dinner at two in the morning, by which time we'd had appetizers, cranberry sauce, sweet potatoes, junk food, and drinks to keep us busy while the turkey was cooking, so that we were too full to eat much of what we were too drunk to enjoy anyway.

John loved his beef and ordered steaks thick and "blue," meaning one step from raw; you basically show both sides to the grill until they just turn brown. He also liked to have prepared foods delivered from various restaurants in Toronto. If they didn't deliver, he'd tell them to put it in a cab. Sometimes he wasn't sure what he felt like eating, so he'd order from two or three different restaurants at the same time.

When I decided to leave *SCTV* and move back to Chicago, John and his soon-to-be wife Rosemary agreed to take over the house I was renting—where many Second Citizens had lived and laughed and brainstormed over the years—and therefore keep the house "in the family." The lease on their apartment ended a couple of months before I was leaving, so they moved in with me. I gained close to twenty pounds in those two months. Later, at their wedding, as Rosemary was walking down the aisle to marry John, she stopped at my row to ask if I'd picked up my mail.

When I moved back to Chicago, John gave me a hockey puck as a going-away present. Good Canadian that he was, he'd wanted to be a hockey player, but he bunged up his knees badly when he was a kid. They often hurt.

John was kind, caring, talented, and creative; he was deeply ethical, generous to a fault, as large in spirit as he was in size. He was good company, a friend to anyone who needed one, and he gave the best hugs. He is missed.

Backstage Passes

It was the small things that counted to John, the things that said you cared for John Candy the human being, not John Candy the star. And being in a business where it's often only the big things that count, well, John was a man who got hurt a lot. Maybe he had a hard time believing everyone wasn't as true and caring as he was.

—Andrew Alexander

• • •

Of all the people I worked with at Second City, I think John improved the most as an actor. You'd think maybe he wouldn't have to. Just because he had so much going for him, just as far as presence went. A lot of actors I think would have coasted on that, but John didn't. I watched what he could do with a part. How believable he would make it and how interesting he could make it. How he could create a true character. And I really credit him with being one of the best, you know.

—Joe Flaherty

Disc 1, Tracks 12 & 13
Disc 2, Track 1

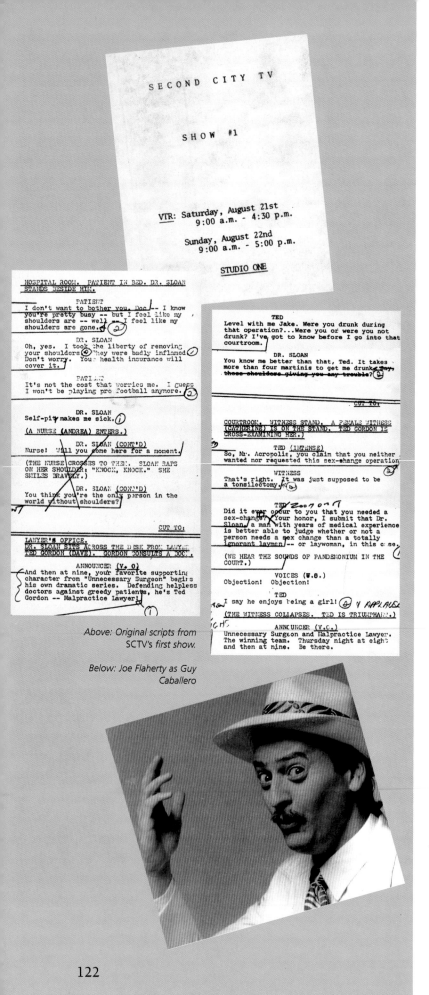

Above: Original scripts from SCTV's first show.

Below: Joe Flaherty as Guy Caballero

like a rabbit") to a backstage episode where his breakdown is becoming apparent, and on to his berserk interruption of a "Masterpiece Theatre" show about Dr. and Mrs. Freud (Eugene Levy and Catherine O'Hara) and a very butch George Sand (Andrea Martin).

The first show also had several parody commercials, mostly done by Dave Thomas; a "Sunrise Semester" lecture on bookkeeping by the very sleazy and sweaty station manager Moe Green (Harold, his character named after the Las Vegas guy who got shot in the eye in *The Godfather*); promos for "Unnecessary Surgeon" and "Malpractice Lawyer"; the first of the many newscasts by Earl Camembert (Eugene) and Floyd Robertson (Joe Flaherty), with Floyd getting all the big news stories and Earl getting very minor stories and deeply resenting it; and, to end the day's programming, a "Words to Live By" with special guest Joni Newton Buffy (Andrea) as a spaced-out folk singer making no sense whatsoever.

"The cast was a young, active group of people who were very strong-minded and confident they knew how to relate to the generation that would be watching them," says Andrew Alexander. "They were, in a sense, their own artistic entity, with their own direction and sense of power. They really took the ensemble mentality from the stage to television."

Throughout the history of *SCTV*, the schedule was always that the writers would work for a few weeks, then they'd shoot for a few weeks, then back to writing, and so on. Of course writing continued during the shooting weeks, mostly rewriting, usually on the set, by the writers who were now the performers; and sometimes new ideas popped up that could be shot on a set already being used. As Harold Ramis describes the original cast:

Not only were they great performers, but everyone sat down at the table to work together. That's how we started every day. Everyone would get their coffee together. We even wrote eight episodes living in the same house in L.A. that Andrew and Len rented for us. We'd meet every day, and there was a swimming pool and a pool table. It was kind of my dream: the comedy house where everyone was funny. You'd sit at that table and John Candy would pull a napkin out of his pocket from a bar the night before. He'd unfold it, and it had an idea, but it was like: "Oh, all I can read is 'Davy Crockett hat.'" You'd try to piece that together for John. He would just keep throwing things in until the scene grew and grew. You knew everything was right because they were going to perform it. There were no false steps. You wouldn't write anything that couldn't be performed because you were already laughing at the table, and that was exactly how it was going to go down. It eliminated a lot of problems.

Global TV produced the first two seasons for a total of fifty-two half-hour episodes, syndicated in the U.S. by Filmways starting in 1977. The show had to be three minutes shorter for the U.S. than for Canada—more time for commercials—which meant that every episode had to be edited twice, often meaning two different versions of the same show. The differing demands of the two lengths, combined with the differing demands of the cast and the producers, did not make for a joyous time in the post-production process, my main job on the show. I left after the first season, and Bernie Sahlins left a half-season later.

When Bernie left, he also took the Second City name with him. It was to have been called "The Second City Television Show" in American syndication, and this put a lot of pressure on Andrew and Len because the syndicator had sold it with that name. (You don't sell a show as *The Mary Tyler Moore Show* and then go back and say it's called "At Home in Minneapolis.") They fought through that one and were able to overcome it in time, but there were some sleepless nights after Bernie took the name back.

Global couldn't afford to keep producing the show, to the great sadness of the crew there, who loved working on the show, hard as it was and long as the hours were (although the extra money may have been part of why they loved it). *SCTV* suffered a year-and-a-half hiatus while Andrew and Len looked for another place to do it. For its third season of twenty-six more half-hour shows, *SCTV* moved to the ITV station in Edmonton, Alberta, carried by the CBC in Canada, with U.S. syndication by Rhodes at different hours in different cities, anywhere from mid-afternoon to after *The Late Late Show*. John Candy was off shooting the pilot for *The Big City Comedy Show*, produced by the Osmonds in Provo, Utah; Catherine O'Hara took a year off; Andrea Martin and Eugene Levy could only commit to a few shows each; Robin Duke, Rick Moranis, and Tony Rosato joined the cast; and John Blanchford took over as director. With few distractions in cold and rather isolated Edmonton, the company melded together quickly. It was like being on the road. Andrew refers to it as a "bunker mentality" that grew up between them.

In 1981, the show went to an hour-and-a-half late night American network slot on NBC, Fridays after Johnny Carson. (Opinion is split as to whether the show worked better in the half-hour or the ninety-minute format.) NBC figured if they could successfully do late-night network programming (11:30 P.M. e.s.t.) on Saturday with *Saturday Night Live*, why not try even later (1:00 A.M.) on Friday? The logic was, perhaps, a little fuzzy, but the show was on an American network, so fine.

Spotlight on Andrew Alexander

*Opposite page top: Martin Short, Eugene Levy, and Andrew
Bottom left to right: Andrew with George Wendt • Andrew
talking things over with Ron West.*

While there is no precise education, formula, or experience that can prepare an individual to lead such a unique organization as The Second City, it is a fact that the individual who does lead it must be pretty unique himself. Andrew Alexander fits this bill. Born in England and raised in Canada, Andrew doesn't share the University of Chicago background of his predecessors. In fact, Andrew's academic background was—in his own words—"terrible."

Instead of studying the classics within ivy-covered walls, Andrew soaked up a wide variety of life lessons and experiences. In 1963, Andrew was shipwrecked in the Pacific Ocean and marooned for seven days in the most desolate region of Baja, California. He was accompanied by his friend Jim Allan, an actress from the New York production of *West Side Story*, a NASA scientist, a child, and a dog. Once rescued, a series of odd jobs would define Andrew's beginnings in business—as a cab driver, the editor of a ski magazine, and advertising salesman for a newspaper chain. In the late 1960s, he even ran a speakeasy. By 1970, Andrew was dabbling in the music industry. He was working with a company called Karma Productions on the Toronto Peace Festival. The festival was supposed to have been anchored by an appearance by John Lennon. However, Lennon wanted the festival to be free of charge, and the whole thing started to collapse. Lennon would go on to write "Instant Karma," an angry anthem in response to Karma Productions' refusal to stage the festival for free.

Andrew's early work in theater included some time in Chicago working in marketing and sales for the Ivanhoe Theatre on Wellington Street. He became a frequent visitor to Second City, developing an eye and an appreciation for the work. He moved on to the Global Village Theatre in Toronto and was involved in a late-night variety show called *Platform* that was a forum for dance, music, poetry, and comedy. It was there that Andrew first met Gilda Radner, who was working in the box office at the time, as well as future Second City alums Dan Aykroyd and Valri Bromfield. Andrew coproduced a number of musicals and plays at this space, including *Spring Thaw* in 1971.

Backstage Pass

I can say now that SCTV probably succeeded because none of us knew what we were doing. Rick Moranis brought that up as a negative. But that's a positive to me. Had we known what was involved—for producers, crew, writers—how hard it was, it would have been frightening. To do it "by the book" would have been really quite difficult. The way we did it was quite anarchistic by comparison. And it worked.

—Andrew Alexander

Although the early days of running Second City in Toronto were often lean ones, with the success of *SCTV,* Andrew was able to elevate the standing of Second City's Toronto branch in fairly short order. Today, due to Andrew's hard work and his solid partnership with Len Stuart, Second City is as much a cultural icon in Canada as it is in America.

But the work of a producer is never done and rarely easy. Recognizing the need for a theater to remain vibrant and essential, Andrew has continued to explore new directions for the company. Whether it's corporate communications, TV shows, Internet-related ventures, or education and outreach, Andrew has rarely sat still and has enjoyed tremendous success. In part, this is due to Andrew's supportive and creative friendship with Second City's co-owner, Len Stuart.

Len Stuart has been intimately involved in the progress of Second City as a business for twenty-five years. A native of Edmonton, Len entered Alberta College and—with typical ambition and drive—became president of the student body of three thousand with his own office and company car. He took a job at Acme Novelty as a shipping clerk and ended up owning the company of 2,600 employees and $200 million in annual revenue. His innovations turned community bingo games into huge revenue centers for government and charity.

Len's partnership with Andrew provided business acumen and secure financing—two rare items in the world of theater. With his businesses well established, Stuart has become a more frequent visitor at Second City. He continues to watch Second City businesses closely. He recently said, "I don't interfere with Andrew's role and leave the dealing with the people inside and the creative direction of the theaters to Andrew. We've hung in through some tough times. It's been a good partnership."

In 1978, Len helped guide *SCTV* through some difficult business transactions with Dr. Charles Allard, a multi-millionaire owner of Allarcom (a large Edmonton-based broadcast company) and Doug Holtby, president of Allarcom, which resulted in *SCTV* being produced in Edmonton for two years. These negotiations, plus the securing of a deal with a major U.S. TV distributor cemented *SCTV*'s future as one of the "100 Greatest TV Shows of All Time," according to *Entertainment Weekly*. Stuart has become more involved in the expanding Second City businesses. He recently invested millions of dollars in a state-of-the-art broadcast studio that is housed in the new Toronto Second City building. He has prepared Second City to continue to become a major TV and Web content provider well into the future. Len recently started the process of establishing a foundation to support and further the work of up-and-coming artists in all creative disciplines.

Len is a brilliant businessman. When I was negotiating for the right to acquire an interest in *SCTV* and have it produced in Edmonton, I was shocked at the knowledge Len had of our industry. You have to remember his background was in printing at the time, so to have the understanding that he did at that time was quite impressive. The deal secured *SCTV* for years to come.

— Doug Holtby

● ● ●

The one constant memory I have of Len is when things looked pretty bleak, he would always say, "No problem," and somehow the problems got solved. I made a sign that I put over my office door with those exact words, a sign that I still keep to this day—"No Problem." I always enjoyed working with Len and respected his straightforwardness.

—Pat Whitley
Co-Producer, *SCTV*

Right (from left): Dade County (Fla.) Police Chief Nick Navaro, Andrew Alexander, Len Stuart, and John Candy

Spotlight on
Dave Thomas

Dave Thomas had been an understudy in the Toronto production of *Godspell* and got into the show later in the run. He joined Second City Toronto in 1975 and was immediately comfortable improvising in front of an audience. He usually played tough-minded characters who were equally tough to melt, and he was a good straight man as well. Dave and Rick Moranis released their LP, *The Great White North*, using their beer-guzzling, purposely clichéd Canadian *SCTV* characters Bob and Doug McKenzie.

It sold more than a million copies and won a Juno (Canada's Grammy). They also played the McKenzie brothers in their movie *Strange Brew*, the highest grossing Canadian film of 1983. Dave was a regular on *Grace Under Fire*, and has been seen in such other movies as *Stripes, Boris and Natasha,* and *The Coneheads*. Dave's also been active as a director, writer, and producer for several movies and TV programs, and he literally wrote the book on *SCTV*.

Dave was totally unselfish about the work, both at Second City and on *SCTV*. He helped others find laughs, find characters, find scenes, often instead of worrying about finding things for himself. Dave returned to the stage show for a while during an early hiatus of the TV show and got to work in several scenes with his good friend Martin Short, including the one as his father turning him on to pot, then scaring him into a paranoid fit.

John, Andrea, and Catherine rejoined the company, and at NBC's request, the show had musical guests, like *Saturday Night Live,* but worked into the show better than on *SNL*. *SCTV* had many conflicts with the network, but the show's writer/performers almost always got what they demanded, running through several network producers in the process. The NBC version lasted two seasons; for a while it was running opposite a similar show on ABC called *Fridays,* which had Second City alum Jack Burns as head writer.

Martin Short joined the cast of *SCTV* during the second NBC season. "When Marty joined," says Andrew Alexander, "it couldn't have come at a better time. He was a shot in the arm. There was some dissension in the air, with NBC pushing for L.A.-based producers, and everyone weighed down by the sheer enormity of work that had to be done every week on an hour-and-a-half show. Marty was a spark, he was new energy, he was terrific. His enthusiasm was contagious. And *SCTV* turned out to be the perfect show for him to mine his comic genius."

Cinemax Cable picked up the show for one more season, this time in forty-five–minute segments with Joe Flaherty, Eugene Levy, Martin Short, and Andrea Martin still on board, with featured players and former Toronto Second Citizens John Hemphill, Mary Charlotte Wilcox, and Valri Bromfield (from the very first cast on Adelaide Street).

Among the other writers who worked on the show over the years were Joe Flaherty's brothers Paul and Dave, Martin Short's brother Mike, Andrea Martin's then-husband (Short's brother-in-law) Bob Dolman, and such Second City alumni as Dick Blasucci, Jim Fisher, and Jim Staahl. Andrew and Len remained executive producers. Producers from the networks came and went, usually totally frustrated; fortunately, Canadian producer Patrick Whitley hung in and kept things together while the network-approved people revolved in and out.

SCTV featured some of the funniest and most bizarre parodies ever shown on TV. In one, I played the beringed hands and small-checked blue-and-white pants of the "savior," serving martinis from a cocktail shaker and adding an olive before giving it to a thirsty Ben Hur in our parody of the movie, with John Candy as Ben doing Curly from The Three Stooges, Dave Thomas and Eugene Levy doing Abbott and Costello as Romans, and Harold Ramis as Mazollo, dying after the cheesiest chariot race ever shot, confessing that Ben's mother and sister (Andrea Martin and Catherine O'Hara) had been turned into—did he say "lepers" or "leopards"? It was "leopards." They were transformed back to human form through the power of more martinis served by the checked pants. (The only other time I almost appeared on camera was at the end of our Chekhov parody, "Waiting for Chekhov," with a bunch of very Chekhovian characters sitting around being bored and wishing they were somewhere else while waiting for Chekhov. Chekhov finally shows up, but it turns out to be Dave as Chekhov from *Star Trek*, who beams them all up. Then I ran onto the set as the show's director wondering what happened and where everyone was. I later cut myself out in the editing room.)

Our first guest stars were Sir John Gielgud and Sir Ralph Richardson. They were in Toronto in a Harold Pinter play, and we asked them if they'd be in our show, which they'd never heard of. To our surprise, they said yes if we wrote something for them they liked. They'd be especially delighted to do a Pinter parody, and wouldn't it be lovely if we dealt with Sir John's love of crossword puzzles and Sir Ralph's love of motorcycles? We wrote about a dozen pieces, including a very funny commercial for a recording of Shakespeare's greatest jokes—naturally using the most obscure ones we could find—and one dealing with England's failing economy by offering the country for sale. The only thing we had trouble with was the Pinter parody with the crossword puzzles and the motorcycles. Something was finally cobbled together set in their dressing room before a performance of their play. Nobody was very happy with it, but it was the only thing the Sirs were willing to do.

Big Jim McBob (Joe Flaherty) and Billy Sol Hurok (John Candy) produced a memorable catch-phrase in their love of blowing up singers they didn't like: "She blowed up good, she blowed up reeeal good!" Joe's Count Floyd, the host of "Monster Horror Chiller Theater" (who was really newscaster Floyd Robertson), also produced a catch-phrase, done in his bad Transylvanian accent: "Oooh, scaaary." Count Floyd's pathetic attempts to make the audience think the movies they showed were scary often included that phrase with the uncertain follow-up, "Wasn't that scary, kids?"

"The Sammy Maudlin Show" was a parody of Sammy Davis Jr.'s short-lived talk show, with Joe as the swinging, fawning host in a huge Afro wig; such guests as Catherine's ultimate bimbo, Lola Heatherton ("I want to bear your children"); and Eugene's sleazy, pretentious ("as a comic, in all seriousness…") Vegas comedian Bobby Bittman ("Howaahya?"); and John as Sammy's fawning, submissive, over-laughing sidekick William B. Williams.

John's lisping and would-be-sinister Dr. Tongue and his grunting hunchback assistant Bruno (Eugene) were usually

Rick Moranis is the only regular *SCTV* performer who never played at Second City. He had written for CBS radio and television and appeared on TV shows such as *90 Minutes Live* and *The Alan Hamel Show*. His friend, Dave Thomas, asked him to do an *SCTV* scene with him in 1980 as a replacement for John Candy. Rick created a number of memorable characters, like the beer-guzzling, hockey-loving canuck, Bob MacKenzie, who hosted "The Great White North" with his brother, Doug (Dave Thomas), and dead-on impersonations of celebrities like Woody Allen, mis-paired with Bob Hope (also played by Dave). His film career since *SCTV* includes costarring, cowriting, and codirecting *Strange Brew* with Dave, as well as having major roles in many other movies such as *Little Shop of Horrors*; both *Ghostbusters* films; *Honey, I Shrunk the Kids*; *My Blue Heaven*; *Club Paradise*; *Spaceballs*; *Parenthood*; and *The Flintstones*.

Spotlight on
Martin Short

Martin Short, before joining the Second City cast in 1977, was well established in the Toronto theater scene, not as an improviser, but certainly as a very funny man who could also sing well and dance a little. He joined *SCTV* late in its run and was soon resident clown. After *SCTV*, Martin went into the TV series *The Associates* and *I'm a Big Girl Now*, then to *Saturday Night Live*, and on to award-winning performances in the Broadway musicals *The Goodbye Girl* and *Little Me*. He's acted in such movies as *Clifford*, *Innerspace*, *Three Amigos*, *The Big Picture*, the *Father of the Bride* films, *Mars Attacks!*, and *A Simple Wish*. He had his own cartoon show as Ed Grimley (a character he created at Second City, brought to *SCTV*, then made famous on *Saturday Night Live*), and had his own syndicated talk show.

Clockwise from above: Short is joined by Robin Williams (left) for an improv set at The Firehall. • Short as the loveable Ed Grimley • Short performs a Second City version of Ed Grimley.

Marty was so strong, like immediately, when he joined the cast. Most people would come in and try to find their place. When you came in, you came in in the middle of the run of a show, you're coming into someone else's roles, roles that another person had invented for the show. Most people would come in and basically try to imitate the person whose roles they're doing and then try to find their own place. Marty came in like a little powerhouse. He just immediately put his own ridiculously strong characters into those scenes. Just such great self-confidence and so funny that he was great to watch (Showtime, 1988).

—Catherine O'Hara

Martin discussed his style of comedy at Showtime's 15th Anniversary Show for Second City Toronto:

I would not say that my work at Second City had intellectual appeal as much as more of a clown quality. The scenes I did, I would always make sure there was enough time, because I would do full costume and hair changes. I would arrive at the theater early, and it was very important that I have my bowl of water and my Dippity-Doo. And I would bring costumes—well, not costumes—I suppose you would call them clothing. You know, shirts from my childhood that I still fit into, tragically enough. (I stopped growing at seven.) Bad pants and unusual jackets that normally you wouldn't keep. But I thought maybe some day. So I always figured that if you walked onstage and looked totally insane, you would get a laugh. And then you were halfway there.

If I thought of a picture of me in Second City, it would be a picture I actually have. It's the whole cast, and we're in the middle of a scene, and someone has said something, and I've clearly broken up, and I'm truly laughing. And that's my memory of doing Second City stage.

I think Marty, when improvising, brought his own reality to the stage. He started by taking over other people's roles. In one scene he played a character—I don't know—it wasn't really Columbo because it was much broader than anything Peter Falk would ever have done. What're you going to do? I mean, fight it? We went with it. It gave the scene a new shape, we got different laughs, it was good, we had fun (Showtime, 1988).

—Dave Thomas

Disc 1, Track 16
Disc 2, Track 1

Spotlight on
Andrea Martin

Andrea Martin, an American from Maine, came to Toronto to be in *Godspell*, then was in a couple of other shows before joining the Second City cast at The Firehall in 1975. A trained actor, she'd had no experience as an improviser and never really lost her fear of it, although she was one of the funniest and most outrageous clowns ever on the Second City stage. The Firehall company did an occasional improv from a subject suggested by the audience where each performer played one of the stages of a joke: transition, set-up, punch line, topper, too far. Andrea always played "too far." Since *SCTV*, she's performed her own one-woman show, *Nude, Nude, Totally Nude*, starred in Broadway musicals, and been in such movies as *Wholly Moses!, Club Paradise, Innerspace, Rude Awakening, Boris and Natasha, Wag the Dog,* and *Stepping Out.*

Andrea talked about her feelings on improv:

I don't think there was one night in all the years I did Second City that I ever felt comfortable doing improvisation. To me, the highlight was the scripted show. With those many weeks of improvisation, finally I got a scene that worked, and then it was like, "Oh thank God, I know the words, and now I can get into the part." I loved any rehearsals anywhere with Sheldon, Bernie, and Del. Anytime we would actually rehearse a scene and set, it was exhilarating. I then felt free to improvise and find.

characters in terrible 3D movies shown in 2D on "Monster Horror Chiller Theater," with 3D non-effects achieved by stupid props being pushed toward the camera and pulled away again.

The polka-playing Schmenge Brothers, Yosh and Stan (John and Eugene), also made a video, "Power to the Punk People Polka," and the HBO pseudo-documentary *The Schmenge Brothers: The Last Polka.*

Harold Ramis did a "Sunrise Semester" as Mort Finkel giving a lesson in do-it-yourself dentistry, using vodka as a painkiller and hurting himself badly until he was eventually too drunk to care. (The crew put real booze in the bottle during the shoot, and Harold ended up actually getting drunk.)

One of John's most frequently recurring characters on *SCTV*, the drunken, bad-tempered, vain Johnny LaRue, like Bob Hope and Woody Allen, was a coward and thought of himself—usually erroneously—as irresistible to women, although he did become the Hugh Hefner of *SCTV* with his own "Penthouse" show. LaRue was also often unable, through his own ego and stupidity, to understand what was going on around him. In the first season alone, for example, food critic LaRue, while reviewing an Italian restaurant at exactly the time and in exactly the place where Al Pacino shoots Sterling Hayden in *The Godfather*, has no idea what's going on or why Harold, as the terrified waiter, is moving around the room crouching behind tables and serving him partially eaten bologna sandwiches. LaRue also had a cooking show in the first season where he presented recipes for poor people, the main ingredient being cat food.

When Harold left the show for *Animal House*, his character Moe Green, the station manager, was kidnapped by Leutonians (also the nationality of the Schmenge Brothers). Moe's job was taken over by Andrea, a screeching vision in leopard jacket and hat, as Edith Prickley (a character she first did at Second City as a mother summoned to a meeting with her child's teacher).

Andrea played harsh-voiced, pants-suited Edna Boil reading the cue cards for her commercials really badly ("Come on down") while Tex (Dave) played the organ, until he ran off on her one day; and in a promo for "The Exorcist of Oz," she turned from Judy Garland as Dorothy into Linda Blair in *The Exorcist* halfway through "Somewhere over the Rainbow." Andrea created talk-show host Libby Wolfson who, like Andrea herself, was very concerned about her appearance and how she smelled; did a promo for Connie Franklin's (read Connie Francis) "20 Depressing Hit Songs"; and played deeply repressed sexologist Cheryl Kinsey on "Sunrise Semester," teaching women how to fake an orgasm.

Catherine was Sister Mary Innocent hosting an exercise show largely involved with self-flaggelation, which Sister Mary clearly enjoyed. And Catherine's commercial for Milk of Amnesia while slowly developing amnesia from having taken a spoonful is one of the best pieces of sustained comic acting I've ever seen—and she did it in one take because we were running out of studio time.

Among Martin Short's characters were former child star Jackie Rogers Jr., Ed Grimley, and his impersonation of Jerry Lewis. (He also did a wicked Katharine Hepburn.)

Dave and Rick Moranis created the check-shirted, beer-swilling, brain-damaged Canadian stereotypes Bob and Doug McKenzie as their response to having to comply with the CBC's requirement for "identifiable Canadian content."

Eugene Levy and John Candy as Stan and Yosh Schmenge

Dave's hostile Asian, Lin Ye Tang, sometimes a host, sometimes a performer, had a slightly different look each time he was in a show; Dave and the makeup people were never satisfied with the look, and kept on experimenting. As angry as Lin Ye Tang often was, Dave's bile really boiled over as the choleric TV editorialist Bill Needle.

Other memorable *SCTV* parodies included *The Andy Griffith Show*, with Eugene doing a lecherous Floyd the Barber, and our own version of John Ford's *The Grapes of Wrath*—"The Grapes of Mud"—with Joe as Tom Joad, Catherine as Ma Joad, Dave as Grandpaw, Eugene as the Reverend, Andrea as the daughter, and Harold as Muley, who also had his own kids' show, which consisted of his whining to the viewers about various slights and mistreatments.

SCTV ran for six seasons between 1976 and 1984, producing 135 episodes in one length or another, and is still in syndication in many major cities (released in 185 half-hour episodes). It received thirteen Emmy Award nominations, and won two Emmy Awards for best writing.

• • •

Spotlight on Catherine O'Hara

Catherine O'Hara started out working in the coat check at The Firehall. Then, in 1974, without any formal training, she successfully replaced Gilda Radner in the cast when Gilda left for New York while the company was playing Chicago. After *SCTV*, Catherine acted in such movies as *After Hours, Heartburn, Beetlejuice,* the first two *Home Alone* movies, *Home Fries,* and did the voice for the female lead in *The Nightmare before Christmas.*

One day early in the first season of *SCTV*, when the show was just getting popular in Canada, Andrea Martin came into the studio laughing. A neighbor had stopped her on the way to work to tell her how much she liked the show, how much she liked Andrea on the show, and how much she liked the other three women too. The other three women were all Catherine (who didn't find the story amusing). That's as good a way as any of defining a great character actor.

Catherine is beautiful, but she has so much diversity in what she can do. She can do frumpy, she can do the vamp. All the others had a background in acting. But with Catherine, she was able to pick it up just by hanging around. She was just drawn to it, as were her brother Marcus and sister Mary Margaret. Some people would call the O'Haras eccentric. They live their lives by their own rules. A close family, mutually supportive, with good values, they have a strong belief in what's right. Catherine brought that to contract negotiations; she just didn't believe in the standard option agreement. I don't think NBC had ever heard anything like it.

Top to bottom: (left to right) Jon Glaser (in pig mask), Adam McKay, Jenna Jolovitz, Scott Allman, Scott Adsit, and Rachel Dratch in Piñata Full of Bees. • Citizen Gates photo shoot (from left to right): Kevin Dorff, cigar store Indian, Scott Allman, Tina Fey, Jenna Jolovitz, Rachel Dratch, and Scott Adsit • Marc Hickox (left) and Doug Morency (right) resprise the classic "Cowboys" scene.

Early on in Second City's history, show titles had little to do with the show's content and were often taken from obscure Shakespearian references, such as *The Seacoast of Bohemia* (a non-existent location from *The Winter's Tale*) and *Alarums & Excursions* (from *King John*: "Alarums, excursions. Enter the Bastard, with Austria's head"…you get the idea).

As Second City developed its comedic and satiric style, the show titles took on more significance—or, at least, more thought was put into making them funny (although they still rarely had anything to do with the content of the shows).

A few of Chicago mainstage show titles:

New York City Is Missing (1964)
Inside the Outsiders or Rainwater for Everyone (1964)
Old Wine in New Bottles (1965)
Justice Is Done or Oh, Calcoolidge! (1970)
Picasso's Mustache (1971)
43rd Parallel or McCabre & Mrs. Miller (1972)
Premises, Premises (1972)
Tippicanoe and Déjà Vu (1973)
Once More with Fooling (1975)
North by North Wells (1976)
Freud Slipped Here (1979)
I Remember Dada or Won't You Come Home, Saul Bellow? (1979)
Exit Pursued by a Bear (1982)
Orwell that Ends Well (1983)
How Green Were My Values (1986)
Jean-Paul Sartre & Ringo (1987)
Kuwait Until Dark or Bright Lights, Night Baseball (1988)
Flag Smoking Permitted in Lobby Only or Censorama (1990)
Economy of Errors (1991)
Truth, Justice, or the American Way (1992)
Are You Now, or Have You Ever Been Mellow? (1994)
Piñata Full of Bees (1995)
Citizen Gates (1996)

Paradigm Lost (1997)
The Psychopath Not Taken (1998)

Some Second City Toronto show titles:
Hello Dali (1974)
Saturday Night Beaver (1978)
To Mock a Kilogram (1982)
Not Based on Anything by Stephen King (1986)
Four Horsemen of the Apocalypse and a Baby (1988)
Inhale to the Chief (1992)

Some Second City e.t.c. revues:
*Disgruntled Employee Picnic or The Postman Always
  Shoots Twice* (1993)
Cardinal Knowledge or Felonious Monks (1993)
Farewell My CompuServe (1996)

And a few Second City Detroit shows:
Kevorkian Unplugged
Viagra Falls

How does Second City come up with these titles? Volume. The following list of titles-that-never-made-it were the result of the actors' brainstorming titles for shows that eventually became the mainstage show *Promise Keepers, Losers Weepers* and the e.t.c. show *River Ants*:

Xenaphobe: Warrior Princess
Pinch Hitler
Zsa Zsa Gabortion
Jehovah's Witness Protection Program
Phyllis Minoxydiller
Fundraisin in the Sun
Tickle Me El Niño
Workers of the World: Just Do It!
Battle Hymn of the Banana Republic
Little Orphan Anthrax
Out of the Mouths of Hot Babes
Co-Ed Naked Cliches from Hell
All of Her Fist
Shirkers of the World, Unite
The Au Pair Went Free Show
What Part of Reno Don't You Understand?
America's Funniest Homophobes
Six Characters in Search of Parking
Seven Brides for Scatman Crothers
Sloppy Seconds Over Tokyo

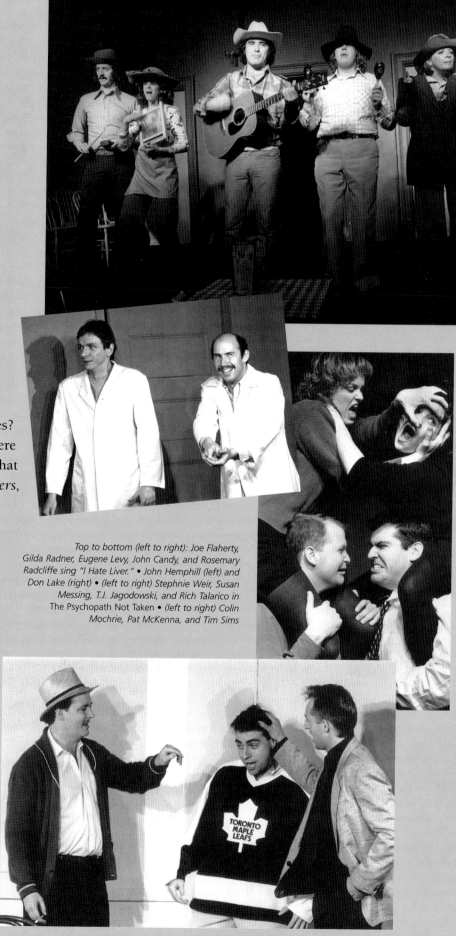

Top to bottom (left to right): Joe Flaherty, Gilda Radner, Eugene Levy, John Candy, and Rosemary Radcliffe sing "I Hate Liver." • John Hemphill (left) and Don Lake (right) • (left to right) Stephnie Weir, Susan Messing, T.J. Jagodowski, and Rich Talarico in The Psychopath Not Taken • (left to right) Colin Mochrie, Pat McKenna, and Tim Sims

7
Chapter

The 1980s

Triumph and Tragedy

To start off with, the 1980s saw the election of Ronald Reagan as president and the murder of John Lennon outside his New York City apartment building. Under Reagan and Bush, the economy grew—the rich got richer as the poor got poorer. Greed was apparently good. By the end of the decade, the economy was in shambles, and the national debt astronomical.

Iran-Contra took a little of the shine off of Reagan's Presidency. Chicago, Philadelphia, and New York were among cities to elect their first African-American mayors. Reagan appointed Sandra Day O'Connor as the first woman on the Supreme Court. The Equal Rights Amendment was defeated. Widespread use of crack cocaine became

Disc 2
Tracks 2–6

Backstage Pass

I remember once we were doing an improvisation on an audience suggestion about *Saturday Night Live* going downhill. Nancy McCabe-Kelly and I were playing a couple watching the show on television and putting it down. We were nailing everybody in it, all their characteristics. Suddenly there was a knock on the door on stage. I went to answer it, and John Belushi walked in. I didn't expect him at all. Well, we went so crazy we never finished the scene (*Chicago Sun-Times*, 1994).

—Danny Breen

Opening page: (left to right)
Bonnie Hunt, Mike Myers,
and Barbara Wallace.

Top to bottom: George Wendt
• Shelley Long

apparent. AIDS, which was only identified early in the 1980s, reached epidemic proportions by 1989.

USA Today *began publication. Among the provocative new books were Allan Bloom's* The Closing of the American Mind, *Stephen Hawking's* A Brief History of Time, *Alice Walker's* The Color Purple, *Jay McInerney's* Bright Lights, Big City, *Salmon Rushdie's* The Satanic Verses, *and Amy Tan's* The Joy Luck Club.

Important new plays included True West, Glengarry Glen Ross, *and* Driving Miss Daisy. *American musicals included* Sunday in the Park with George, Into the Woods, *and* Little Shop of Horrors. *But the British musical took over Broadway with* Les Miserables, *and Andrew Lloyd Weber's* The Phantom of the Opera *and* Cats.

Innovative films were scarce in the 1980s, but a few of the better ones included David Lynch's Blue Velvet, *Martin Scorcese's* Raging Bull, *and Spike Lee's* Do the Right Thing.

CNN and MTV began broadcasting. The last episode of M*A*S*H *was the most watched show in the history of TV.* Dallas, Dynasty, *and* Miami Vice *ruled the airwaves, otherwise.* Late Night with David Letterman *started its run, as did* The Simpsons.

CDs were introduced in 1985 and, by the end of the decade, had replaced vinyl LPs. New wave crossed over where punk never did. Michael Jackson, Prince, Madonna, Van Halen, and Guns n' Roses topped the charts. U2 and R.E.M. went from college-radio staples to stadium rockers.

It was a time of conservatism and conspicuous consumption—kind of like when Second City started.

By the end of the 1970s, Second City had found a new and wider popularity, which kept building through the 1980s. We were even becoming a tourist attraction, and by the mid-1980s, you had to call nearly two months in advance to secure a Saturday night ticket. Of course, this was at least in part because of the celebrity being achieved by so many Second City alums.

Along with *SCTV* and *Saturday Night Live*, many alumni had a major effect on American entertainment—writing, directing, and starring in some of the highest-grossing and popular works of the decade.

John Belushi and Dan Aykroyd's movie *The Blues Brothers* opened in 1980, with John Candy also prominently in the cast. It not only became a hit movie, it also spawned a best-selling album and concert tour. (John Belushi told older folks like me not to see it unless we went on a Saturday night to the downtown theater where it was playing and see it with the audience it was meant for. He was right.)

Harold Ramis directed *Caddyshack*, featuring Bill Murray, Brian Doyle-Murray, and a gopher. Bill and Harold starred in *Stripes*, with John Candy, Dave Thomas, and Joe Flaherty also in the cast. *Ghostbusters*, one of the highest-grossing movies of all time, was co-written by Dan and Harold, starred Bill, Dan, and Harold, and featured Rick Moranis from *SCTV* in a supporting role. (*Ghostbusters II* came out in 1989.) John Candy drew a lot of attention with his role in *Splash*, and went on from there to become a major movie star.

Cheers began its long and popular run on NBC, making stars of Shelley Long and George Wendt. Betty Thomas became a regular on the long-running and influential police drama *Hill Street Blues*. And Jim Belushi, Robin Duke, Tim Kazurinsky, Tony Rosato, Mary Gross, Brian Doyle-Murray, Martin Short, and Mike Myers joined *Saturday Night Live* in the 1980s.

Second City e.t.c.

Behind Second City, Bernie Sahlins and Joyce Sloane had fixed up a space for Paul Sills to hold workshops and do Story Theater shows. In 1981, after Paul left town, they redid it into a cabaret space for Practical Theater, a comedy company made up of such recent Northwestern University graduates as Paul Barrosse, Julia Louis Dreyfus, Brad Hall, Richard Kind, Gary Kroeger, and Tom Virtue, who'd been performing in their forty-seat storefront space named the John Lennon Auditorium. (They kept calling me their director, but what I usually did was come to rehearsals, laugh, and sometimes say, "You can't do that.") Most of them were quickly gobbled up by *Saturday Night Live*. (When Bob Tischler and Dick Ebersol from *SNL* came to see the Practical show, they were unhappy at having to pay for their tickets. Joyce told them, "The kids need the money. Take it out of your limo budget.") Practical soon went out of business, and Richard Kind and Tom Virtue moved over to Second City.

In 1982, Bernie directed the mainstage company in *Glenna Loved It or If You Knew Sushi* with an extremely talented company that included Danny Breen, Meagan Fay, John Kapelos, Lance Kinsey, Nonie Newton-Breen, and Rick Thomas. Unfortunately, that was the year we had to close the weekend Second City we'd opened in 1976 at the Chateau Louise Resort Theatre in Dundee, Illinois, as a more permanent booking for some of the talented and underemployed touring company people. A lot of good people were therefore hanging around Second City in the early 1980s with no place to perform on a regular basis and tired of doing

Top to bottom: A coupon for a Second City e.t.c. performance • Jane Morris (left), Jeff Michalski (middle), and Steve Assad (right) act out a scene in Mirrors at the Border. • *(left to right) Kevin Crowley, Joe Liss, and Bonnie Hunt perform in a scene from* Kuwait Until Dark.

Backstage Pass

Richard Kind had this terrific ability to play sympathetic, sweet, frightened, and not-caring—all at the same time. I cast him in a CBS pilot called *110 Lombard Street*, after the address of The Old Firehall in Toronto. He brought a great scene with him from mainstage that we renamed "Kidder," about a wealthy man whose philosophy of life was, "Never kid a kidder." In Chicago, it went by a name we couldn't use on TV (just replace "kid" with the worst word you can imagine). Mike Myers played his daughter's rather unqualified suitor in the scene. The cast also included people like Bonnie Hunt, Ryan Stiles, and Don Lake. It's too bad the time slot eventually went to Pat Sajak.

—Andrew Alexander

Richard Kind reacts with hilarious shock during a scene with Dan Castellaneta (left).

touring company gigs. Since the Practical space was empty, Jane Morris and Jeff Michalski organized a group of touring company people, including Bill Applebaum, Jim Fay, Carey Goldenberg, Susan Gauthier, and pianist/musical director Ruby Streak. They asked Bernie and Joyce if they could put on the Touring Company show there. Bernie said OK. It was called The Second City e.t.c., and was to be used as an overflow theater when the mainstage show was sold out. But Bernie said they could only do old material, not their own stuff. According to Mark Belden, the following is what led to e.t.c. creating an original show:

It's 1981 and Bernie Sahlins' friend Larry Edwards has a basement apartment he needs to rent. Bernie asks around and finds a couple of touring company actors, Jim Fay and Jeff Michalski, and sets them up in this apartment. They bring in a third guy, a standup comedian, and the three of them sign a one-year lease. Over the course of the next year, so many comedians, actors, girlfriends, acquaintances, drunks, and druggies use this apartment that it is completely ruined. One day Jimmy Fay decides he's had enough and moves. Desperate for cash to pay for their part of the rent, the other two let a former mental patient move in. He proceeds to punch holes in all the walls and start fistfights. Eventually, the original lessees all move out to get away from the madman and the trashed apartment. He, in turn, brings in some of his friends to share the rent. Meanwhile, the Edwardses are living above all this, with no idea of what's going on in their basement. Finally, during the last month of the lease, Mrs. Edwards ventures down to ask the nice boys she rented to if they want to renew for another year. She knocks on the door two days in a row, and no one answers. The third day, still nobody answers, so she tries the doorknob. It turns. She opens the door; it's off its hinges and falls in. She looks around the apartment, runs upstairs, and calls the police. She thinks the apartment has been broken into and vandalized while the actors were on the road. When it turns out that not one of the people on the lease is still living in the apartment, she is outraged, and it all ends up in Bernie's lap. Needless to say, Bernie is extremely pissed off, and Michalski and Fay languish in the touring company far longer than anyone ever has before, the frustration of which leads them to write the first Second City e.t.c. revue, Cows on Ice.

While Bernie was up in Toronto in September 1982, Joyce let them open *Cows on Ice*, the show of original material they'd developed out on the road, and invite the critics.

Joyce recalls the opening of *Cows on Ice*:

I said, "Okay, you can open it, but I don't want to know about it!" The night they opened, I went out of town. They got great reviews; it was really a terrific show. Everything was going just great. Bernie comes back, and would you believe it? On the way in from the airport, the driver hands him an old newspaper, and Richard Christiansen's fabulous review for the show is in that paper. So he comes in: "Who did this? I'm going to fire the whole company if you don't tell me who did it! I'm calling Christiansen. You're lucky he's out of town!" Jane Morris comes to me and says, "I'm going to quit because I'll tell Bernie I did it." I said, "Just wait. It'll blow over." So that went on for about two days, ranting and raving. He got over it, and they've been doing their own shows back there ever since. Everybody asks why it was called "e.t.c.". "Experimental Theater Company" is a definition that I hear very often. But when I gave it the name, I didn't really have anything in mind. It doesn't really mean anything.

Rave reviews and good houses ensured the longevity of the e.t.c. show, which will celebrate its twentieth anniversary as a full-time theater, doing its own revues, in 2001. The progress of a Second City entertainer/performer in Chicago is now usually from the Training Center to one of the three touring companies to e.t.c. to mainstage.

Although it originally depended on the overflow from Second City for most of its audience, by the end of the 1980s, e.t.c. had its own following. Maybe because of its back-of-Pipers-Alley location, maybe because of its slightly younger, slightly raunchier audience, e.t.c.'s companies were perceived for quite a while as being willing to take more risks in style and subject matter than one was likely to find on the mainstage. Some of it was strongly political—especially when Ron West and Michael McCarthy were in the company for shows like *America Lite*. Some of it was strongly personal—like Jane Morris' graphic and hilarious description of what it feels like to give birth. Minority and gender issues were also often dealt with in a tougher, harsher way—which is not to say that there weren't many moments of silliness and pure lunacy as well.

Because of the audiences it appeals to and the kinds of material one can create for them, some performers have refused to leave e.t.c. for mainstage, and some have been hired for bigger things straight off the e.t.c. stage, like Horatio Sanz (*Saturday Night Live*) and Ken Campbell (*Herman's Head*).

Spotlight on
Richard Kind

Richard Kind, originally from Trenton, New Jersey, joined the Second City Chicago mainstage in 1983. Before that he'd been a member of the Practical Theater Company with Julia Louis-Dreyfus and Brad Hall, among others. At Second City, Richard was a clown, usually playing loud-mouthed, intrusive characters. He made exaggerated faces and could "mug" with his body as well, which was as flexible and expressive as his face. One of Richard's many talents is his ability to stick his entire fist into his

mouth. Since leaving Second City Chicago and Second City in Santa Monica, he's done lots of TV and film work, including regular stints on Carol Burnett's short-lived *Carol and Company*, *Mad About You*, and *Spin City*. His films include roles in *johns*, *Stargate*, *Mr. Saturday Night*, and the voice of Molt in *A Bug's Life*. Richard remains an avid golfer and uses almost any excuse to visit his friends in Chicago.

Dead, Gone, Dead

Second City had a lot to mourn during the 1980s. Original founder Howard Alk passed away in January 1982. In March of that same year, Second City's most famous alum, John Belushi, died of a drug overdose. It's hard for anyone to describe the shock and horror that the loss of John Belushi had on Second City. Not only is it difficult to lose a loved one, but when that cherished member of your family is an international celebrity, and the circumstances of his death lend themselves to tabloid coverage, the media feeding frenzy that follows is immediate, uncontrollable, and devastating.

I was at home when the phone rang, and a former student, now a radio newscaster, was on the other end of the line. After identifying himself, he asked me if I had anything to say about John Belushi's death. I asked if he was joking, and he assured me he wasn't, and did I have anything to say? I was fighting tears and muttered a few words about not knowing about it when I heard him say, "Hold it, you're on the air." I hung up quickly.

Joyce Sloane was sitting in her office when she received a call from a friend in the press notifying her of John's death. Within minutes, the phone began ringing off the hook and the media started arriving at the theater. Joyce, still in shock, posted two staff members at the foot of the stairs to stop the journalists from entering the building. Still, some slipped through.

Several funerals and memorial services followed. In Chicago, there was a very long Greek Orthodox ceremony, after which the mourners descended to the basement for shots of whiskey—a tradition. Then Joyce and Bernie and Jane Sahlins flew to Martha's Vineyard for the private funeral. Arriving in Martha's Vineyard, they couldn't find a car to rent; apparently, the media had reserved all the cars on the tiny island. So Joyce, in her inimitable fashion, found a restaurant on the grounds of the airport and convinced the short-order cook to let them borrow his car. The service took place in a stark white New England church. The shutters had to be closed so the press wouldn't see in. James Taylor sang "Lonesome Road" at the graveside as the news helicopters buzzed overhead.

Then the group traveled to New York for a memorial service at St. John the Divine Cathedral. That night, Bernie and Jane took Jim Belushi and his wife Sandy to dinner in Greenwich Village. On the way back, Jim asked the limo driver to stop for a moment at the White Horse Tavern. Jim and Will Aldis had done a Second City scene about two brothers meeting at the White Horse. In the

Top to bottom: The cast of No, No, Wilmette (clockwise from left): Joe Flaherty, Judy Morgan, John Belushi, Jim Fisher, Roberta Maguire, Brian Doyle-Murray, and Dan Ziskie • John Belushi engages in swordplay.

Opposite page: Jim Belushi

scene they talk about life, family, and death. After several drinks they begin talking about poets, which the younger brother (Will) wants to be: ⒸⒹ

Jim: Now look, I'm older'n you, right?

Will: Yeah?

Jim: Now you listen to me.

Will: Okay?

Jim: I'll tell ya what's important. A degree's not important, man. Alright? Livin' right and dyin' right's important. Understand?

Will: Yeah.

Jim: See this bar here, Mr. Lit?

Will: Sorta.

Jim: You see it. You know who Dylan Thomas is?

Will: Yeah, I know—

Jim: Hunh?

Will: Yeah, sure!

Jim: See that stool right on the end there?

Will: Yeah?

Jim: Dylan Thomas died right there, man.

Will: Really?

Jim: Yeah.

Will: What happened?

Jim: He came here in 1953, right, to do a tour.

Will: Yeah.

Jim: An, ah, he was an alcoholic. You knew that.

Will: He was a poet.

Jim: He was a poet, right. You gotta be an alcoholic, sure, right. So he was sick, right? So he came here—he was sick, right—and he went to the doctor. The doctor told him, "Dylan, you drink any more, you're gonna die." So he came right here, man. Sat right there. Piled twenty-seven shots of white grain alcohol like this—like a Christmas tree, right? Sat there—boomp, boomp, boomp, boomp, boomp, right? His head hit the bar. Went into a coma. Went over to the hospital across the street. Died, man. Sheet over the head. Dead, gone, dead. Right fucking there, man.

Bernie and Jim entered the White Horse and ordered a couple of Rolling Rock beers. They sat in silence until Jim spoke softly, "Dead, gone, dead." They finished their beers and left.

John was just thirty-three years old.

Backstage Pass

A friend of mine came into my office just after we'd heard about John's death. She also happened to write for a popular national magazine. She expressed her regret and sat with me. I was just beside myself with grief. Eric Forsberg, Josephine's son, whom I had known since he was a baby, came in with a single red rose for me. That did it. We were crying and hugging, and then I noticed that my friend had taken her notebook out and was recording everything that was said. She wasn't a friend—not that day—she was a reporter looking for a good story. It just made me sick. I was mostly worried for John's brother Jim. At the time he was in *The Pirates of Penzance* downtown and was planning to perform. I went to the theater and stayed in the dressing room the whole night, just so he would have someone there for him.

—Joyce Sloane

Spotlight on
Dan Castellaneta

Dan Castellaneta, commonly regarded as a great improviser, joined Second City Chicago in 1986 after several years in touring companies and at e.t.c. He was a great ensemble player as well as being very funny. When Tracey Ullman came to Chicago in 1987 to check out the cast, she immediately spotted Dan. He left to do her show, where he developed the

voice of Homer Simpson for some animated shorts on the show. *The Simpsons* began airing in 1989 as a separate half-hour animated sitcom and is still running. Dan has used his extraordinary voice on a number of other animated shows such as *Cow and Chicken*, *All Dogs Go To Heaven*, *Hey Arnold*, and *The Tick*. His film credits include *Nothing In Common*, *The War of the Roses*, *The Client*, *Love Affair*, *Forget Paris*, *Space Jam*, and *My Giant*. Dan also regularly performs in theater, creating his own one-man shows and improvising with Second City alumni in Los Angeles.

Transitions

Not every attempt at expansion has been as successful as e.t.c. In 1980, Second City Toronto opened in Edmonton, Alberta, at a glitzy rock 'n' roll palace called Lucifer's, where—as in the early days at The Firehall—we had to work in front of a wall of amplifiers and a draped drum kit. It lasted only two years.

However, from 1983 to 1992 Second City had a home in the three hundred-seat Corner Stage theater in London, Ontario, produced by Lyn Okkerse (Andrew Alexander's sister) and her husband Peter. London offered us a rather sophisticated audience; however, because of its small size, we had to put up a new show every three or four months. Since London was planned as a place where performer/writers and directors could get seasoning before moving on to The Firehall in Toronto, doing that many shows a year certainly gave it to them. While they were in existence, both Edmonton and London served as stepping stones between the Canadian Touring Company and The Firehall in Toronto.

Del Close left Second City in 1983. He and Bernie Sahlins finally decided that their disagreements about improvisation as a means or an end, and what kind of show a Second City show should be, could no longer produce a fruitful partnership. Bernie took over as director as well as producer. In 1984, he moved the Chicago company—Meagan Fay, Mike Hagerty, Isabella Hoffman, John Kapelos, Richard Kind, and Rick Thomas—to the Village Gate in New York for what turned out to be a short run of their show *Orwell That Ends Well*.

In December 1984, many alumni from Playwrights, Compass, and Second City—including Alan Arkin, Ed Asner, Shelley Berman, Severn Darden, Barbara Harris, Robert Klein, Harold Ramis, David Shepherd, Martin Short, Paul Sills, David Steinberg, Betty Thomas, Dave Thomas, George Wendt, and Fred Willard—returned to Chicago (on specially chartered jets no less) for Second City's twenty-fifth anniversary. A private show for friends and family took place on the mainstage with a mixture of performances by alumni and the current cast—Mindy Bell, Jim Fay, Mike Hagerty, John Kapelos, Richard Kind, and Mona Lyden. Severn Darden and Shelley Berman did a brilliant improv together. No one wanted the evening to end, but it finally did at around two in the morning. *Newsweek* said in 1984: "By now, virtually anyone who likes to laugh knows about Chicago's Second City." *Time* called Second City the "capital of comedy" in 1985.

The next night, to help celebrate the occasion (and pay for the jet planes and hotel accommodations), HBO shot a live TV special of old scenes with alumni and current company members

Spotlight on
Michael Gellman, Bruce Pirrie and Sandra Balcovske•••

Michael Gellman joined the Second City cast in 1974, after working for Dudley Riggs in Minnesota. He got particularly good at doing a dead-on impersonation of President Nixon. After leaving the company, Michael began teaching and directing at Second Cities in Chicago, Toronto, London, Ontario, and Detroit. He's still one of the key teachers at the Training Center.

Bruce Pirrie grew up in Toronto's suburbs, then attended suburban York University for a degree in film and English. *SCTV* and The Firehall's productions inspired him to take Second City classes in the early 1980s. He was invited to join the touring company, then made his mainstage debut as an actor/writer in *I've Got a Sequel*. He appeared in several Firehall shows and then directed *Four Horsemen of the Apocalypse and a Baby*, *A Nightmare on Sussex Drive*, and *Jolly Rogers Cable or Pirates in Men's Pants*. Bruce carries on the Second City TV legacy as a writer and director for *The Red Green Show*, which features plenty of Second City talent—including Pat McKenna as Cousin Harold. Bruce is also a widely recognized face from Canadian television commercials.

A native Albertan of Russian descent, **Sandra Balcovske** was an established presence in local theater before joining the short-lived Second City company in Edmonton. After relocating to Toronto, Sandra appeared as an actor and writer in *Waiting for John Doe*, then became one of Second City's top directors. Among the shows she directed are *Andy Warhol, Your Fifteen Minutes Are Up*; *When Bush Comes to Shove*; *Shopping Off to Buffalo*; *Tory*; *Party of Two*; and *Tragically OHIP*. Sandra was also artistic director of Second City Toronto for several years. She continues to work in film and theater in Toronto as a writer-director and maintains close ties with Second City and its alumni network.

working together, which ran on HBO and the CBC in Canada. In 1988, many alumni returned to Toronto for a similar celebration of Second City's fifteenth anniversary at The Old Firehall and, to help celebrate the occasion, a Showtime/CBC TV special was shot.

In 1985, shortly after the twenty-fifth anniversary, we lost the last of the originals; Bernie sold all of Second City to Andrew Alexander and Len Stuart. As Bernie put it, never again would he be the one who was told when the copier was broken. (Joyce said she was always the one who was told anyway, so what was he worrying about?) Legend has it that the deal was made on a napkin at the front bar of the Chicago Second City. The deal also included Bernie continuing as director. Andrew became executive producer and moved Joyce from associate producer to producer and partner.

Top to bottom: Richard Kind (left), Jim Fay (middle), and Dan Castellaneta (right) play codgy old men. • Barbara Wallace, Steve Assad (middle), and Mike Myers (right) perform in Kuwait Until Dark.

Andrew and Len immediately began to expand Second City's non-theatrical business. By then there had been a noticeable increase in the number of young people moving to Chicago and Toronto to try and get into the cast, so Andrew decided it was time to establish official Second City training centers first in Chicago, then in Toronto. Far more expansion lay ahead; a more diversified entity was emerging.

In 1987, we opened a company in the Chicago suburb of Rolling Meadows near O'Hare Airport, giving us three companies in the Chicago area all doing their own material. It was called Second City Northwest and, under the guidance of producer

Cheryl Sloane, became—like the place in London—an excellent training ground for performers and directors before moving to a mainstage. At that point a performer's usual route became Training Center to one of the touring companies to Rolling Meadows to e.t.c. to mainstage. Rolling Meadows closed in 1996 when its lease ran out, and the space became a cafeteria for Motorola. But in 2000, we returned to the northwest suburbs with summer seasons for the touring companies at the Metropolis Performing Arts Center in Arlington Heights.

Also in 1987, after twenty-three years, pianist/musical director Fred Kaz left the Chicago mainstage for good to direct a show at Second City

Northwest. He then moved to L.A. and worked in the show we opened in Santa Monica in 1989. In honor of Fred's retirement, Andrew and Len threw a huge party in L.A., attended by alumni of almost every generation, and provided Fred with a lifetime pension and a boat. Fred was replaced in Chicago by Ruby Streak.

Catherine O'Hara, John Candy, and Eugene Levy all did guest-director stints at Second City Toronto during the 1980s. (Dave Foley, Kevin McDonald, and Scott Thompson of *The Kids in the Hall* were in the Toronto touring company briefly.)

Andrew and Joyce asked Betty Thomas to test her wings as a director with *Kuwait Until Dark*, after Bernie decided he didn't want to direct any more Second City shows in 1988. "I realized that I had no one left to talk to," said Bernie. "The new generations were all weaned on television. That was their frame of reference. The original group had come out of the University of Chicago, then the Beat Generation, even the so-called 'Next Generation' were a group that came from a theatrical and literary base. They were children of the television age, sure, but they were intellectual about it."

We were still trying to expand into television. After a few one-shot TV shows—a 1988 CBC and ABC *SCTV* retrospective, and some failed pilots, some by Bernie, some by Andrew—Andrew and Len opened a Second City at the old Mayfair Theatre in trendy Santa Monica in 1989 on what was then the rather desolate promenade. (Bad timing—today the promenade is a busy center of shops, restaurants, and nightlife.) The casts were primarily made up of alumni, some based in L.A., some imported from Toronto and Chicago, including Andrea Martin, Robin Duke, Mike Hagerty, Bonnie Hunt, Richard Kind, Don Lake, and Ryan Stiles. Andy Dick spent some time there as a member of the touring company.

The Santa Monica theater had two goals: one was to have a Second City cabaret in Los Angeles where alumni would have a place to show the industry their talents in the best environment possible. "I had no illusions about opening in L.A.," says Andrew. "I had seen many of our incredibly talented people leave the stages in Chicago and Toronto only to fall through the cracks in L.A. I knew it was going to be difficult, but I was confident that we could develop a unique creative environment that would work for the performers." The second goal was to springboard ideas for TV shows. In association with Ron Howard's Imagine Films, they developed the parody talk show *My Talk Show* in 1990, starring Toronto alumnae Deb McGrath and Linda Kash, which was syndicated in over 90 percent of the country. It didn't build an audi-

Spotlight on
Aaron Freeman

Aaron Freeman, after years of touring companies (and being fired twice), left Second City to establish himself as one of Chicago's most prominent African-American political humorists. Aaron created *Council Wars*, a parody based on the problems Mayor Harold Washington was having with a group of Chicago aldermen at the City Council, as well as co-writing and starring in *Do the White Thing*. He wrote a book,

Confessions of a Lottery Ball; hosted his own National Public Radio show called *Metropolis*; and continues to host his own locally televised talk show, *Talking with Aaron Freeman*. Aaron also writes an online column for the *Chicago Tribune* (as well as doing many of its radio ads) and *The Jim Lehrer News Hour*. In 1999, he directed *The Return of the Hip Messiah* at Second City's Donny's Skybox, tucked up at the top of Pipers Alley, two floors above Second City e.t.c.

Spotlight on
Ryan Stiles & Colin Mochrie

Ryan Stiles and Colin Mochrie joined the Toronto Second City mainstage in 1986 and 1988, respectively. They were both in the original British version of *Whose Line Is It Anyway?* Ryan also was in the Second City in Santa Monica and began appearing in small roles on a number of TV shows and movies, such as *Hot Shots* and *Hot Shots, Part Deux*. He's now a regular on *The Drew Carey Show*, and both he and Colin are regulars on the U.S. version of *Whose Line Is It Anyway?*, which has also featured a number of other Second City alumni including Stephen Colbert, Ian Gomez, and musical director Laura Hall. Colin also hosts Comedy Network's Supertown Challenge, directed by Bruce Pirrie.

Ryan's a tall, rangy guy and a bit of a loner. He's an American who came to work for us in Vancouver when we were at Expo '86 (The World's Fair). He was in the cast there, then moved to Second City Toronto. A terrific

improviser, Ryan has "a look" that is helpful in a lot of cases. He was hilarious in a scene he did with Dana Andersen as Gorbachev, with that red wine stain on his forehead, and Ryan as an educator with a pointer using the stain as a map to geopolitical crises. On stage, he could exploit his size to hilarious effect. Over the years, two of the best improvisers were Ryan and Colin. They both wound up as huge stars in England doing *Whose Line Is It Anyway?* while they were still doing Second City in Toronto. They couldn't walk down the street in England without getting mobbed. When Drew Carey and Ryan were starting the U.S. television version, they said they had to have Colin with them. ABC fought it until they actually saw him work. Now he's a huge star here, too.

Backstage Pass

Apparently, one night Ryan Stiles made Deb McGrath (Colin Mochrie's wife) laugh so hard during a scene, she peed her pants on stage. The stage was carpeted, so it left an icky smell lingering for a while.

—Tamara Bick

Opposite page, clockwise from top left: Ryan Stiles • Colin Mochrie • Ryan Stiles and Dana Andersen take a rest. • Ryan Stiles writes Chris Barnes a ticket at The Second City in Los Angeles.

Above: Colin Mochrie plays a man of action. • Right: Colin Mochrie in Bye Bye Lingual or Just Say Non • Far right: Ryan Stiles as "Honest Abe" Lincoln

Backstage Passes

Bonnie could nail me in a second. Andrew and I were walking back from an advertising meeting and I was carrying one of our cane-back chairs that we were showing to the agency. Bonnie was leaving the theater as we were entering. "Oh look," she said, "Andrew's given Kelly a raise."

—Kelly Leonard

● ● ○

Mel Gibson was coaxed into doing the improv set and finally said, "Okay, I'll just do it real fast, a quick in and out," and he wound up doing an hour and just loving it. In 1974, Peter Cook and Dudley Moore were performing in Toronto and came over to Second City to do an improv set with Dan Aykroyd, John Candy, Gilda Radner, and Eugene Levy. Peter and Dudley were terrified, truly terrified. And Peter, I think, had to fortify himself with a couple of bottles of red wine so that when it came time to do the set, he was well past improvising. Dudley had been into the wine too, but he managed to get by on impishness and mugging. Dan was sensitive to what was going on and saw an opportunity to show a couple of Brits how you fly without a net. He was just brilliant that night. Somehow they all got through it. I don't think the audience ever guessed what was going on.

—Andrew Alexander

● ● ○

Keanu Reeves saw the show one night in Toronto, came backstage, and said in awe, "Wow, dudes, you guys change really fast!"

—Tamara Bick

ence, although critically acclaimed, and was not renewed for a second season. Second City L.A. eventually fell victim to the apathetic L.A. theater audience. Furthermore, the comedy boom that had spurred the opening of hundreds of clubs around the country was in full retreat. Too many clubs, too many comedy acts on cable, and a slowing economy soon caused the closing of many, if not most of the comedy clubs everywhere. Andrew reflected on the closing of Santa Monica:

I took a group to California including Bonnie Hunt, Don Lake, Jane Morris, John Hemphill, Chris Barnes, and Ryan Stiles. We had a deal with CBS to develop sitcoms. We had offices that we rented in a storefront right next to the theater. We had a big table for everybody to sit around, and everybody would come in about eleven in the morning, and there were muffins and coffee—the whole concept was to come up with ideas for sitcoms. When we had honed those different ideas, we would invite the network to come in and watch them on stage after we'd done the regular show. Well, the conflicts there were pretty severe with everybody. Looking back on it, I can see we were asking them to be satirists by night and prime-time sitcom writers by day. And there was an inherent conflict in that. We were asking them to put away their teeth and aim for the middle.

Andrew and Len, still confident in the philosophy that it is important to have a place for our alumni to play and showcase their talents, have reopened on Melrose Avenue in Hollywood. This venture, with an emphasis on the Training Center, is less dependent on L.A. audiences.

Celebrities

Former Second City performers often refuse to improvise with the cast when they come back to see a show, especially if they haven't done it in a while. Some alums, like Mina Kolb, Avery Schreiber, and Tim Kazurinsky can always be counted on to join the improv set when they're at the show.

On the other hand, some celebrities who come to see the show while in Chicago do agree to improvise with the cast during the set. Many of them have never worked without a script before and are usually terrified, but the cast invariably cushions them beautifully. Among those who've joined the cast on stage are Don Adams, Milton Berle, Michael J. Fox, Mel Gibson, Sara Gilbert, Arye Gross, Tom Hanks, Sean P. Hayes, Helen Hunt, Michael Palin, Jonathan Pryce, Brooke Shields, Kristy Swanson, Sinbad, Steven Weber, and Robin Williams.

Spotlight on
Bonnie Hunt

Bonnie Hunt joined the Chicago Second City cast in 1986. While still in the company, Bonnie got a small part as a waitress in *Rain Man*, in a scene with Dustin Hoffman and Tom Cruise. When she left Second City, she went to Hollywood and made a big hit on the talk shows, especially David Letterman's. She's been in such movies as *Dave*, the two *Beethoven* movies, *Jumanji* with Robin Williams, *Jerry Maguire*, and *The Green Mile* with Tom Hanks. Bonnie was a regular on the sitcom *Grand*, and starred in two unsuccessful CBS sitcoms produced by Letterman's company, *The Building* and *The Bonnie Hunt Show*. Both shows had former Toronto Second Citizen Don Lake as co-writer and fellow actor; Bonnie's friend and former Second City Chicago company member Holly Wortell was also in the casts. In 2000, Bonnie and Don co-wrote the screenplay for *Return to Me*, which was also the first feature film Bonnie directed. It starred David Duchovny and Minnie Driver, with Carroll O'Connor, Jim Belushi, and Bonnie. Second City alums Tim O'Malley and Holly Wortell were also in it. Bonnie's an incredibly quick-witted improviser with a wide range of characters, most of them strong and fast on the comeback. With *The Building*, she became the first woman to write and star in her own series.

Bonnie, describing the difference between sketches and scenes to the *Chicago Tribune* in 1999, said, "I think sketches might be a better description of what *Saturday Night Live* was doing then. But we really tried to do what we called scenes…. [A scene] tells a story, a beginning, middle, and end, and is driven by character…" She later went on to say, "The great thing about Second City is you're trained there by the audience. You kind of develop that sixth sense after years of performing about how to ride that roller coaster when you're telling a story through characters" (AP, 2000).

Top to bottom: Bonnie Hunt in a scene with (from left to right) Kevin Crowley, Rick Hall, and Barbara Wallace • Bonnie Hunt • Hunt receives a warm embrace from Dustin Hoffman and Tom Cruise on the set of Rain Man.

Spotlight on
Mike Myers...

Top to bottom: Mike Myers •
Myers at The Second City Toronto

Opposite page, top to bottom:
Myers plays Anne of Green
Gables. • Myers dons dreadlocks for
a scene with Bonnie Hunt (left) and
Barbara Wallace (right).

Mike Myers was born and raised in Toronto. Even before getting into Second City, he was already known by the performers there as someone willing to be as outrageous as necessary in order to get a laugh. When he auditioned for Second City on his last day of high school, he'd already done some commercials and some acting around town. He'd wanted to join since he was four years old and was hired immediately for the touring company. He toured for a year and a half, then moved to the Toronto mainstage from 1986 to 1988, and joined the Chicago mainstage company in 1988. Mike wasn't pushing to go to Chicago, but Andrew asked him to go. He went into a cast with Bonnie Hunt and Richard Kind, and it was a little tough for him. He was a Canadian entering a structure, and you could see people in the touring company saying, "Why are you bringing this guy in?"

At Second City, he did Wayne, Dieter (the German filmmaker he first did on stage with Dana Andersen as Brock), and a lot of other characters who later showed up on *Saturday Night Live*. The story goes that Chicago producer Joyce Sloane gave Mike the night off in Chicago from performing in the Betty Thomas-directed revue *Kuwait Until Dark* so that he could attend The Second City Toronto's Fifteenth Anniversary show. Mike worked with Martin Short during the show, who then called *Saturday Night Live* producer Lorne Michaels and told him, "You've gotta hire this guy." In 1989, Mike joined the long list of Second City performers who've made the transition to *SNL*. He made the first of the two box-office smash *Wayne's World* movies while still on the show. Mike's also starred in such films as *So I Married an Axe Murderer*; *Mystery, Alaska*; the two *Austin Powers* movies; and portrayed Steve Rubell in the film *54*. His popularity just continues to grow.

Underneath that nice, polite guy was an individual who really knew what he wanted to do and was hard-working and creative. You could compare Mike a bit to Eugene Levy in that he's guarded, he's cautious, and a scientist about his work, a student of comedy. At the same time, he also brought a fresh, youthful energy and characters that were new. And he was savvy about what he wanted to do with his characters. "I wanted him to do Wayne for *110 Lombard*, the special we did with CBS," recalls Andrew Alexander. "I remember having a discussion with him on the set one day and saying, 'You know, it would probably work better if you did this bit as Wayne.' And he very politely declined. The same year he went to *Saturday Night Live* and Wayne became a huge hit."

Mike, reminiscing about Second City, said: "I miss the luxury of being able to perform eight shows a week, six nights a week. So that within a given performance that you run for six months, it's almost like a laboratory. OK, tonight I'll pause a millisecond here, or I'll throw in this new joke here. And, of course, the improv aspect is something that I'm going to miss."

Backstage Passes

Mike and I were in the Toronto touring company and were performing a scene called "Job Interview." I was a nervous applicant and Mike was the boss interviewing me. At one point, Mike was to reach up and flick my nose. This is where the scene fell apart: instead of flicking my nose, he accidentally stuck his finger *up* my nose. There we were, in front of a packed house at The Firehall, filling in for the mainstage company, with Mike's finger up my nose. True professionals that we were, we giggled through the entire rest of the scene, our lines barely audible. The audience, realizing what had happened, roared with laughter. It was the first time I cracked up on stage, but not the last.

—Kevin Frank

When I got to mainstage in Toronto, it was pretty easy to get inhibited as a performer. I always talk about the feeling of "ghosts" around you in The Firehall. I think this is why people like Mike Myers got so far ahead—because he didn't give a shit if he sounded like Martin Short. He just went out there completely uncensored and did his own stuff, regardless of whether it was familiar or not.

—Linda Kash

Top to bottom: Tim Meadows (left) and Chris Farley (right) are joined onstage in Chicago by Milton Berle. • John Kapelos plays the guitar as Meagan Fay accompanies on the violin in a scene from Orwell That Ends Well.

Opposite page: Gilda Radner, who died in 1989 at the age of forty-two, shares her loving charm with Eugene Levy during a scene.

This, according to Ron West, is what it was like working with one guest improviser:

In addition to being a festering pit of disease, backstage Chicago is a locker room where obscenity, bad taste, and sexism are the ruling junta. Pre-Academy Award Helen Hunt was in town shooting a TV movie. Mitch Rouse brought her backstage and said, in effect, this blonde woman who's on TV wants to do the improv set. We only sort of knew her. We were planning the set in the green room. John Rubano said something to Helen that involved four words I can't write here, the gentlest of which is "lick." I cringed. Helen, recognizing the test before her, said four other words I can't write here, the gentlest of which was "shit." We laughed, and the junta of obscenity, bad taste, and sexism gave her full membership in the club you can't get into. We all loved Helen after that. And she improvised pretty well all that week. It didn't matter though. She had passed the more crucial back-stage test. I held Helen's hand during one scene, one of the best moments I ever improvised. Her palms sweat when she gets nervous, incidentally.

Old Wine, New Bottles

By the end of the 1980s, with *SCTV* in syndication and Second City's alumni selling more and more movie tickets and boosting more and more TV show ratings, we were better known than ever. Although our theaters were still mostly selling out—months ahead on weekends—and the touring companies were still spreading the message around North America, a small percentage of the media and our regular audiences began to accuse us of being old hat, predictable, formulaic. Whether it was a matter of taking shots because we were king of the hill or a case of hubris, it wasn't unusual for the tag line "Second City, Second Rate" to appear over reviews of our shows. One Chicago critic referred to our material as "etch-a-sketch"; one in Toronto said we were "a place to go for roast beef with your mom." E.t.c. was being proclaimed as the newer, hipper place, but even it was starting to get accusations of being tired.

Much of the criticism was unfair—and irrelevant to most of our audiences—but not to some critics and quite a few people who thought they should be the ones performing and directing the shows. Critics who'd been praising us since 1959 were wearying of the lights-up, lights-down sketch comedy we'd made famous, and they were no longer as impressed by the performers' ability to improvise. (Bernie Sahlins has a saying: "Once you've seen all the Second City shows, you've seen one of them.")

Perhaps worst of all, we were beginning to be compared to ourselves; "It's not as good as it used to be" became a recurring refrain. Tony Adler, then a critic for Chicago's alternative newspaper *The Reader*, saw our dilemma in 1990 this way: "The typical *Reader* review of any current Second City show starts out talking about the great old shows of legend—the ones nobody actually could have seen, where Mike Nichols and Gilda Radner did patient/therapist routines while Severn Darden and John Belushi ran drills for the U of C football team. The review then explains why the current show is a complete, pathetic betrayal of everything those old shows stood for."

Losing Gilda

Gilda Radner died in 1989 at the age of forty-two. Three years earlier, she had been diagnosed with ovarian cancer.

"I had just returned from seeing Gilda in California," recalls Joyce Sloane, "and I was telling a friend how great she looked and how we all thought that she would pull through this thing, that the doctors had gotten all of the cancer. My friend said to me, 'That's what they told Steve McQueen.' My blood ran cold. I think I realized, for the first time, that we would lose her."

Although she struggled bravely, in the end, like so many others have, she succumbed to the disease. She was survived by her husband, Gene Wilder, and left behind a wonderful autobiography, *It's Always Something*. Dan Aykroyd, who had lost his best friend, John Belushi, just seven years earlier, and who had shared the struggles at Second City Toronto and the fame and fortune of *Saturday Night Live* with her, said of Gilda, "I loved her like a sister."

Gilda had a child-like quality that came through many of her characters and endeared her to everyone who saw her. Her passing was a hard blow to the entire Second City family at the end of a decade filled with successes, failures, opportunities, changes, and tragedies.

Gilda fought [cancer] the way she fought everything else. She never complained. She bore what she bore in silence and was very strong. Her husband Gene Wilder was incredibly supportive and wonderful.

—Lorne Michaels

Gilda was possessed of the spirit of the theater. When she left to join *Saturday Night Live*, it was an exciting time. Gilda, in her short time at Second City, had a tremendous impact on all of us. She was so good, so human. Her death was devastating for the entire Second City family.

—Andrew Alexander

Spotlight on
Death Onstage
and Off . . .

Since Second City has always been like a large, extended family, when one of our family dies, it leaves a hole in a lot of hearts.

Second City was dealt consecutive blows when performer Jim Fay and Natalie Taylor, wife of Chicago mainstage stage manager Craig Taylor, died within weeks of each other in 1987. Still in his early thirties, Jim was in the mainstage company but had taken some time off. He died alone at home of a heart attack, his wife and son gone for the day. Natalie, a staff member of Second City and even younger than Jim, was bathing her and Craig's young daughter Samantha when she lay down on the floor and didn't get up, felled by a brain aneurysm. The short time between these events was simply devastating to the theater. We had to bring in counselors to deal with the grief of the staff and performers. "We lost Jim Fay and Natalie Taylor in the same few weeks," recalls cast member Rick Hall. "It made us all realize how close we had become."

Some of the Compass and Second City alumni who are gone from us:

Howard Alk

Bill Alton

Jon Anderson Jr.

J.J. Barry

John Belushi

Roger Bowen

John Brent

Mona Burr Cunningham

John Candy

Del Close

Robert Coughlan

Bob Curry

Severn Darden

Don DePollo

Brenda Donohue

Tom Erhart

Above: (standing, left to right) Murphy Dunne, Martin Harvey Friedberg, Ira Miller, J.J. Barry, and Burt Heyman; (on floor) Carol Robinson and Peter Boyle

Opposite page: (left to right) Michael Gellman, Deborah Harmon, Mert Rich, Betty Thomas, and Don DePollo in the scene "Funeral."

Jim Fay
Chris Farley
Sid Grossfeld
Anthony Holland
Gilda Radner
Fritzie Sahlins
Diana Sands
Tim Sims
Viola Spolin

At Second City, we've always understood that if you can't laugh at death, what can you laugh at? On stage, we've had scenes set in heaven and hell, we've had a surprise party for an old man who dies of a heart attack when he enters and everyone jumps out and yells "Surprise!" We've had Avery Schreiber as a union man ascend to heaven on a very creaky pulley, and we've had Death himself in several scenes, usually losing out in his attempt to take someone to the great beyond.

Another funeral scene, besides the Van Camp's Beans one, featured Judy Graubart, Alex Canaan, and Sandra Caron as mourners, David Steinberg as the pontificating rabbi, Robert Klein as the funeral director who sang "If Ever I Would Leave You" from *Camelot*, and Fred Willard as an intruder who just liked going to funerals and taking photos of the deceased and the mourners, which he proceeded to do.

The fortieth anniversary show had a blackout set at a funeral. As the minister begins the service, a cell phone is heard. Finally, Stephnie Weir, as one of the mourners, realizes where the sound is coming from, opens the coffin lid, takes a cell phone out of the corpse's pocket, answers it, listens for a moment, and says, "He's dead." *Blackout*.

Backstage Pass

The birth of the famous funeral sketch (later ripped off by Mary Tyler Moore's writers as a funeral scene in which a clown in a peanut costume was crushed by an elephant attempting to shell him, and was voted the best comedy scene of the century or something like that) was when the cast returned from attending the funeral for a friend of Joyce Sloane's. Del said he'd always wanted to do a scene where someone died from getting his head stuck in a gallon can of Van Camp's Beans. Joe Flaherty suggested what it would be like if you couldn't stop laughing. We all chose parts. That night we improvised the scene that is verbatim the classic it remains today!

—Jim Fisher

157

8

Chapter

The 1990s and Beyond

Changing the Form

After the war in Iraq and the recession of the early 1990s, Bill Clinton defeated President George Bush in the 1992 election on the unofficial platform, "It's the economy, stupid," thus ushering in an eight-year comedic boon the likes of which the U.S. has never seen. The economy also improved. Clinton managed to slither his way out of one scandal after another—mostly sexual—until, as the result of a totally unrelated independent prosecutor's investigation, he was forced to admit that he did something "wrong" involving White House intern Monica Lewinsky, a cigar, and semen stains on a dress. He was impeached but managed to keep his position. And for a while, Jay Leno's and David Letterman's monologues virtually wrote themselves.

Disc 2
Tracks 7–15

The Soviet Union collapsed; Germany unified. The former Yugoslavia was torn apart by war. White minority rule in South Africa ended. And progress was made on peace in Northern Ireland and the Middle East…Well, sort of.

The Branch-Davidian cult's encounter with the FBI left more than eighty members dead. The Unabomber, Montana hermit Ted Kaczynski, was arrested and convicted. Home video revealed L.A. cops savagely beating Rodney King after a traffic stop. After the cops were acquitted, major riots erupted throughout L.A. A few years later, O.J. Simpson was acquitted of the murders of his ex-wife, Nicole Simpson, and her friend, Ron Goldman, by an L.A. jury, but was found guilty in the civil suit.

Douglas Coupland's Generation X, Neil Sheehan's A Bright, Shining Lie, Frank McCourt's Angela's Ashes, Charles Frazier's Cold Mountain, and J.K. Rowling's Harry Potter series were among the decade's more popular and influential books. Important plays included Angels in America and the musical Rent.

Among the groundbreaking films of the 1990s were Pulp Fiction, Fargo, The Blair Witch Project, American Beauty, and Being John Malkovich. And on TV, everybody was watching Seinfeld and Friends. The dramas ER and The X-Files gained followers, and HBO garnered critical acclaim for The Larry Sanders Show, Oz, and The Sopranos. Ellen Degeneres came out on an episode of her sitcom, Ellen.

Seattle grunge broke out with Nirvana, Soundgarden, and Pearl Jam, and the Chicago alternative music scene grabbed national attention with Liz Phair, Urge Overkill, and Smashing Pumpkins. Gangsta rap and country became big, as did boy-groups like 'N Sync and Backstreet Boys. Kurt Cobain killed himself with a shotgun.

A sheep named Dolly was cloned. People around the world erroneously celebrated the coming of the new millennium—which doesn't come until the year 2001—in 2000. The Y2K computer bug didn't.

Second City alumni wrote, starred in, and directed some of the most visible film and TV comedies of the 1990s. *Groundhog Day*, directed by Harold Ramis and cowritten by Harold and Brian Doyle-Murray, was a huge hit for star Bill Murray; it also had

Opening page (from left to right): Chris Farley as "Motivational Speaker" Matt Foley, with Jill Talley, Bob Odenkirk, Holly Wortell, and Tim Meadows

This page (from left to right): Chris Farley, Tim Meadows (top), Holly Wortell (bottom), Judy Scott, Dave Pasquesi, Joe Liss, and Joel Murray

appearances by alums Brian, Ken Campbell, Robin Duke, Dave Pasquesi, and Rob Riley. *Wayne's World* and *Austin Powers: International Man of Mystery*, written and starring Mike Myers, opened and enjoyed overwhelming success—both movies spawning sequels. Second City alum Bob Odenkirk and comedian David Cross created and starred in HBO's *Mr. Show*. Chris Farley became a star on *Saturday Night Live* and in movies. Other Second Citizens who made it on *SNL* included Tim Meadows, Dave Koechner, Nancy Walls, Horatio Sanz, and Rachel Dratch. Adam McKay was named head writer in 1996, Tina Fey in 1999. The U.S. Comedy Arts Festival in Aspen, Colorado, honored the cast of *SCTV* in 1999, and A&E broadcast *The 149th½ Edition of the Second City*, an hour retrospective. Yet, when the decade started out, Second City was still struggling to find a fresh approach.

New Directions

In 1989, when Del Close returned to Second City Chicago to direct *The Gods Must Be Lazy*, he hired an extraordinary group of people to be in the show: Chris Farley, Tim Meadows, Joel Murray, Dave Pasquesi, Judy Scott, and Holly Wortell, with Joe Liss remaining from the preceding cast. Not only were they an excellent performing company and a talented group of improvisers, but Judy was the first African-American woman in a mainstage show. With Tim, it was the first time that more than one African-American of either sex was in a show.

The Gods Must Be Lazy wasn't universally admired; like Del himself, it was pretty dark, often misogynistic, and occasionally confusing to many in our audiences. It seemed unfinished, and actually it was; Del pronounced the show ready to open two weeks prior to opening night, all but blowing off the final two weeks of previews and rehearsals. And Bernie Sahlins wasn't around anymore to finish it for him.

But the show was a harbinger of things to come. It had an edge that many who'd been criticizing us felt had been missing for too long. For them, the "formula" at least wasn't as apparent as it had been recently. Furthermore, part of what was occasionally confusing to our more traditional and formerly content audiences was that not everything was as neatly plotted out as they were expecting; the scenes weren't always the traditional beginning-middle-end ones they were used to. Along with his personal worldview, Del had also brought a little of the more fragmented structure of his improvisational "Harold" to the show, the long form (about an hour) he'd invented at The Committee in San Francisco and taught at the ImprovOlympic in Chicago. The

Tim Meadows

Tim Meadows is originally from Michigan. He joined Second City's mainstage in *The Gods Must Be Lazy* in 1989 and soon built a reputation for being soft-spoken, gentlemanly, and a true ensemble player, always eager to make his partner look good. He followed his good friend Chris Farley to *Saturday Night Live* in 1991, where he's had one of the longest runs in the show's history. He's created many memorable characters on *SNL*, including Leon Phelps (the Ladies' Man), and Lionel Osbourne, host of the pub-

lic affairs show "Perspectives." In 1993, Tim got an Emmy nomination for his writing on *SNL*. He's been in such movies as *Wayne's World 2*, *The Coneheads*, and *It's Pat*, and has a new film based on his Ladies' Man character.

Spotlight on

Chris Farley

Chris Farley was a sloppy clown. He was hired for the Second City stage in 1989 by Del Close, with whom he'd studied. On Fox News Chicago in February of 1996, Chris said of himself, "When I was at Second City I was always jumping out of a window, jumping from offstage to onstage or from onstage into the audience." At Second City, he was renowned for throwing himself off the walls, whether it was as a most unpleasant male stripper or the "freak of nature" whale boy who squirted water from his head (a football helmet covered in pink foam with a straw attached to a hand pump). Bob Odenkirk developed the scene "Motivational Speaker" **CD** after Chris' character Matt Foley (who lived "in a van down by the river") showed up in an improv set. (The scene was later done pretty much intact on *Saturday Night Live*.)

The wild party boy image didn't always match the real Chris; he was very polite and—when he wasn't "on"—could be extremely shy. He was a devout Catholic, attending mass daily at St. Michaels Church a few blocks behind Second City in Old Town. Chris

*Above: Chris Farley as "Motivational Speaker" Matt Foley
• Left to right: Tim Meadows, Farley, Dave Pasquesi, Holly Wortell, Joel Murray, and Joe Liss*

Opposite page: Farley and Tim Meadows play a pick-up game of basketball. • Left to right: Jill Talley, Chris Farley, and Tim Meadows

went from Second City to *Saturday Night Live* in 1990, and from there on to stardom in movies like *Tommy Boy*, *Black Sheep*, and *Beverly Hills Ninja*, as well as being in such films as *Wayne's World*, *Airheads*, *The Coneheads*, *Billy Madison*, *Dirty Work*, and *Almost Heroes*. Chris never forgot his roots; he returned often to Second City to perform with the casts during the improv sets. He even attended Second City's annual Christmas party just days before his untimely death in 1997. Some would say he died of living too much like his idol John Belushi. His family established the Chris Farley Foundation to help kids stay away from drugs.

Backstage Passes

Chris liked to compare himself to John Belushi. John was Chris' idol. I tried to explain to him that the character John played in *Animal House* was just a character. John wasn't like that offstage. I even introduced Chris to John's wife Judy and asked, "Would a lovely woman like this marry him if he were the character from *Animal House*?" But Chris idolized him. He adored him, as a whole generation did.

—Joyce Sloane

● ●

I was in the audience the first time Chris did his Matt Foley character. His friend, Matt Foley, a soft-spoken Catholic priest, was also in the audience, and Chris thought it would be fun to use his name for such an outrageous character. Chris destroyed the place that night. He was, of course, capable of brilliantly subtle performances too, but when he went for pure, raw laughs, I've never seen anyone better.

—Brian Stack

Backstage Passes

"Tourist trap" is not a term we want associated with what we do, so we shook things up for a while, although I think the core values are the same. Continuity is important, but so is keeping it alive. This is live theater; there's always going to be a certain fragility to it. We made changes that some Second City people didn't like. We brought in new staff and new directors.

—Andrew Alexander

• ● •

Tom Gianas honed a directing style that included a strong political agenda and revues in which the individual scenes were less important than the vision of the entire show. These strengths were not always as clear to the actors in the middle of the process as they were in the final analysis.

—Anne Libera

• ● •

When I came in to direct my first Toronto show, I talked to a lot of people who had directed; I wanted to do some homework first. I was told the biggest mistake you could make was to go in with a theme as structure because the cast will resent you. They'll think you're imposing your will, and they'll reject it. But it takes a lot of guts to go in blank. The best advice I got was from Sandy Balcovske: "Don't be afraid to spend an entire day just talking." And for the first couple of days of rehearsal we did that—talked about what was going on in the world, what we were interested in, what our passions were…

—Bob Martin

"Harold" is a recurring, intersecting series of scenes, monologues, and blackouts improvised on the spot by the cast from a series of audience suggestions, including a topic.

The Gods Must Be Lazy was Del's last Second City show, and we were unsure where to go next creatively. While business was still booming in Chicago and Toronto, we were still facing the critics' laments that Second City had become "old hat," "predictable," and "formulaic." Even the phrase "tourist trap" had been slapped on us.

The Second City National Touring Company (from left to right): Jeff Rogers, Rachel Dratch, Joe Dempsey (standing), Renee Albert, and Charlie Hartsock

Producer Joyce Sloane had a difficult task ahead of her after Del left; she needed to find new artistic leaders that would help Second City regain a bit of the fire that our critics felt was still lacking in the current revues. Both Joyce and Andrew were fans of alum Nate Herman, who'd expressed an interest in directing, so they took a chance and let him direct the next show, *It Was Thirty Years Ago Today*, in 1989. After that he became the director of the e.t.c. shows for a while. Nate is what you would call eccentric. He has a maniacal laugh, laser wit, and is given to crushing his eyeglasses in his hands when he's unhappy about something. Among the many legendary Nate Herman stories (which are almost as numerous as those about Severn Darden and Del) is the time when frustration led him to throw a giant flower pot out of the second floor box-office window, narrowly missing Tim Meadows as he walked down the street on his way to rehearsal. Another story about Nate is the one in which, while working as a bus driver in California, he was so frustrated with the whining of his passengers that he pulled the bus up to a stop light, opened the door, and walked out, leaving the passengers in the driverless bus in the middle of the street. Nate is smart and funny and has vision. The e.t.c. revues *America Lite* and *Ameri-Go-Round* that he directed were both concept shows with strong political themes and several scenes that were connected, either literally or thematically. Both shows worked. Nate and his casts were laying important experimental groundwork for what was soon to happen to the Second City form.

Amazing as it may seem, there've been very few directors in the forty-year history of Second City. Paul Sills, Alan Myerson, Bernie, Del, and I did the bulk of the directing chores in Chicago until the late 1980s. Toronto in the 1970s was mostly directed by Bernie, Joe Flaherty, Del, or me; in the 1980s mostly by Sandra Balcovske, Bruce Pirrie, and John Hemphill with a few guest shots by alumni. It wasn't until Bernie quit directing Second City in early 1988 that we started having to conduct searches and trial runs for new directors. Besides Nate, among the new blood who've directed on our mainstages in America and Canada since then are former Second City performers Pete Burns, John Hildreth, Chris Earle, Linda Kash, Bob Martin, Betty Thomas, and Ron West, current Second City performer Kevin Dorff, and non-vets Tom Gianas, Mick Napier, Jeff Richmond, Norm Holly, Anne Libera, Noah Gregeropolous, and Pete Zahradnick. And for old blood's sake, I did one new show and the thirty-fifth anniversary retrospective.

Putting the scenes into a running order has always been the hardest task for the director. When Paul Sills made a running order for the first act of our early shows, one of his main concerns was to make certain that the audience got familiar with all the performers and their individual personalities. Then the second act would have some scenes that allowed the performers to be seen in completely different ways from what the audience had come to expect. At the same time, Paul, like every director after him, was also concerned with keeping the momentum going in each act. That part was a bit easier in the early days, since the shows then had a different and more leisurely pace and flow, with longer and fewer scenes and less concern with constant laughs.

Paul Sills' concept of a running order, based as much as possible on the credentials of the actors, changed over the years. Bernie, for instance, when he took over as director, had come to believe that you should put a lot of your best and smartest and, if possible, most politically relevant stuff up front to establish the credentials of the show more than of the actors. Now we do a little of both.

Even with usually no more than twelve or fourteen pieces in the early shows to put into an order, it was still hard to find the

Spotlight on
Tom Gianas

Tom Gianas performed for four or five years in a comedy troupe around Chicago. "Audiences and I came to an agreement that I should focus on directing," said Tom. "Joyce agreed with that and hired me. That's how I became a director." Starting in 1990, Tom directed Second City shows in both Chicago theaters, at Second City Northwest, and in Detroit. (One of Tom's unbreakable new rules as a post-*SCTV* Second City director: no TV parodies—too easy and *SCTV* did it better than we ever could.)

His fifth and, unfortunately, last Chicago mainstage show was the brilliant and form-breaking *Piñata Full of Bees*. Since then, Tom's been a writer for *Saturday Night Live*, Michael Moore's *The Awful Truth*, and various other TV projects.

Spotlight on Mick Napier

Mick Napier grew up in Kentucky and went to Indiana University, intending to study veterinary medicine. He took an interest in improv, however, from reading Jeff Sweet's book about Second City, *Something Wonderful Right Away*, and formed his own improv group at school. Mick came to Chicago after graduation, where he flunked out halfway through the Second City Training Center program. He did, eventually, go on to complete the program and teach in it as well. At the same time, he was working out at ImprovOlympic, until he began feeling too restricted by all the rules of how to perform a "Harold." He and a couple of other rebels opened their own place, eventually known as The Annoyance Theatre, a place for a wilder, more free-flowing, no-holds-barred kind of improv. Mick's approach eventually also led the Annoyance to producing scripted shows through improv, including two long-running hits, *The Real Live Brady Bunch* and *Co-Ed Prison Sluts*, as well as such shows as *That Darned Anti-Christ* and *Manson: The Musical*.

Mick directed Second City shows at Second City Northwest in the early 1990s, then left to direct *Exit 57* on Comedy Central, and David Sedaris' play *One Woman Shoe* off-Broadway, both with Second City alum (and David's sister) Amy Sedaris. He came back to Second City to direct *Citizen Gates* on the mainstage in 1996, started directing at e.t.c. as well in 1997, and won Jeff Awards for best director and best revue for his mainstage show *Paradigm Lost*, also in 1997. Mick has continued directing some of the shows in both spaces, including the much-praised fortieth anniversary show, *Second City 4.0*.

"The first time I saw a show at Second City," said Mick, "Mike Hagerty was asking for suggestions for an improv set. He was asking for occupations, so I said, 'Cracker salter,' and he laughed. I remember thinking, 'My God, I just made that guy laugh,' and that was very romantic for me. And ten years later I'm directing it, which is romantic and frightening—and wonderful."

order that would build and sustain momentum from scene to scene in each act without ruining some scenes by putting them too near scenes they shouldn't be near—whether for content, pace, style, frequency of actor appearance, or whatever other reason you can figure out. These days, there are a lot more pieces to deal with, partly because the average piece is shorter. There are also more pieces because of the breaking up of longer pieces and spreading them through the show in the form that Del began to explore in *The Gods Must Be Lazy*, and that Tom Gianas found the key to in 1995 with *Piñata Full of Bees* as an excellent way of doing a Second City show.

I walked backstage one night recently, and Mick Napier was juggling about forty little cards with scene names on them that all had to go into one show—a mind-numbing task.

New Waves

One of the by-products of our thriving training program and the relatively few slots available to performers at Second City is that many performers trained by us start their own comedy troupes. Joyce found Tom Gianas working with one of those upstart ensembles and hired him to direct *Flag Smoking Permitted in Lobby Only* in 1990. By then, Joe Liss and Joel Murray had left for L.A. and Judy Scott for Toronto. Tom added Jill Talley and his friend Bob Odenkirk to the cast of Chris Farley, Tim Meadows, Tim O'Malley, Dave Pasquesi, and Holly Wortell.

In the early 1990s, Second City Chicago—with three Equity stages, three national touring companies, training and corporate interests, and frequent TV projects—had only six full-time employees and two typewriters. The box office still took reservations on an answering machine, and when that wasn't on, a frazzled box-office employee answered all the calls.

Mick Napier has enlarged and expanded upon the new form that was developed in *Piñata Full of Bees*—tying the sketches of a show together thematically and building a more theatrical vision for Second City, utilizing sets, music, choreography, and intricate lighting concepts to create a cohesive visual whole. I'll never forget the preview of *Paradigm Lost*. Mick asked me not to attend because he was trying something "insane." I stayed anyway and was treated to one of the greatest nights of theater in my life. What Mick had done was to take every scene in the show, cut them all in half, mix them throughout the show, and add a throughline that would somehow try to make sense of what was going on—and he accomplished this in one afternoon's rehearsal. Since that night, Mick's genius doesn't surprise me anymore.

—Kelly Leonard

I had the chance to see Mick Napier do a rehearsed pitch to the Fox network for a new show he's been working on. "Tell us about yourself," they said. He replied, "I hate sketch comedy, I don't know where my life is actually going. I chain-smoke, drink hard, and am sexually perverse." He positioned himself pretty clearly. He's brought some of that edginess to the cast.

—Andrew Alexander

Top row: Rich Talarico, Jerry Minor, Rachel Hamilton, Aaron Carney, Rebecca Sohn, Jeff Richmond, and Mick Napier; bottom row: Horatio Sanz, Laura Krafft, and Matt Dwyer

Spotlight on
Bob Odenkirk

Bob Odenkirk grew up in Naperville, Illinois, about a half hour west of Chicago. He did one show at Second City in Chicago in 1990. Before that, he'd been doing stand-up and some writing for *Saturday Night Live*. Bob was brought into the mainstage cast by his friend, director Tom Gianas, without having even been in a touring company first. This caused a

lot of friction, and it unfortunately took a while before Bob was able to feel welcome. He helped create some excellent material during his brief stay with us, including the first of Chris Farley's "Motivational Speaker" scenes. Bob's now best known as one of the stars and co-creators (with David Cross) of *Mr. Show*, which premiered on HBO in 1996. Bob was a regular on *The Larry Sanders Show*, as Larry's weasely agent Stevie Grant, and was also a cast member of *The Ben Stiller Show*. Bob's latest project is *Run, Ronny, Run*, for which he produces, writes, and stars.

Andrew was beginning to see the need for changes not only artistically, but in the way Second City was operating as a business. With the Santa Monica Second City closed, he uprooted his family again—he'd only recently moved them from Toronto—and moved to Chicago, putting himself and Joyce in day-to-day contact for the first time. On the surface, Andrew and Joyce couldn't be less similar: he's an English-born Canadian, with a cool and reserved exterior and a small circle of friends; she's a Chicago-born Jewish mother who counted literally thousands of actors as her extended family, often giving them a couch to sleep on and a job when they needed money. (At one point, I gave Andrew a book on middle-European Jewish ghetto psychology to help him understand Joyce's roots and where she was "coming from.")

There are similarities between Joyce and Andrew, however. They're both stubborn, driven, and talented leaders. They both devoted their adult lives to Second City, often putting it in front of personal and professional gain. And each of them had a vision for what Second City was and should be. With some inevitable kinks as Andrew established his own brand of leadership at Second City, the combination of Joyce's mother-hen approach and Andrew's entrepreneurial spirit created a more dynamic Second City, which still retained much of the "Ma & Pa" quality that had served the theater so well until then.

In fall 1992, Andrew brought in Kelly Leonard as associate producer, to learn the ropes and help guide the Chicago Second City, with Joyce continuing as producer emeritus, offering her vast knowledge and insight as the company began to grow and change.

For the next three years, Second City would undergo a strange, exciting, and occasionally uncomfortable transition as Andrew, Kelly, and Joyce worked to move the theater in a new direction.

After doing more or less traditional shows at several of the Second City theaters, in 1995, Tom Gianas directed the form-breaking *Piñata Full of Bees*, our eightieth revue, and Kelly's first show as producer. *Piñata* didn't come out of thin air, of course. There'd been Del's show, Nate Herman's shows at e.t.c., Tom's earlier shows, all in various ways pushing out the boundaries of the form. And the innovations going on in the improv community outside Second City were also part of it. The Del-Bernie feud over improvisation as an art form or a writing technique was lost on the new performers being trained by both Second City and ImprovOlympic. They loved improvisation, they loved good writing, and they saw no reason why the two couldn't exist side by side. Or even together. But to achieve this new mix, the form would have to change. Needless to say, we never intended to turn into a full-fledged improv theater. But the long-form improvisations did serve as an inspiration to Tom and his cast.

Even though the shows were selling better than ever, Andrew saw the need for change and gave permission to cast and director to experiment with the tried and true form of a Second City revue. Like Del had done with his ensemble for *The Gods Must Be Lazy*,

Tom ignored the Touring Company-to-Northwest-to-e.t.c.-to-mainstage pecking order and built an ensemble that he felt could provide the vision for a new kind of show. The cast included veteran performers Scott Adsit, Scott Allman, and Jenna Jolovitz (who'd all

Left to right, top: Adam McKay, Scott Adsit, and Rachel Dratch (with cello); bottom: Jenna Jolovitz, Scott Allman, and Jon Glaser

gone more or less the traditional route), along with new-school improvisers Jon Glaser, Adam McKay, and Rachel Dratch. This mix of theatrically trained writer/actors and almost solely long-form, improv-based performers was the perfect combination.

As they began to create and stage new material, Tom had the set from the last revue completely dismantled, leaving only a bare stage that reached to the back brick wall. Props and costumes were hung in full view of the audience, cast members sat onstage and watched while their fellow performers played out their scenes, and music director Ruby Streak began bringing in sampled music to augment the scenes and blare during transitions. She also worked with the actors to score scenes themselves, putting a bass guitar, drums, and even a cello onstage.

Piñata was, to a large extent, a two-act variation on Del's "Harold," using the form, but rehearsed and set rather than improvised on the spot. The results were a show that not only looked different than any Second City revue in history, but also had an anarchistic political edge that hadn't been seen on the mainstage since the late 1960s or early '70s, from its opener in which Uncle Sam is put on trial by figures with flashlights and gas masks, to its closer, "Passion," about a man on a quest to get Americans to understand the lies our corporate and consumer

Spotlight on
Adam McKay

Adam McKay is originally from Pennsylvania. He came to Chicago and studied with Del Close at the ImprovOlympic, where he soon became enamored of Del's long-form improv "The Harold." Adam was also involved with an early version of The Upright Citizens Brigade. He joined the Touring Company in 1993, e.t.c. in 1995, and moved to the mainstage the same year for *Piñata Full of Bees*. He was hired as head writer by *Saturday Night Live* in 1996 and is still writing and creating short films for the show. (He's also the son-in-law of Byrne and Joyce Piven, having married their daughter, Shira. Second City truly is a small world.)

At Second City, Adam specialized in bizarre juxtapositions between his characters and their environments: white-bread suburban gang members, zombies who run into old friends from high school, Noam Chomsky substitute-teaching public school.

Backstage Passes

I remember thinking that I must be the most attractive job candidate around. Here I was, just out of college, on my first interview, and I land a job with Bernie Sahlins' Willow Street Carnival, a new and exciting theater troupe, and, in the meantime, get to work at the legendary Second City. I arrived at the front bar of Second City on a Friday night—certain that I'd be put to work in the marketing department or something—and Alison Riley, the house manager, said, "You can start tonight, follow me." She walked me through the mainstage theater and into the kitchen: "There's the sink, there's the dirty glasses, rinse and dry." I washed glasses for six straight hours. My hands were raw. The only noble thing about that experience was that I found out that David Mamet had been a busboy at Second City.

—Kelly Leonard

● ● ●

The job of the Producer at Second City is an amalgam of priest, firefighter, and magician. The job requires the skill of being able to spot, encourage, and, above all, listen to the young performers. Producers must have the ability to develop new directors that share the vision of what constitutes a strong Second City show, but, at the same time, preserve the integrity of what Second City has meant in the past. The very nature of the spontaneity of the work and the process requires a producer to be constantly reacting to emergencies—actors that get sick and can't perform on opening night, a show that five nights before the opening is getting very few laughs. The best producers are able to deal with all the financial and business issues of running a theater as well as the deeper artistic concerns. We've been lucky with Sally Cochrane, Lyn Okkerse, Kelly Leonard, Cheryl Sloane, Joe Janes, and Nancy Marino to find producers who embrace these and other qualities that have led The Second City over the last two decades.

—Andrew Alexander

culture have perpetrated on them. The scene ended with the cast asking audience members to surrender their Blockbuster Video cards because of the company's censorship practices and monopoly of the industry. The cards that were given up—and many were each night—were then cut up in small pieces and thrown over the audiences' heads from a simulated water tower built above the entrance from the theater to the back bar.

Left to right: Scott Adsit, Jenna Jolovitz (bottom), Tina Fey (top), and Kevin Dorff

The show was glued together by frequent returns to Noam Chomsky (played by Adam McKay) teaching a grade school class the "real" history of America, including the slaughter of Native Americans, racism, and commercialism gone wild. A large part of the attitude of the show surely came from Adam. His interest in radical politics, rap music, and the cultural fringes gave the show a radical air. He also was able to galvanize the ensemble into taking incredible risks. In the scene "Gump," CD for instance, Adam played a low-level human resource director who, in the course of a standard company-wide psychological exam, learns that the company's vice president (Scott Adsit) is legally retarded. Scott, an excellent actor, played the "challenged" corporate executive with a perfect blend of stupidity, smugness, and an undeservedly enlarged ego.

Occasional improvs remained in the show, like when Rachel Dratch came out as a young girl, tossed a ball to members of the audience, and asked them questions as if they were one of her parents. The people would answer the questions and toss the ball back. Soon Rachel was having conversations with several members of the audience—one as her father, another as perhaps her father's mistress or her mother's new husband—always with the ball tossed back and forth from the stage to whichever person Rachel wanted to talk to next.

The road to the final product wasn't an easy one. Many audiences (and performers) walked out of the theater shaking their

Spotlight on Kelly Leonard, Sally Cochrane, and Lyn Okkerse

Kelly Leonard, the son of famed Chicago radio and television broadcaster Roy Leonard, began his Second City career as a dishwasher. After a brief stint as a production assistant for Bernie Sahlins' short-lived Willow Street Carnival Theater, Kelly was hired into the box office by manager Anne Libera. Kelly and Anne married in 1996 and have a wonderful three-year-old named Nick. As Kelly quickly rose through the ranks, Andrew Alexander made Kelly his assistant in 1991 and associate producer in 1992. He was promoted to full producer in 1995.

In 1983, with her husband Peter, **Lyn Okkerse** opened The Second City at The CornerStage in London, Ontario. The theater produced twenty-seven shows in nine years. In 1993, when Second City partnered with Olympia Entertainment in Detroit to open a Second City in the Motor City, Lyn took the reigns as producer there for five years. In 1997, Toronto Second City built a new theater, and Lyn moved to Toronto to support the new venue as producer. Lyn is on the committee of Gilda's Club Toronto.

Sally Cochrane was born in Germany to British parents and emigrated to Canada at the age of four. While a student at the University of Toronto, she waitressed part-time at The Second City. Upon earning her master's degree in 1978, Sally returned to Second City as full-time general manager, eventually becoming the producer, a position she held until 1996, when Sally elected to become a full-time mom (and Second City lost a great producer). Sally lives in Toronto with her husband, Patrick Whitley, and their two children. She met Patrick at Second City in 1980. Patrick was a producer on *SCTV*.

Top to bottom: Kelly Leonard • Lyn Okkerse • Sally Cochrane

171

Spotlight on
Rachel Dratch

Rachel Dratch is a squeaky little clown. After being in touring companies for several years, she was ready to quit when she got cast in the mainstage revue *Piñata Full of Bees* in 1995. Although she can play many different characters successfully, as with most of the best clowns, the audience immediately recognizes her— even behind the mask she wore in a scene as an annoying little girl bugging visitor Jim Zulevic. Rachel has a tiny frame and a high, squeaky voice from which she's able to produce an impressive amount of sound. During her time at Second City, she twice won Jeff Awards as best actress in a revue. Rachel joined the cast of *Saturday Night Live* in 1999. She'd been watching and dreaming about being on the show since third grade.

Some Second City performers have an enviable advantage over their fellow ensemble members: the audience is in love with them. In the late 1980s and early '90s, it was Chris Farley; later, it was Rachel. Although these two performers are opposites in almost every arena—he was huge, she's tiny; he bounced off the walls, she seemed to float right through them—they both had the audience eating out of the palms of their hands.

Much of Rachel's comedy revolves around her size. In *Promise Keepers, Losers Weepers*, she played a five-hundred-pound woman (with the aid of two male cast members underneath a tremendously large mu mu) out to protect the interests of feminism. In *Piñata Full of Bees*, her rendition of Led Zeppelin's "Whole Lotta Love" on the cello brought the house down each night. Her portrayal of the first woman ever to play for the Chicago Bulls was a big hit—especially the evening Steve Kerr and Luc Longley of the then-championship Bulls showed up for the show. And, of course, the character she created in "Wicked" **CD** made its way onto *Saturday Night Live*. "Rachel's humor is so joyful and never at anyone's expense," says fellow Second City alumna Tina Fey. "It is so refreshing. It's always just silliness and joyfulness." Rachel continues to work together with Tina on *SNL*.

In *Paradigm Lost*, a darkly shrouded Rachel Dratch plays the recorder as Jim Zulevic, Tina Fey, and Kevin Dorff look on.

heads. Kelly Leonard, Scott Adsit, and Rachel Dratch discussed the initial reactions to this new kind of Second City show:

Kelly: Chicago theater critic Tony Adler sought me out after a preview and said, "This stuff is amazing—but aren't you worried about committing commercial suicide?" (or words to that effect). No such concerns were ever voiced by Andrew. He knew we needed unflinching support if we were to pull it off.

Rachel: In one of those "in your face" moves that Tom Gianas is fond of, in the middle of a scene during the improv set one night, Scott Adsit walked out and tearfully announced that the President had been shot. The audience totally believed it and gasped, then went silent.

Scott: I brought a TV out onstage so they could stay and watch live coverage on the news. Instead of that, the TV showed sports bloopers. The cast all came out and were each won over by the hilarious sports bloopers. We laughed at the TV while the audience watched us. About ten percent of them got it and laughed, sixty percent were bewildered, and thirty percent got it and were furious. We stayed onstage laughing at sports bloopers until the entire audience had left.

Rachel: They hated us. As Scott Allman said of their response, "You could hear a mouse shit."

Kelly: I had to write many letters to customers rightfully outraged by the material. I guess you don't get to magic places without taking some chances and failing. Tom Gianas understands this better than anyone.

The kinks were worked out, the hard edges made more accessible and the reviews for *Piñata* were tremendous, as was the audience reaction. Within a few months, both Adam McKay and Tom Gianas were hired onto the writing staff of *Saturday Night Live*, and Jon Glaser was hired away to work on the short-lived *Dana Carvey Show* and then *Late Night* with Conan O'Brien.

Critics and audiences loved the new direction Second City was taking with *Piñata*. But the challenges to the old Second City form didn't end there. Del's ImprovOlympic had developed a

Piñata was the show that kind of changed the style of the shows at Second City. We basically didn't do any blackouts and kept the lights up the whole time. And we tried to make scenes connect into each other and have things come back, and just have the show be more connected as a whole instead of just a plain revue. What we did was we had a bunch of first halves of scenes in the first act, and then they would resolve themselves in the second act. I guess it made the audience be more patient with us and then they got a bigger payoff (*Chicago Tribune*, 1999).

—Rachel Dratch

A scene from Paradigm Lost *(from left to right): Jenna Jolovitz, Rachel Dratch, Scott Adsit, Kevin Dorff, Jim Zulevic, Tina Fey*

Jeff Richmond and Tina Fey

We've seen how often couples get formed at Second City. Jeff Richmond and Tina Fey were already a couple when Tina got hired as an actress in the touring company and Jeff was hired to play piano for Second City e.t.c. Who knew that, just five years later, Jeff would be one of Second City's key stage directors, and Tina would be the first female head writer in *Saturday Night Live* history. In addition to their incredible talent, they're really nice people. Jeff's background in musical theater has brought a colorful vitality to the shows he's directed—all of which have been nominated for Joseph Jefferson Awards. Tina's wry sensibility and top-notch improvisation really helped make her shows on the mainstage some of the best in recent history. In 1999, Jeff directed Tina and Rachel Dratch in a two-woman revue called *Dratch & Fey*. A hit in Chicago, the show was remounted in the summer of 2000 in New York to more rave reviews. Great things lie ahead for this pair.

number of exciting young improvisers, and other local troupes such as Jazz Freddy and Ed were making a splash performing improvised plays. So Kelly performed a raiding party on all the talent that had been working in black-box theaters for little if any money. He hired performers such as Kevin Dorff, David Koechner, Brian Stack, Miriam Tolan, and others. He even produced our own long-form improvisational show, *Lois Kaz*, directed by ImprovOlympic vet Noah Gregeropolous in the e.t.c. space on off-nights. The show was an instant smash and made many of our critics sit up and take notice.

Although Tom Gianas was gone, Second City found an equally innovative director in Mick Napier. 1996's *Citizen Gates* was an election year hit, with really strong political satire. It also featured the first gender-equal cast in Chicago mainstage history. But it was Mick's next show, *Paradigm Lost*, that established him as one of the most exciting young directors in town. The cast included Scott Adsit, Kevin Dorff, Rachel Dratch, Tina Fey, Jenna Jolovitz, and Jim Zulevic. The show centered around the dreams and nightmares of a corporate executive (Jim) who's in a coma. Like *Piñata*, the show presented a number of shifting realities and recurring characters. The second act opened with an improvised day of programming on National Public Radio—all based on the audience suggestion of a household object. *Paradigm Lost* won Jeff Awards for best production, for Mick as best director, and for Rachel and Scott as best actress and actor.

Paradigm Lost was chosen to appear at the U.S. Comedy Arts Festival in Aspen, Colorado. It was also the subject of the documentary *Second to None*, made by HMS Media; camera crews were allowed to follow the show through the rehearsal period all the way to its opening night. *Saturday Night Live* came knocking again toward the end of the show's run, and Tina Fey was hired onto its writing staff. Within two years, she became the first woman head writer in the history of *SNL*.

Acrobatics All the Way Out

We lost some people forever in the 1990s. Viola Spolin, Paul Sills' mother and the true founder of improvisational acting in North America, died in 1994. Viola's contributions to all the generations that have come after her is incalculable. Her "games" brought an entirely new way of thinking about acting and comedy into existence. She is and will always be the teacher.

John Candy died the same year as Viola. He had been working with Andrew and Len in an effort to get a license in Canada to operate a comedy cable channel while he was in Mexico for

Wagons East, the film he was shooting at the time of his death. John's death was both shocking and devastating. Memorial services were held in L.A. and Toronto, both attended by throngs of friends, family, and fans—all friends, the way John looked at things.

Kelly Leonard remembered first hearing the news:

I was at a hotel in the suburbs looking at a new potential location when a hotel employee came in and said there was an emergency phone call for me. My wife was at the theater and said, "John Candy just died. The press is calling—they're at the front door, and Andrew's locked himself in his office." I hustled back to the theater and could barely enter through the front door, as it was blocked by camera crews and newsmen. John was one of Andrew's very best friends, and Andrew was more distraught than I have ever seen him. We created a short statement for the press and decided to say nothing more.

"I was privileged to be asked by Rose Candy to deliver one of the three eulogies given at John's funeral in 1994," said Andrew. "John and I—like many others—had gone through some rough periods when he was not happy with me, nor I with him. So I was thankful that three years before John died, we were able to put all of the rough times behind us and continue the wonderful friendship."

The funeral procession left the Church on Sunset Boulevard and proceeded south on one of the busiest highways in the world, the 405 freeway. The California Highway Patrol and LAPD had closed the highway travelling south to accommodate the cortège to the cemetery that was about two miles north of LAX airport. The police holding their hands to their chest, while blocking all of the exit ramps, was an emotional and stirring tribute to this lovable, wonderful Canadian who captured the hearts of everyday people. This was an unheard-of gesture in L.A. and one that none of us can ever forget.

Severn Darden died in 1995. Although he didn't achieve a national level of celebrity, he maintains an almost mystical level of fame at Second City. He was the first true Second City eccentric.

Severn worked as one of our workshop instructors out in Los Angeles. He had no problem relating to the generation that was coming up and had a

Severn Darden at Second City's twenty-fifth anniversary

Backstage Passes

During a scene called "Orchestra," cast members were stationed throughout the audience as students in a classroom (with audience members treated as fellow students). The teacher, Ron West, was onstage, and we "students" had to get our section of the classroom/audience to participate. On opening night, Irv Kupcinet [famed *Chicago Sun-Times* columnist] was seated in my section. Actually he was sleeping in my section. I raised my hand and told the teacher, "William is asleep in class again." The audience laughed while "Kup" continued his repose. Most of the people there recognized him, which made it all the more entertaining. We proceeded to spend quite a bit of stage-time joking about the drowsy "William." At one point, he jolted awake (perhaps poked by his wife Essie) and laughed gamely along with the audience, unaware that he was the butt of the joke. He must have had a great dream because the next day we received a nice write-up with no mention of the columnist's siesta! (It's a Second City tradition on opening night to take bets backstage as to how long "Kup" will last before falling asleep.)

—Jill Talley

● ● ●

Severn Darden was once part of a group hired to brainstorm a new advertising campaign for Coca-Cola. The story goes that he sat quietly for a half hour or so, chewing on his handkerchief as he usually did, then made one of the two following suggestions, depending on who's telling the story: "How about 'Eat Coca-Cola'?" or 'First thing: change the name." In either case, he then left the room and didn't return.

—S.P.

Backstage Passes

In 1983 or early '84, I interviewed Joyce Sloane for my college radio station (for my own ends, let's be honest), and she was great. While hanging out after the interview, I ran into Del Close, whose name I recognized from Second City programs and his credit on *Saturday Night Live*. He had just left Second City and was happy to do an interview also. I spent about three hours at his apartment—I still have part of the interview on tape. It changed my life.

—Bob Odenkirk

● ● ●

It was so much fun to be around John Candy. He laughed so much.

—Martin Short

Left to right: Jill Talley, Tim O'Malley, Bob Odenkirk, Holly Wortell, Chris Farley (top), Tim Meadows (bottom), and Dave Pasquesi

lot of fun with a young improv group called The Modernaires, as well as working with a group called The Post-Modernaires, which included Mina Kolb and Paul Dooley. Severn had returned for Second City's twenty-fifth and thirtieth anniversary celebrations, to see old friends, to reminisce, and to entertain. He was a true original.

The 1997 annual holiday party at Second City—always a fun and wild time—seemed especially happy. Even alumnus Chris Farley stopped by to pay his respects. While it was great, as always, to have Chris come by, he didn't look good. His latest trip to Minnesota to treat his alcohol addiction hadn't taken. He was extremely overweight, and there was a certain sadness about him.

Kelly recalls how he learned of Chris' death:

Chris' brother, John, was in the touring company at the time, and he was late for an important rehearsal. I was a little pissed, and I knew he'd been staying with Chris at the John Hancock building. When I called the apartment, Ted, Chris' assistant, answered the phone. I asked for John, and Ted said in a rushed and strange voice, "The police are here. I can't talk. John will call you." And he hung up. I actually didn't think much about it. But not two minutes later a local radio station called me looking for confirmation that Chris was dead. I spun around in my chair to see two news vans pull up in front of the theater. Having been through this with John Candy, I had some idea of what to do. I called Andrew, and we worked on a statement to the press. The mainstage cast was rehearsing in the theater—many in the cast were friends with Chris—I told them what had happened. As we were talking, Joyce walked in from the parking lot. She knew from our faces.

Like his idol John Belushi, Chris' overwhelming appetites destroyed him. "He's like the third one," Del Close said in *USA Today*. "There's John Belushi, John Candy, and him, but I frankly expected him to survive. There was the weight, and there were the drugs, but he didn't seem doomed to me." Dan Aykroyd, in *Time*, remembered a conversation he had with Chris during the summer: "When I saw him in bad shape, I brought up John Belushi and River Phoenix. I laid into him about what kind of pills and powders show up at nightclubs that are lethal. I said it many times to him: he was playing with death if he did this, and look who went before him. I can't buy that he wanted to emulate Belushi this much."

That evening, as camera crews and morbid curiosity seekers still surrounded the building, Kevin Dorff—a longtime friend of

Chris'—addressed the audience following the regular performance: "At this time we would like to say on behalf of The Second City, how saddened we were today by the news of the death of our friend Chris Farley. Shakespeare said, 'Brevity is the soul of wit.' Chris Farley had the soul of a comedian, and, sadly, his life was too brief. As someone who knew him, worked with him, and learned a lot from him, I can tell you that while he was here he made a lot of people laugh—right here on this stage and on others—and I know that this was his greatest joy, and he had a very happy life for that reason. While we here at The Second City family will miss him, our sympathies and our best wishes go to his family in Wisconsin and here in Chicago to whom he is irreplaceable and will always be, of course. Now, that being said, I should tell you that there will be a brief break before we do Chris' favorite part of the show: the improv set."

Second City chartered a bus from its home on Wells Street to attend Chris' funeral in Madison, Wisconsin. Actors and staff traded stories of Chris during the long drive. Lorne Michaels, Dan Aykroyd, Chris Rock, George Wendt, Tom Arnold, John Goodman, Adam Sandler, Tim Meadows, Rob Schneider, and hundreds more assembled to say good-bye.

Del Close died of emphysema in 1999. When it was clear that Andrew's parody *My Talk Show* wasn't going to be picked up for more episodes, he had Del and Bruce Pirrie create a series of monologues that would interrupt the show in progress. They called Del's character "Ozzie Mandius." One monologue on death has particular resonance now that Del is gone:

I was reading in a newspaper the other day about a skydiver who dived out of an airplane and did aerial acrobatics for several thousand feet. When he pulled the ripcord, the main chute did not open. Then he pulled the emergency chute cord, and that did not open. And then what did he do? He did flips and acrobatics head over heels at the top of his ability all the way into the ground. Splat. Now that's my kind of guy. That's kind of a metaphor for life, isn't it? I mean we're all going to hit the ground—splat—eventually, aren't we? So what I'm going to do is follow that guy's example and do acrobatics all the way out.

More Expansion

At the same time that the show's form and content were evolving, Second City, under Andrew's steady guidance, began expanding in all different directions, frequently meeting resistance.

Andrew set up a team of young artistic administrators to help expand our training, corporate, touring, and resident theater

Amy Sedaris, originally from North Carolina, joined the Second City mainstage in 1992 after playing in the Touring Company and at Second City Northwest. She left to create the Comedy Central series *Exit 57* with fellow Second City performers Stephen Colbert, Paul Dinello, and Mitch Rouse, directed by Mick Napier. The show received five

Cable ACE nominations during its two-year run. Then the group re-formed to create *Strangers with Candy*, also for Comedy Central, in which Amy, Paul, and Stephen star. Amy has appeared in several plays off-Broadway, including the Obie Award-winning *One Woman Shoe* (directed by Mick), *The Most Fabulous Story Ever Told*, and *Country Club*. She can also be heard frequently on National Public Radio, working with her writer/performer brother David.

Amy was one of the few Second City character actors who liked to wear wigs for almost all of her characters. She created what have been called by Kelly, "huge, obscene, crazy characters—hicks, grannies, even a doomed squirrel. This was a very beautiful, waifish woman who would make herself really ugly onstage in order to get a laugh. She could contort her face in any way." "Gothic and grotesque" is another way to describe her characters, among the most startling of which was a dead-on impersonation of Ross Perot.

Ian Gomez and Nia Vardalos

Ian Gomez joined the Northwest company in 1991, then moved to the e.t.c. stage in 1992. He and his wife, Nia Vardalos, also in those companies at that time, both caught the eye of L.A. casting directors and talent scouts before they even had the opportunity to "move up" to the Chicago mainstage. Ian and Nia left for L.A. straight from e.t.c. Nia is the author of the L.A. hit one-woman play *My Big Fat Greek Wedding*, based on the couple's wedding, which Tom Hanks is making into a feature film. She also can be seen frequently on commercials and sitcoms. Ian also has been on many TV shows, as well as being a regular or semi-regular on *The Drew Carey Show*, *Whose Line Is It Anyway?*, *Felicity*, and *Norm*. He's been in such movies as *EdTV*, *'Til There Was You*, and *Rookie of the Year*. (Ian is the stepson of Charlie Rubin, one of the owners of Square East, where Second City played in New York in the 1960s.)

divisions. Individuals were given autonomy to shape and grow their divisions. Kelly's job was to increase the role of the touring companies while finding the right mix of artists to inspire the work of the resident stages; Martin de Maat and Anne Libera set about to expand the Training Center's scope and size; and Joe Keefe, a former touring and resident company performer himself, flexed his entrepreneurial muscle in creating Second City Communications—a separate company that would service the corporate sector.

Joe Keefe started Second City Communications in Chicago in 1992. Since then, he, Wendy Morrison, and Nancy Marino (who has since moved into a consultancy role) in Toronto have developed it into a large and financially successful separate division of Second City Enterprises. Its main purpose is to create entertainments (commonly known as "industrials" or "trade shows"), videos, and workshops for business organizations. It also does training seminars, using improv techniques to help people communicate, gain confidence, think freely, and act fast. It's known at Second City as BizCo—for "business company"—just as the touring companies are known as RedCo, BlueCo and GreenCo, and the mainstage resident company is known as RezCo. (E.t.c. is just e.t.c.)

Second City's first Industrial ever, early in the 1960s, was created for introducing distributors to the concept of 7-Up as the Un-Cola. The actors bitched a lot about how we were selling out, until they saw the size of their checks. Since then, they've mostly bitched about how much money they *should* have made.

In 1992, we also had the first of what are now yearly bookings at the English Theatre in Vienna, Austria. In 1995, Second City made its debut at the Edinburgh, Scotland, Fringe Festival. And in 1996, we made our Kennedy Center debut in Washington, D.C., with our Chicago mainstage show *Truth, Justice, or the American Way*, directed by Tom Gianas.

By 1997, the changes that had been so burdensome toward the beginning of the decade were finally paying off. Business was thriving, and the shows were exciting, unpredictable, and full of talented actors.

Motown and Diversity

While *Piñata Full of Bees* was changing the very nature of what a Second City show could be, another kind of revolution was taking place at Second City, but not in Chicago or Toronto. In September 1993, we opened a Second City in Detroit in a unique business partnership with the Illitch family (Little Caesars, the

Detroit Red Wings, and Detroit Tigers), across from the site of the new Tigers stadium in Detroit's once-devastated downtown, which was rapidly being restored. While the experience of creating social and political satire in a city just beginning urban renewal is itself noteworthy, Detroit is especially important as the first Second City theater to produce racially integrated casts from day one.

Second City has almost always created scenes on the race issue. From the earliest revues, we have explored racism from the white left and the white right. What we were mostly unable to do was explore race from the minority perspective, since pitifully few minority performers of any kind have been on our stages in Chicago or Toronto. It was, in fact, the efforts of our white performers to address issues of race that got Andrew going, as he recalls it:

I was living in L.A. when the Rodney King riots happened. Two days later, I flew back to Chicago, and the cast—all white, no minorities—were struggling with how to deal with this issue. It struck home. We were sitting in Chicago—its downtown population is fifty percent African-American—and we didn't have any African-Americans on stage. And, beyond that, we didn't really have a system for encouraging them to take part. In Detroit, we've been much more successful in attracting African-Americans. When half of the cast is composed of minority actors, it's much more relaxed, the race-related material comes much more quickly, there's a sense of safety, there's a broader scope. (You can also see this in our e.t.c. cast in Chicago right now.) We do a lot of material in Detroit that's about race issues. It's a very diverse cast, and there's a point of view there that's a little more visceral. There was one particular show we did, Steam Cleaning While You Walk, *directed by Tom Gianas, that was almost all race issues. And I worried about it. I was mainly concerned that the show was so unevenly balanced that it would actually hurt some terrific material. Anytime you focus on one issue you run the risk of diluting the content. Anyway, the NAACP was considering boycotting us; they thought the show was divisive. We had to explain how the material was developed and how it was created by African-American actors.*

The original cast of Second City Detroit, (top to bottom, left to right): Colin Ferguson, Jackie Purtan, Andrew Newberg, Tim Pryor, Robin Bucci, Angela Shelton, Jerry Minor, Suzy Nakamura

179

Backstage Pass

Left to right: Brian Stack, Horatio Sanz, Jerry Minor, and armless mannequin

We had to be very clear about our intent, especially given the lack of representation in our history.

The auditions in Detroit were cast with an eye toward racial equality. The twelve or so finalists worked with Second City Training Center Director Anne Libera over an intensive three-week period. Out of this group, eight were chosen to make up the first cast—Robin Bucci, Colin Ferguson, Jerry Minor, Suzy Nakamura, Andy Newberg, Tim Pryor, Jackie Purtan, and Angela Shelton, with pianist/musical director Mark Levenson imported from Second City Northwest, John Holtson stage-managing, and Norm Holly directing. Andrew brought Lyn Okkerse in from Canada to produce the Detroit company and, almost immediately, the difference was felt. No longer was it only a matter of discussing race in "white" terms. Even inter-race issues such as the friction between light-skinned and dark-skinned blacks became possible subject matter for satire.

Second City Detroit is still running strong and has its own touring company and its own Training Center. Thus, it also has its own built-in Training Center-to-Touring Company-to-mainstage route—except that, for at least some of the performers in Detroit, mainstage there is sort of a hoped-for stepping stone to e.t.c. or mainstage in Chicago, where they're more likely to be "discovered."

Among the talented actors to come out of Detroit, Larry Campbell recently got a pilot deal with NBC, Colin Ferguson was seen in *Tales of the City*, Jerry Minor has been on *Mr. Show* and *The Martin Short Show*, and now writes for *Saturday Night Live*, and Angela Shelton is hosting a Chicago TV talk show.

In Chicago, Andrew decided to try an Outreach Program and asked alumnus Aaron Freeman to start it. The Outreach Program's mission was—and still is—to broaden the diversity of Second City's stages through more aggressive talent searches, specialized workshops, and other community-based efforts. Aaron described the changing state of race at Second City over the years:

The late Bob Curry is generally considered to be the Jackie Robinson of Second City. In 1966, he was the resident company's first Negro improviser. I was the second, ten years later. Bob was brilliant and fearless and was famous for getting naked at any time for no particular reason. The joke was that despite being painfully funny, Bob was so weird that it took a decade before the company would hire another black actor. I feared that joke. I worried that the hopes and dreams of all future brown improvisers rode on my funny bone; that if I wasn't really great, Second City would not hire a dark face for another decade.

My only experience with racism as workplace policy was at The Second City. From the time I joined the touring company in 1977 until 1980, I was not allowed to play the "blood relative" of any cast member. Since I was the "company Negro," this severely limited my choice of roles. This policy did not come down from the top. It was a judgment made by the touring company director at the time. He reasoned that, while our audiences had no problem accepting a twenty-five-year-old playing eight, they would never buy a brown man as his father. At the time I did not protest. As a twenty-one-year-old actor getting his first shot with the most prestigious comedy troupe in America, I wanted to make no waves. After a couple of years, Bernie Sahlins heard about the policy. His response was, "I will not be a party to such blatant racism." When I left, I was immediately replaced by Tim Meadows, who thrived and went on to fame and fortune on SNL and in Hollywood. The modern Second City boasts a bumper crop of dark funny folk. They play whatever roles they can or want, including management. Bob Curry would be proud; so would Martin Luther King.

Because it continued to be frustrating finding minority performers to sign up for auditions at Second City Chicago, after Aaron found himself too short on time to be able to continue the work, Andrew hired Frances Callier, an African-American Touring Company performer and a teacher at and director of the Training Center, to continue the Outreach Program, including scholarships and summer workshops at the Training Center. After about six or seven years, we've had some success, and our minority representation on stage today is considerably better. By

Frances Callier

Spotlight on

Horatio Sanz

Horatio "Raj" Sanz, after being in touring companies for several years, joined the e.t.c. company in 1996. Although he's always shied away from any sort of limiting classification as a minority performer, Raj was an important figure as a Latino cast member of e.t.c., helping us increase a diversity in the cast we'd

been so lacking in for so long. Raj never made it to mainstage. I'm not even sure he wanted to, he was having such a good time at e.t.c. He joined the *Saturday Night Live* cast in 1998, the first Second City performer to be hired for it straight out of e.t.c. Raj liked to push the boundaries of taste whenever possible, and the audience allowed him extraordinarily loose boundaries. There was Tony Royce, the sleazy owner of the Lucky Deal used car lot in Melrose Park, Illinois. After witnessing a horrible plane crash outside his car lot, Royce is interviewed by local reporters and uses the opportunity to help promote his dealership "on Mannheim Road." And there was the guy crushed between cars in a subway accident trying to say good-bye to his wife by cell phone, the disgustingly sexist lounge singer, and many more, all riotously funny.

Ruby Streak and Bob Derkach

Any director, producer, or actor at Second City will tell you that the musical director provides the essential backbone of a revue. For decades, Second City

has been blessed with two musicians that have created an amazing catalogue of songs

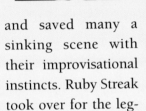

and saved many a sinking scene with their improvisational instincts. Ruby Streak took over for the legendary Fred Kaz in the 1980s and hasn't missed a beat. In particular, her innovations during the *Piñata Full of Bees* period provided a whole new soundscape for our shows. Bob Derkach has played an almost identical role for the ensemble in Toronto, finding a delicate balance in both scoring scenes and writing original songs.

Additionally, both Ruby and Bob provide a level of consistency and experience as Second City ensemble members come and go. They have literally seen it all and their perspective is incredibly unique and undeniably essential.

"It's been a real asset to have Ruby and Bob on board," says Andrew Alexander. "Not only are they both tremendous artists, but they also serve a director function both during rehearsals and the long runs of our shows."

the end of 1998, e.t.c. had assembled the most diverse cast in the history of the theater. Directed by Jeff Richmond, this ensemble received local theater award nominations and critical acclaim for *The Revelation Will Not Be Televised* and *History Repaints Itself*.

Former Training Center Director Ed Garza assembled a group of gay sketch comedy performers—another group notably absent from past Second City casts (at least openly)—and helped create GayCo Productions. This group has received excellent notices for its revues *Whitney Houston, We Have a Problem* and *Everyone's Coming Out Rosie*, both also directed by Jeff Richmond.

Andrew now looks to a bright future for diversity at Second City:

From left to right: Jim Zulevic, Adam McKay (bottom), Dee Ryan, Jimmy Doyle, Jenna Jolovitz, and John Hildreth (bottom) in a scene from e.t.c.'s One Nation Under Fraud

In Chicago, we've come to the point where we believe the only way we're going to be successful is going into the community and building a theater. We've met with Dorothy Tillman, a very active and visible African-American alderman in Chicago. She's part of a group trying to reestablish Bronzeville on the South Side. We've been awarded a large grant to help build a theater there that will be totally devoted to doing the kind of work Second City does, but in the black community, co-owned and operated by African-Americans. It has to start right at the grass roots.

Which is exactly what we did to begin with, back at The Compass in 1955.

Farewell to The Old Firehall

By the late 1990s, The Second City had regained the kind of critical acclaim that was its hallmark in the early 1960s, and Andrew and Len Stuart's plan for expansion had not only become a reality, it was still expanding. The Chicago and Detroit theaters were thriving, touring productions could be seen all over the world, and Second City Communications had become its own burgeoning corporate entity. The New York and Los Angeles training centers opened in 1998. The one in Cleveland opened in 1999 in preparation for the opening of a resident theater there. In 1998, almost two hundred thousand people visited the two Second City Chicago stages alone. To help manage all the business brought by this growth, Andrew and Len appointed Roy Lister president of The Second City Inc. In 1999, under the supervision of Martin de Maat, Francis Callier, Moira Dunphy, and Janis Rae, our training centers in Chicago and Toronto offered more than one hundred classes a week. The training center in Cleveland already has more than two hundred students. In 1999, the casts of Chicago's and Toronto's mainstages and the e.t.c. joined together to perform at Montreal's Just for Laughs Festival. In 2000, the three Chicago touring companies began the first of their summer runs at the Metropolis Performing Arts Centre in Arlington Heights, Illinois.

But there were problems in Toronto. Much has been written about the bohemian charms of The Old Firehall. However, by 1997, it had become clear that it was no longer the best place for Second City in Toronto: too small, too technically under-equipped, too far from where "the action" in the city had moved by then. So, Andrew and Len moved Second City Toronto across town to its current, larger, far-better-located new space at 56 Blue Jays Way. Achilles Ciconne keeps the building maintained, and has since he was sixteen. He's much happier in the new space. It has state-of-the-art lighting and sound capabilities, a beautiful lobby and theater space, a large curved stair-case leading out of the lobby into the theater, and large, mounted photos of former performers all over the walls. The building has a TV studio and post-pro-duction facility. It also has the added bonus of a smaller performance space called The Tim Sims Playhouse, named after a performer who died too young; it's run by his widow, Lindsey Leese, who was in the Firehall company with Tim. (Fittingly, The Old Firehall was turned into the Gilda's Club of Toronto.)

"The last night at The Firehall," says Sandra Balcovske, "there were a half dozen of us who stayed later than anyone else, probably five or six in the morning. We thought about writing something on the wall, and we started to write down people's names, couples who had met there, who had kids, people who'd had relationships inside the company. It turned into an incredible family tree."

56 Blue Jays Way, the new home of The Second City Toronto

Bonnie Hunt

Greg Holliman

Kathryn Greenwood

Bonnie Hunt was a nurse prior to and during some of her time at Second City. Her father had made a deal with her—Bonnie would attend nursing school as something to fall back on, and if she hated it, she could leave. Sadly, her father passed away during this period. She wasn't enjoying school and later said, "I felt I was going for him." A patient she was caring for who was dying of cancer talked on and on about a guy he worked with and what a wonderful person he was. Finally, Bonnie figured out the patient was talking about her own father. She finished nursing school, and then began her career as one of the funniest women in show business.

Greg Holliman currently portrays Principal Blackman on *Strangers With Candy*, but Greg got his start studying with The Second City. Greg would go on to tour with the company, but never ended up on a resident stage (our loss). In his early Second City days, Greg would often come to classes on roller skates, wearing a red bow tie. His incredible likeness (in height and looks) to Michael Jordan led him to be a stand-in for the star on numerous commercial shoots. A little known fact about Greg is that he came to Second City via the Jehovah Witnesses, where his parents had him walking door to door delivering the spiritual message of the Witnesses. Not your normal Second City background, but...

At twelve years old, **Kathryn Greenwood**'s grandmother took her to The Old Firehall to see The Second City. She was blown away by the whole feel of the place: the ambience of the cabaret space and the informal brilliance of the show. Kathryn left the theater that night with two goals: one, to become a member of The Second City, and; two, to marry Martin Short. (One out of two isn't bad.) Kathryn quit her day job in the office of a pro-choice organization to join The Second City Touring Company. She became a member of the Toronto mainstage in 1990. She is active in stage, television, and film. To date, she is still is not married to Martin Short.

Bob Martin's mother came to see him perform at The Old Firehall. Once. She was in her seventies, very British, very proper—she had no understanding of what Second City was, nor could Bob begin to explain it to her. She was also easily offended by anything sexual on stage (although, like all old British women, she loved drag queens). He tried to prepare her by saying that she might not get all of the material in the show, but that she would love the improv set. In the end, she didn't get anything in the show, and Bob played a six-foot talking penis for the entire fifty-minute set. She went home with Bob's sister, and Bob went home and leafed though Freud's *Jokes and Their Relation to the Unconscious*.

Jenny Parsons has been a part of many death-defying improvs. "There's nothing like it," she says. One night in the early 1990s in Toronto, she was part of a cast that got an audience suggestion of "balls." Backstage, the cast put together a list of scenes based on various suggestions, and Kathy Greenwood came up with an idea for a blackout. So the cast went out, and all the guys said, "Man, that sure took a lot of balls to do that." "Yup, you've sure got a lot of balls." And Kathy said, "Yup, that sure took a lot of *labia*." They stood there in the deafening silence as the audience sat stunned. As the lights went out, you could see the whites of the performers' eyes and smell the flop sweat. Then, in the dark, a sudden explosion of laughter from the audience. They were howling and cheering. It was then that Jenny felt that she and her fellow actors had survived something together—an exhilarating, unifying moment.

The most interesting aspect of **Chris Farley**'s first days at Second City were the exact opposite of what you might expect. The man who would literally bounce off the walls to generate laughs, showed up to his first rehearsals exactly on time with a pad and pencil, and waited quietly for the director's instructions. Chris was often like that. He would always make a point of saying hello to a fellow actor's parents when they came to the show. His off-stage charm was legendary, even if it did have a touch of cheekiness to it. Chris would often try to sweet-talk the box office into giving him extra tickets for the show. He used all his charm one day to try to get Joyce Sloane to give him the night off so he could attend his family's annual Fourth of July party. When Joyce wouldn't budge and said, "That's what being an actor is, Chris. You have to understand that." Chris replied, "I understand it, but I'm afraid my Dad never will." Joyce gave him the night off.

Bob Martin

Jenny Parsons

Chris Farley

Outro

Two blackouts from the early 1960s may sum up Second City's point of view about the world and the people in it as well as anything can:

A man in ancient garb enters a fairly darkened stage carrying a lit lantern and looking around. He knocks on a door (we had doors onstage then). It's opened by another man, also in ancient garb.

Man 2: Who are you? What do you want?

Man 1: I am Diogenes. I'm looking for an honest man.

Man 2: (As he reaches toward the lantern) Oh yeah? What're you doing with my lantern?

Diogenes looks embarrassed as the lights black out.

And:

A man in rags comes crawling across the stage as the piano underscores his pain. He finally reaches the door, reaches up from the floor, and knocks. The door is opened by a man in ancient garb.

Man 2: What do you want?

Man 1: I am the Prodigal Son. I've come home. Where are my parents?

Man 2: They moved (and he slams the door).

Black out.

On December 16, 1999, Beethoven's and Noël Coward's birthdays, we celebrated forty years of The Second City in Chicago, the longest run in the history of the city; it even beats the New York run of *The Fantasticks*, which opened nine months later and will probably close sooner. Rather than put on the star-studded anniversary events of years past, we decided to take a more reflective approach. Alumni were invited back for a weekend of seminars, film festivals of old material, and a brunch saluting Bernie Sahlins, Joyce Sloane, and me. Furthermore, to honor not only the past, but the future as well, Second City and e.t.c. each opened new revues on consecutive nights directed by Mick Napier and Jeff Richmond, respectively. Both shows were enthusiastically received by alumni and critics alike. Second Citizens from many different generations came in, including David Shepherd, Joyce Piven, Jo Forsberg, Barbara Harris, Mina Kolb, Alan Arkin, Avery Schreiber, Fred Kaz, Robert Klein, Harold Ramis, Joe Flaherty, Tim Kazurinsky, Tony Rosato, Richard Kind, Mike Hagerty, Tim Meadows, Ron West, Tina Fey, and Tom Gianas.

The outside (above) and inside (below) of The Second City theater today

The first night of the four-day weekend, the opening of the new mainstage show, I walked into the theater and saw people from the last forty-eight years of my professional (and personal) life—all the way back to when I was a sixteen-year-old student at the University of Chicago—as well as my brother and sister-in-law, all in one room. That's a lot of years, a lot of memories, all crashing in at once. It was exhilarating and terrifying at the same time, and it was one of the only times in my life when I can remember having a full-out anxiety attack. I covered it, I think. I greeted and hugged and chatted with many people before the show started, even though I don't have a clue as to what I said or did. It took about fifteen minutes into the first act (and a large scotch) before I could focus. From then on it was all just exhilarating.

Perhaps Bernie Sahlins summed up Second City's significance best:

It's not comedy's role to change the world. Man is the only animal that laughs, and comedy's single role is to evoke the laughter that celebrates our unity as moral creatures. Comedy informs us that we are not alone, that us kings, peasants, presidents, priests, and penitents, we're all in the same boat. Our laughter is at once a protest and an acceptance of our common destiny. It's a sign of our victory over all that oppresses and constricts. As my friend Ted Cohen said, "When we, as a community, laugh at the same thing, that is a very special moment. It is the realization of a desperate hope that we are enough like one another to sense one another and to be able to live together." That's exactly why Second City's still here after forty years, and may it continue to bring us together in that hope.

Clive Barnes once said in the *New York Times* that "the entire recent tradition of American theatrical satire can be summed up in three words: The Second City." We are indeed the single most important influence on comedy in North America in the last half of the century. In fact, our techniques, based in Viola Spolin's improv games, have had a major influence on acting, directing, and writing in general, in theater, in movies, and on TV. It's amazing that we've lasted, it's amazing that we've expanded into the "empire" we're now often called, and probably most amazing of all is how many talented people we've found and nurtured and sent on their way, ready to find their careers. (These days we mostly don't even have to look; they find us.) Even many who didn't make it to "fame and fortune" have managed to make a good living in our hard and harsh business. Second City teaches you to land on your feet, or at least get a laugh as you're falling on your face. ● ● ●

Through the years, Second City has been a surrogate parent to the many who have traipsed through its doors. No matter where you roam, returning to Second City is always like coming home. Bernie, Andrew, Del, Fred, Sheldon, and Joyce are some who settled in, who put to work their knowledge and skills to keep the doors open.

—Judy Belushi Pisano

From the fortieth anniversary celebration (from left to right): Sheldon Patinkin, Joe Flaherty, Harold Ramis, Mick Napier, Jeff Richmond, Tom Gianas, and Jeffrey Sweet

back WORD
back back

back
back

by James Belushi

My brother, John, was in the company when I was sixteen years old. I went to see the show, and it was the best show Second City has had in the last forty years. The cast had John, Harold Ramis, Brian Doyle-Murray, Jim Fisher, Joe Flaherty, Eugenie Ross-Leming, and Judy Morgan. Fred Kaz at piano. Those names are tattooed on my arm. That was in 1970. The show contained many of the sketches that were done for the next twenty years in the touring company: "Funeral," "Hamlet," "Brest Litovsk." **CD**

It was the single funniest show I had seen in all my life.

At that moment, I wanted to be here. I wanted to be part of this. So, from that moment, my whole agenda was to be in the Second City resident company. Six-and-a-half years later, I started at Second City.

Between 1970 and 1976 I did everything I could to prepare myself. I started my own improvisation group in high school. I read Viola Spolin's book, *Improvisation for the Theater*, and I saw each new show at least six times. I studied the rhythms of every show and sucked up as much as I could. I was totally possessed by improv.

I majored in speech, but I had my improv troupes at College of DuPage and Southern Illinois University. We played horrible bars, cancer benefits—not a lot of laughs at the cancer benefit. Plus, I did a lot of theater in college.

My brother didn't give me any pointers. But that was good, I had to do it all myself. That's the way I look at it. I didn't study with anyone at Second City. I learned improvisation kind of the way you learn to drive a motorcycle, by grinding the gears and shifting into the wrong gears and slowly learning to do it right, so that by the time I got to Second City, I had learned the patter.

And then there was an enormous leap of growth when I got into the touring company. There, I was finally getting a chance to do the scenes I had seen over and over and over. So rehearsal was a breeze.

Also, George Wendt taught me a lot about comedy that first year in the touring company. When I got into the touring company, I had one

more semester to go for college. I remember I auditioned in May. My first gig was June 6, 1976. I still have the check stub. I remember I did a lot of material on the Bicentennial.

Then I was student teaching at Lyons township when I was performing in the touring company. In the second semester I was going to school at the University of Illinois in Chicago, doing eight shows a week at Chateau Louise during the winter of 1977, which was one of the harshest winters in Chicago history.

Joyce Sloane made my mom a promise that they wouldn't put me in a resident company until I finished college. And she made me finish my degree. Then Joyce rented me a car so I could go down to Southern Illinois University to pick it up.

When I stepped onto the mainstage, my two biggest surprises were that girls liked me more and how bad I felt when I had a bad improvisational set. We had some great shows, and some great sketches: "Benny the Denny's Chef," a little musical number Fred Kaz wrote for us, that I would do just before intermission. Fred was worried that he had created a butcher. I was totally out of breath by the intermission. It took me the whole intermission to get my breath back. And then there was the "White Horse Tavern" **CD** scene. It was about the romanticizing of suicide by the great literary artists.

But what I remember most fondly from that period was Joyce Sloane. She was it. She did a lot of things for a lot of people. She gave herself up to the people in that theater. She gave us confidence, strength, and support. Gave me money; I didn't have money. She gave me her car. She took me to the dentist. She was the heart of that theater. And Fred was the soul.

What I learned at Second City was a certain confidence. Like George Wendt once said, "In an audition, they give you a page of the script and point out three places they want laughs. We would deliver seven." It was confidence with characters and why some things worked and some didn't.

last WORD...

by Harold Ramis

I first saw Second City in the summer of 1967. I had just come back to Chicago after college in St. Louis at Washington University. I'd gotten married after I graduated and tried graduate school for about a week and then moved back to Chicago. I was working as a full-time substitute teacher in the Chicago public schools. My first wife and I went to see Second City, and I really liked it. The actors were so accessible, they were almost in your lap. I had this mixed feeling about the show: this is great, this is really funny. But I can do *that*. I've heard other people say that. In fact, when I was onstage, Betty Thomas was a waitress at Second City. I know she would look up onstage and say, I can do *that*.

I enlisted in the workshop with Josephine Forsberg. I took twelve classes with her. And I performed in the company of her children's theater. An opening came up in the touring company, which Forsberg also directed. I honestly felt the place in the company should go to me. It wasn't just blind ambition. I thought I was doing good work. But she picked someone else. And I thought, well, I'm done. She doesn't see what I do. There was no angry blowup, no confrontation. Just me thinking, I'll go somewhere else. So I went around the corner to the Old Town Players Theater in St. Michael's Church. I said I had done a little improv, and they said they wanted someone to teach improv. So I started doing workshops there for a number of weeks, and we put on a public performance.

In the meantime, I started writing freelance features for the *Chicago Daily News*. I had approached Richard Christiansen, who edited the "Panorama" Sunday supplement, and I hounded him until he gave me some freelance work. After a while, he was publishing everything I wrote.

In the summer of 1968, I sent some of my pieces to *Playboy*. They hired me to be the "Party Jokes" editor. That was their entry-level position. I took that and continued freelancing at the *Daily News*.

One day, Richard Christiansen called me and said a friend of his, Michael Miller, was the new director at Second City, and he wanted me to meet him. I'd pretty much given up on Second City. I called Michael Miller, and he said, all right, come down Saturday night for the second show. He said, you'll go in the improv set. I hadn't been onstage in months. I figured, this is it, either you do it or you don't. After the second show, we took suggestions. We went backstage. I volunteered for a number of pieces and went out and did them. Michael Miller was forming a new touring company, and, after seeing me improvise, he said, all right, you're in. It was there I first met Brian Doyle-Murray and Joe Flaherty.

This was in 1968, and Chicago was erupting. We had the race riots in the spring of 1968, the Democratic Convention in the summer, and then a year later the Chicago Seven trial. Abbie Hoffman used to come to The Second City then. He improvised with us as an alibi during the trial. When the Weathermen were in the streets, he was with us. He actually played Judge Hoffman onstage, which was cool.

In the touring company we had started working up our anti-war material. Bernie Sahlins booked us into West Point. Our act was greeted with stony silence. Another time Joyce Sloane booked us into a nightclub in Louisville, Kentucky. We had a lot of sacrilegious material and anti-war material in the show, and they hated us. Someone threw a glass at the stage, I remember. We rewrote the show. We basically took a lot of *Playboy* party jokes and acted them out onstage. It was the only safe thing we could think of. We also worked up a country western song called, "If I'd a Known She Was Dead I'd Never Have Asked Her to Dance."

I worked at *Playboy* through 1968. Then Bernie Sahlins decided to move the current resident company to New York and moved us in as the new resident company. We worked up a show and called ourselves "The Next Generation." We were the long hairs. We looked like hippies, but we weren't really, and we weren't very good. We had a couple of good pieces. We improvised well. But our stuff was rough. I remember one of the columnists from the papers came in, saw the show in previews, and wrote, "If this is the 'next generation,' let's have the old generation back."

Our first shows were poorly attended. Sometimes, there were as many of us onstage as there were in the audience. The first show wasn't very good. The second show we got a little better. After the third show, things started getting good. It was fun.

I felt lucky to be at Second City during that time. It was the best job you could have in Chicago. What Second City taught me was how to play well with others. Those who get it, learn that.

Second City also makes it possible for performers to experience every actor's nightmare—to be in a play and not know what play you're in or what your dialogue is. We do that every night by choice at Second City. We go out there and put ourselves in the actor's nightmare. It inspires a general feeling of delightful hysteria.

Resident Stage Actors, Directors, Musicians, Stage Managers, and Producers

The Compass Players, Playwrights Theatre Club, and Second City New York

1955–1959

Alan Alda
Jane Alexander
Howard Alk
Alan Arkin
Larry Arrick
Ed Asner
Sandy Baron
Rose Arrick
Lloyd Battista
Walter Beakel
Shelley Berman
Haym Bernson
Roger Bowen
Hildy Brooks
R. Victor Brown
Jack Burns
Mona Burr
Loretta Chiljian
Del Close
Robert Coughlan
Barbara Dana
Severn Darden
Kornel Michael David
Bob Dishy
MacIntyre Dixon
Paul Dooley
Andrew Duncan
Tom Erhart
Theodore J. Flicker
Barbara "Bobbi" Gordon
Mark Gordon
Philip Baker Hall
Larry Hankin
Valarie Harper
Barbara Harris
Jo Henderson
Mo Hirsch
Kenna Hunt
Henry Jaglom
Lee Kalcheim
Linda Lavin
Martin Lavut
Sid Lazard
Mickey LeGlaire
Richard Libertini
Ron Liebman
Freya Manston
Allaudin Mathieu
Elaine May
Paul Mazursky
Anne Meara
Lucy Minnerle
George Morrison
Mike Nichols
Tom O'Horgan
Robert Patton
Nancy Ponder
Diana Sands
Reni Santoni
Linda Segal
Suzanne "Honey" Shepard
David Shepherd
George Sherman
Peg Shirley
Paul Sills
Viola Spolin
Leslie J. Stark
Jerry Stiller
Ron Weyand
Collin Wilcox
Mary Louise Wilson

The Second City Chicago

1959

Howard Alk
Roger Bowen
Severn Darden
Andrew Duncan
Barbara Harris
Mina Kolb
Allaudin Mathieu
Sheldon Patinkin
Bernard Sahlins
Paul Sills
Eugene Troobnick

1960

Alan Arkin
Paul Sand
Joyce Sloane

1961

Bill Alton
John Brent
Hamilton Camp
Del Close
Melinda Dillon
Anthony Holland
Zohra Lampert
Alan Myerson
Joan Rivers
Avery Schreiber

1962

Mona Burr
Dennis Cunningham
Dick Schaal

1963

Jack Burns
MacIntyre Dixon
Ann Elder
Judy Harris
Melissa "Sally" Hart
Richard Libertini
Omar Shapli

1964

Ian Davidson
Eugene Kadish
Fred Kaz
Harv Robbin
David Steinberg

1965

Joan Bassie
Robert Benedetti
Alex Canaan
Sondra Caron
Josephine Raciti Forsberg
Judy Graubart
Robert Klein
David Paulsen
Fred Willard

1966

Bob Curry
Sid Grossfeld
Sandy Holt
Jon Shank
David Walsh
Penny White

1967

J. J. Barry
Peter Boyle
Martin Harvey Freidberg

Burt Heyman
Lynne Lipton
Ira Miller

1968

Murphy Dunne
Michael Miller
Carol Robinson
Eugenie Ross-Leming

1969

David Blum
Martin de Maat
Brian Doyle-Murray
Jim Fisher
Joe Flaherty
Nate Herman
Pamela Hoffman
Roberta Maguire
Judy Morgan
Harold Ramis
Eric Ross
Cyril Simon
Paul Taylor

1971

John Belushi
Dan Ziskie

1972

David Rasche
Ann Ryerson

1973

John Candy
Stephanie Cotsirilos
Tino Insana
Bill Murray
Jim Staahl
Betty Thomas

1974

Dan Aykroyd
Cassandra Danz
Don DePollo
Michael J. Gellman
Allan Guttman
Deborah Harmon
Richard Kurtzman
Eugene Levy
Raul Moncada
Rosemary Radcliffe
Gilda Radner
Mert Rich
Doug Steckler
Paul Zegler

1975

Bernadette Birkett
Miriam Flynn
George Wendt

1976

Will Aldis
Eric Boardman
Steven Kampmann
Shelley Long
Jim Sherman

1977

Cynthia Cavalenes
Larry Coven

1978

Jim Belushi

Tim Kazurinsky
Audrie Neenan
Lawrence J. Perkins
Maria Ricossa

1979

Danny Breen
Mary Gross
Bruce Jarchow
Nancy McCabe-Kelly

1980

Meagen Fay
Lance Kinsey
Rob Riley

1981

Susan Bugg
John Kapelos
Rick Thomas

1982

Nonie Newton-Breen
Craig Taylor

1983

Bekka Eaton
Ed Greenberg
Michael Hagerty
Isabella Hoffman
Richard Kind

1985

Andrew Alexander
Mindy Bell
Jim Fay
Mona Lyden
Len Stuart

1986

Dan Castellaneta
Rick Hall
Bonnie Hunt
Maureen Kelly
Harry Murphy

1988

Joe Liss
Mike Myers

1989

Chris Farley
Tim Meadows
Joel Murray
David Pasquesi
Judith Scott
Holly Wortell

1990

Tom Gianas
Bob Odenkirk
Tim O'Malley
Jill Talley

1991

Fran Adams
Cynthia Caponera
Steve Carell
Michael McCarthy
John Rubano
Ron West

1992

Paul Dinello
Kelly Leonard

Ruth Rudnick
Amy Sedaris

1993

Stephen Colbert
David Razowsky

1994

Scott Adsit
Scott Allman
Jackie Hoffman

1995

Rachel Dratch
Jon Glaser
Jenna Jolovitz
Adam McKay

1996

Kevin Dorff
Tina Fey
Mick Napier
Lyn Pusztai

1997

Jim Zulevic

1998

Rachel Hamilton
T.J. Jagodowski
Susan Messing
Jeff Richmond
Tami Sagher
Rich Talarico
Stephnie Weir

1999

Ed Furman
Beth Kligerman

2000

Craig Cackowski
Sue Gillan
Angela Shelton

The Second City Toronto

1973

Dan Aykroyd
Andrew Alexander
Valri Bromfield
Brian Doyle-Murray
Jayne Eastwood
Gino Empry
Joe Flaherty
Fred Kaz
Gilda Radner
Bernard Sahlins
Gerry Salsberg
Sam Shopsowitz
Joyce Sloane

1974

John Candy
Todd Jeffrey Ellis
Piers Gilson
Allan Guttman
Eugene Levy
Catherine O'Hara
Sheldon Patinkin
Jim Patry
Rosemary Radcliffe

1975

Carol Cassis
Ben Gordon

Andrea Martin
John Monteith
Dave Thomas

1976

Peter Aykroyd
Brenda Donohue
Len Stuart

1977

Del Close
Robin Duke
Steven Kampmann
Martin Short
Dave Thompson
Peter Torokvei

1978

Scott Baker
Sally Cochrane
Cathy Gallant

1979

Maggie Butterfield
Don DePollo
Don Dickinson
Melissa Ellis
Derek McGrath
Tony Rosato
Kim Sisson
Mary Charlotte Wilcox

1980

Tom Baker
Gabe Cohen
Steve Ehrlick
John Hemphill
Kathleen Laskey
Denise Pidgeon
Wendy Slutsky

1981

Ken Innes
Jerrold Karch
Deborah Kimmett

1982

Michael J. Gellman
Don Lake

1983

Donald Adams
Bob Derkach
June Graham
Bruce Hunter
Ron James
Madelyn Keane
Debra McGrath
Lyn Okkerse
Peter Okkerse
Bruce Pirrie
Jane Schoettle
Blaine Selkirk
Adrian Truss

1984

Sandra Balcovske
Karen Poce

1985

Dana Andersen
Bob Bainborough
Kevin Frankoff
Linda Kash
Dorothy Tenute

1986
David Huband
Jeff Michalski
Mike Myers
Deborah Theaker
Mark Wilson

1987
Tamar Malic
Ryan Stiles
Audrey Webb

1988
Neil Crone
Wendy Hopkins
Lindsay Leese
Colin Mochrie
Alana Shields
Tim Sims

1989
Patrick McKenna

1990
Kathryn Greenwood
Karen Hines
Gary Pearson
Ed Sahely

1991
Christopher Earle
Nick Johne
Jenny Parsons
Judith Scott
Peter Sherk
Brian Smith

1993
Andrew Currie
Jackie Harris
Steve Morel
Paul O'Sullivan
Jonathan Wilson

1994
Lori Nasso
Janet Van De Graaff

1995
Tamara Bick
Kerry Garnier
Albert Howell
Nancy Marino
Teresa Pavlinek

1996
Jennifer Irwin
Mollie Jacques
Bob Martin
Jack Mosshammer

1997
James Carroll
Marc Hickox
Melody Johnson
Arnold Pinnock
Angela Shelton

1998
Gavin Crawford
Tracy Dawson
Andrew Dollar
Mary Pat Farrell
Jerry C. Minor
Doug Morency
Lee Smart
Gina Sorell
Jennifer Whalen

1999
Paul Bates
Lisa Brooke
Kevin Dorff
K. McPherson Jones

2000
Geri Hall

The Second City e.t.c.
1983
Bill Applebaum
Rob Bronstein
Don DePollo
Jim Fay
Susan Gauthier
Carey Goldenberg
Jeff Michalski
Jane Morris
Bernard Sahlins
Joyce Sloane
Ruby Streak

1984
Steve Assad
Dan Castellaneta
Isabella Hoffman
Maureen Kelly
Harry Murphy

1985
Andrew Alexander
Len Stuart

1986
Mark Belden
Mindy Bell
Kevin Crowley
Kevin Doyle
Joe Keefe
Barbara Wallace

1987
Chris Barnes
Madeleine Belden
Joe Liss

1988
Laura Hall
Judith Scott
Jill Talley
Holly Wortell

1989
Mark Beltzman
Dan Gillogly
Nate Herman
Michael McCarthy
Ruth Rudnick
Ron West

1990
Fran Adams
Steve Carell
Tom Gianas
John Rubano

1991
Rose Abdoo
Megan Moore Burns
Peter Burns
Ken Campbell
Jeff Garlin
Dave Razowsky

1992
Scott Allman
Stephen Colbert
Ian Gomez

Jackie Hoffman
Jenna Jolovitz
Kelly Leonard

1993
Scott Adsit
Michael Broh
Jimmy Doyle
Norm Holly
Nia Vardalos

1994
John Hildreth

1995
Adam McKay
Jeff Richmond
Aaron Rhodes
Dee Ryan
Brian Stack
Miriam Tolan
Jim Zulevic

1996
Neil Flynn
Laura Krafft
Jerry C. Minor
Horatio Sanz
Peter Zahradnick

1997
Aaron Carney
Matt Dwyer
Rachel Hamilton
Mick Napier
Rebecca Sohn
Rich Talarico

1998
Craig Cackowski
Kristin Ford
Noah Gregoropoulos
Tami Sagher

1999
Ali Farahnakian
Martin Garcia
Sue Gillan
Beth Kligerman
Jack McBrayer
David Pompeii
Lyn Pusztai
Klaus Peter Schuller
Angela Shelton
Trey Stone
Michael Thomas

The Second City Detroit
1993
Andrew Alexander
Robin Bucci
Colin Ferguson
John Holtson
Mark Levenson
Jerry C. Minor
Suzy Nakamura
Andrew Newberg
Lyn Okkerse
Tim Pryor
Jackie Purtan
Angela Shelton
Len Stuart

1994
Tom Gianas
Nancy Hayden
Todd Stashwick

1995
Peter Burns
John Farley
Joshua Funk
Dionna Griffin
Grant Krause
Emily Rose Merrell
Ed Smarron
Chris Smith
Rico Bruce Wade

1996
Larry Campbell
Kim Greene
John Hildreth
Chad Krueger
Anne Libera
Trey Stone

1997
Eric Black
Margaret Exner
Andrew Graham
Brandon Johnson
Keegan-Michael Key
Joe Latessa
Catherine Worth

1998
Michael J. Gellman
Elaine Hendriks
Marc Evan Jackson
Mary Jane Pories
Ron West
Nyima Woods

1999
John Edwartowski
Shatha Faraj
Joe Janes
Antoine McKay
Maribeth Monroe
Mary Vinette
Marc Warzecha

2000
Dexter Bullard
Cheri Johnson
David Razowsky

The Second City Northwest
1988
Fran Adams
Andrew Alexander
Jon Anderson
Mark Beltzman
Bill Cusack
Fred Kaz
Tim O'Malley
David Pasquesi
Ruth Rudnick
Cheryl Sloane
Joyce Sloane
Len Stuart

1989
Steve Carell
Christina Dunne
Jim Jatho
Sean Masterson
John Michalski
David Razowsky
John Rubano
Claudia Smith-Special
Faith Soloway

1990
Ken Campbell
Kevin Crowley

Amy Sedaris

1991
Scott Allman
Stephen Colbert
Paul Dinello
Ian Gomez
Jackie Hoffman
John Holtson
Megan Moore-Burns
Mick Napier
Charlie Silliman
Nia Vardalos

1992
Scott Adsit
Tom Gianas
John Hildreth
Norm Holly
Mark Levenson
Aliza Murrieta
Aaron Rhodes
Mitch Rouse
Jim Zulevic

1993
Peter Burns
Deborah Goldberg
Karol Kent
Kelly Leonard
John Thies
Tracy Thorpe

1994
Renee Albert
Pat Andrews
Bernadette Birkett
Martin Brady
Matt Dwyer
Jennifer Estlin
Pat Finn
Michael Gellman
David Koechner
Ron West

1995
Michael Bloom
Anne Libera
Theresa Mulligan
Todd Stashwick
Nancy Walls

The Second City London
1983–1992
Donald Adams
Andrew Alexander
Dana Andersen
Elizabeth Baird
Sandra Balcovske
Jack Banks
John Bynum
Luc Casimiri
Alan Catlin
John Costello
Catherine Creary
Martin de Maat
Patrick Dubois
Kevin Frankoff
Michael J. Gellman
Mike Goran
Kathryn Greenwood
Allan Guttman
David Healey
Karen Hines
Shari Hollett
Wendy Hopkins
Bruce Hunter
Todd Jeffrey-Ellis
Linda Kash

Madelyn Keane
Joe Keefe
Peter Keleghan
Deborah Kimmett
Elvira Kurt
Lindsay Leese
Frank McAnulty
Patrick McKenna
Steve Morel
Sue Morrison
Barbara Muller
Lori Nasso
Lyn Okkerse
Jenny Parsons
Bruce Pirrie
Karen Poce
Ed Sahely
Jerry Schaefer
Jane Schoettle
Devon Scott
Paul Scott
Blaine Selkirk
Tim Sims
Brian Smith
Marilyn Smith
Rob Smith
Len Stuart
David Talbot
Deborah Theaker
Adrian Truss
Nia Vardalos
Audrey Webb
Jonathan Wilson
Mark Wilson

The Second City Edmonton
1979–1982
Andrew Alexander
Bob Bainborough
Sandra Balcovske
Lorraine Behnan
Gabe Cohen
Bob Derkach
Don Dickinson
Robin Duke
Michael J. Gellman
Christine Henderson
Sparky Johnston
Gerald Karsh
Gail Kerbel
Keith Knight
Don Lamont
David Mann
Jeanette Nelson
Jan Randall
Mert Rich
Carol Sinclair
Kevin Smith
Veena Sood
Doug Stratten
Len Stuart
Adrian Truss

Selected Bibliography

Christiansen, Richard. 1994. "Thirty-Five Years of Second to None." *Chicago Tribune*, 13 November, Arts & Entertainment.

Coleman, Janet. 1990. *The Compass: The Improvisational Theatre that Revolutionized American Comedy*. Chicago: University of Chicago Press.

Johnson, Allan. 1999. "Reliving 40 Years of Second City Through Performers' Eyes." *Chicago Tribune*, 12 December, Arts & Entertainment.

Kurtin, Kelly. 1999. "Laughing Matters." *Where Chicago*, December.

McCrohan, Donna. 1987. *The Second City: A Backstage History of Comedy's Hottest Troupe*. New York: Perigee Books.

Rosenthal, Marshall. 1972. "Stamped with His Own Brando." *Chicago Daily News*, 15 April.

Showtime. 1988. *The Second City Toronto 15th Anniversary*. Produced and directed by Eugene Levy.

Spolin, Viola. 1963. *Improvisation for the Theater: A Handbook of Teaching and Directing Techniques*. Evanston, Ill.: Northwestern University Press.

Sweet, Jeffrey. [1978] 1986. *Something Wonderful Right Away*. Reprint, New York: Limelight Editions.

Weber, Bruce. 1999. "Industrial Strength Comedy." *New York Times*, 21 December, The Living Arts.

Index

Acknowledgments

First of all, thanks to the many alumni who filled out those less-than-adequate questionnaires we sent around. To those of you who didn't get any of your answers quoted, I'm sorry, and blame the editors.

There are undoubtedly errors of both commission and omission in this book (there always are). If the alumni of Playwrights, Compass, Second City, and all that's come after catch any, let me know. (Hopefully the book will sell so well that it'll need a second edition, and I can make corrections.) What you consider to be errors in judgment don't count.

The following people need special thanks for work beyond the call of duty: Brian Boland, Karyn Bugelli, Matt Cullison, Peter Feniak, Mike Ferbache, Josephine Raciti Forsberg, Aaron Freeman, Tom Gianas, Kelly Haran, Jack Helbig, Mary Beth Hughes, Jordan Jacobs, Joe Keefe, Beth Kligerman, Mike Konopka, Anne Libera, Jim McMahon, Rich Nixon, Lyn Okkerse, Tim O'Malley, Dominique Raccah and the Staff of Sourcebooks, Felice Rose, Scott Silberstien, Cheryl Sloane, Caroline Syran, and I'm sure I've left some out, for which I apologize.

Andrew Alexander and Bernie and Jane Nicholl Sahlins deserve thanks, of course, with a special thanks to my dear friend Bernie Sahlins, without whom I wouldn't have the life I have.

Joyce Sloane and her incredible memory have both been invaluable.

I agreed with almost all of the suggestions made by my editors at Sourcebooks, project editor Alex Lubertozzi and editorial director Todd Stocke. They're truly amazing.

And finally, Kelly Leonard has worked himself into exhaustion helping to get this book together. It couldn't have been done without him, for which there's no way to thank him.

photoCREDITS

Chapter 1

1 Courtesy of Mickey Pallas, Courtesy of Mickey Pallas, William Allaudin Mathieu Collection, Courtesy of David Shepherd; 2 Courtesy of the *Chicago Maroon*; 3 Courtesy of Joyce and Byrne Piven, Courtesy of Joyce and Byrne Piven; 4 Courtesy of Joyce and Byrne Piven, Courtesy of Joyce and Byrne Piven; 5 David Shepherd Collection; 7 Courtesy of David R. Zimmerman; 8 Courtesy of Joyce and Byrne Piven; 9 Courtesy of Joyce and Byrne Piven, David Shepherd Collection; 10 Courtesy of Mickey Pallas; 12 David Shepherd Collection; 13 David Shepherd Collection; 15 Courtesy of Mike Brosilow; 16 William Allaudin Mathieu Collection; 17 David Shepherd Collection; 18 Courtesy of Norris MacNamara; 19 Courtesy of Mike Brosilow; 20 Courtesy Ted Flicker; 21 Roger Bowen Collection; 22 Robert A. Martin Collection.

Chapter 2

26 Courtesy of Morton Shapiro; 27 Courtesy of Morton Shapiro; 29 Courtesy of Mickey Pallas, Courtesy of Mickey Pallas; 31 William Allaudin Mathieu Collection; 32 Courtesy of Mickey Pallas; 34 Courtesy of Andrew Duncan; 37 Courtesy of Morton Shapiro; 38 Courtesy of Robert Lightfoot, William Allaudin Mathieu Collection.

Chapter 3

44 Courtesy of Morton Shapiro, Courtesy of Morton Shapiro; 45 Courtesy of Mike Brosilow; 46 Courtesy of Morton Shapiro; 47 David Shepherd Collection; 49 Courtesy of Leon L. Lopez; 50 Courtesy of Jennifer Girard; 51 Courtesy of Mike Brosilow; 52 Courtesy of Morton Shapiro; 53 Courtesy of Mickey Pallas; 55 Courtesy of Mickey Pallas.

Chapter 4

59 Metro News Photos; 61 Courtesy of Morton Shapiro; 62 Courtesy of Mickey Pallas, Courtesy of the Royal Alexandra Theatre; 64 Courtesy of Archie Lieberman; 65 Courtesy of Mickey Pallas; 67 Courtesy of Archie Lieberman; 69 Courtesy of Archie Lieberman; 70 Courtesy of Mike Brosilow; 71 Courtesy of Fred Schell; 72 Courtesy of Alex Canaan; 73 Courtesy of Robert Lightfoot; 74 Courtesy of Robert Lightfoot, Courtesy of Robert Lightfoot; 76 Courtesy of Jay King; 77 Courtesy of Jennifer Girard, Courtesy of Jennifer Girard; 78 Courtesy of Jennifer Girard.

Chapter 5

82 Courtesy of Dick Klein; 87 Courtesy of Dick Klein; 88 Courtesy of R.C. Lieberman; 89 Courtesy of R.C. Lieberman; 90 Courtesy of Dick Klein, Courtesy of Dick Klein; 91 Courtesy of Dick Klein; 96 Courtesy of Dick Klein; 101 Courtesy of Dick Klein; 102 Courtesy of Dick Klein, Courtesy of Dick Klein; 103 Courtesy of Jay King, Courtesy of Dick Klein; 104 Courtesy of Jay King, Courtesy of Dick Klein, Courtesy of Dick Klein; 107 Courtesy of Jay King; 108 Courtesy of Jay King; 109 Courtesy of Jay King, Courtesy of Jay King; 110 Courtesy of Leon M. Lopez/Daily News; 111 Courtesy of Marc Hauser, Courtesy of Jay King; 112 Courtesy of Jay King, Courtesy of Jay King, Courtesy of Jay King; 113 Courtesy of Jay King, Courtesy of Jay King.

Chapter 6

116 Courtesy of Norman Seeff; 120 Courtesy of Hugh Wesley; 124 Courtesy of Rob Waymen; 126 Courtesy of Rob Waymen; 127 Courtesy of Rob Waymen, Courtesy of Rob Waymen; 130 Courtesy of Hugh Wesley; 131 Courtesy of Hugh Wesley, Courtesy of Hugh Wesley; 134 Courtesy of Jennifer Girard, Courtesy of Jennifer Girard; 135 Courtesy of Mike Brosilow, Courtesy of Lisa Ebright, Courtesy of Mary Ellen Matthews, Courtesy of Mickey Pallas.

Chapter 7

136 Courtesy of Rick Alexander; 138 Courtesy of Joyce Sloane; 139 Courtesy of Jennifer Girard, Courtesy of Jennifer Girard, Courtesy of Jennifer Girard; 141 Courtesy of Jennifer Girard; 142 Courtesy of Dick Klein, Courtesy of Dick Klein; 144 Courtesy of J.B. Spector, Courtesy of Jay King; 146 Courtesy of Jennifer Girard, Courtesy of Jennifer Girard; 147 Courtesy of Jennifer Girard; 148 Courtesy of Rick Alexander, Courtesy of Rick Alexander, Courtesy of Rick Alexander; 149 Courtesy of Rick Alexander, Courtesy of Rick Alexander, Courtesy of Rick Alexander; 151 Courtesy of Jennifer Girard, Courtesy of Robert Potter, Courtesy of Joyce Sloane; 152 Courtesy of Rick Alexander, Courtesy of Rick Alexander; 153 Courtesy of Rick Alexander, Courtesy of Rick Alexander; 154 Courtesy of Jennifer Girard; 155 Courtesy of David Street; 156 Courtesy of Robert Lightfoot; 157 Courtesy of Jay King.

Chapter 8

158 Courtesy of Jennifer Girard; 159 Courtesy of Jennifer Girard; 161 Courtesy of Mary Ellen Matthews; 162 Courtesy of Jennifer Girard, Courtesy of Jennifer Girard; 163 Courtesy of Jennifer Girard, Courtesy of Jennifer Girard; 165 Courtesy of Brian Perkinson; 166 Courtesy of Jennifer Girard and Mike Brosilow; 167 Courtesy of Jennifer Girard; 169 Courtesy of Jennifer Girard; 171 Courtesy of Mike Brosilow, Courtesy of Mike Brosilow, Courtesy of Mike Brosilow; 172 Courtesy of Jennifer Girard, Courtesy of Brian McConeky; 174 Courtesy of Mike Brosilow; 177 Courtesy of Jennifer Girard; 178 Courtesy of Jennifer Girard; 181 Courtesy of Carlos Sanz; 184 Courtesy of Second City; 186 Courtesy of Jennifer Girard; 187 Courtesy of Mike Brosilow.

Audio Credits:

Audio Engineering and Archival Restoration: Mike Konopka, Thundertone Audio
De-Noising: Craig Harding, September Audio
Colossal Mastering: Dan Stout

Some photos courtesy of:

Mike Brosilow (773) 235-4696
Jennifer Girard (773) 929-3730
Marc Hauser (773) 486-4381
Jay King (630) 845-9912
Dick Klein dklein@iols.com
Robert Potter (312) 226-2060
J. B. Spector (773) 276-0642